PENGUIN BOOKS

RIPE

Annie Hawes, originally
Her previous book, *Extra*

Ripe for the Picking

ANNIE HAWES

PENGUIN BOOKS

PENGUIN BOOKS

Published by the Penguin Group
Penguin Books Ltd, 80 Strand, London WC2R 0RL, England
Penguin Putnam Inc., 375 Hudson Street, New York, New York 10014, USA
Penguin Books Australia Ltd, 250 Camberwell Road,
Camberwell, Victoria 3124, Australia
Penguin Books Canada Ltd, 10 Alcorn Avenue, Toronto, Ontario, Canada M4V 3B2
Penguin Books India (P) Ltd, 11 Community Centre,
Panchsheel Park, New Delhi – 110 017, India
Penguin Books (NZ) Ltd, Cnr Rosedale and Airborne Roads,
Albany, Auckland, New Zealand
Penguin Books (South Africa) (Pty) Ltd, 24 Sturdee Avenue,
Rosebank 2196, South Africa

Penguin Books Ltd, Registered Offices: 80 Strand, London WC2R 0RL, England

www.penguin.com

First published 2003
3

Set in 11/13 pt Monotype Bembo
Typeset by Rowland Phototypesetting Ltd, Bury St Edmunds, Suffolk
Printed in England by Clays Ltd, St Ives plc

For Patrizia, Greta and Miki

A rickety three-legged stepladder, the home-made kind you use for pruning olive trees, stands in the middle of my kitchen. From out here under the grapevines, all I can see of the ongoing operation is a pair of stout boots perched high on its creaking rungs; above the boots, a pair of wrinkled corduroy trousers fading off into the shadow of the beams above. The sound effects are pretty impressive, though. A series of knowledgeable huffings, puffings, proddings and scrapings; a sudden outbreak of loud buzzing; a heartfelt call upon the Madonna from somewhere in the region of the grizzled moustache on high. A great shower of powdery sawdust falls to the worn terracotta tiles below. Can there be a whole nest of bees up there? The suspense is too much to bear. I nip across the terrace and stick my head through the door. How's it looking?

Euh! mutters Franco the expert in tones of deepest pessimism.

Porca miseria! he adds dramatically, as a hail of splintery fragments rains down upon my head, accompanied by another burst of wild buzzing.

I wipe the sawdust from my eyes and return chastened to the pleasant shade of the vines, where my neighbour Anna is waiting with me to hear Franco's verdict. She is wrapped in her usual voluminous apron, and naturally she is not just sitting about doing nothing as she waits. No native of the village of Diano San Pietro would sink so low. She has already made a quick tour of the olive trees nearest the house, checking for any sucker shoots I may have missed; and alas for my reputation, she has found several, which she has whisked off the trunks with an expert snap of the fingers. Now she is busy picking surplus leaves off my vine pergola, wherever she feels that a touch more sunshine needs to get on to the bunches of grapes gently ripening below. The shade from the vines, as far as I'm concerned, is a lot more important than the grape harvest they will provide, but I don't bother arguing. I have, as it happens, become relatively competent at looking after my own crops and garden after so many years; I've been living in this house ever since my sister and I came across it while on a holiday job in the plant nursery down at the bottom of the valley – and discovered to our amazement that the building, along with its surrounding terraces of olive trees, was on sale for no more than our joint two months' wages. An irresistible bargain; and one that set us up for a decade-long steep learning curve in the matter of the customs and lifestyle of an olive-farming community in this north-western corner of Italy, right up against the border with the South of France. But public opinion in San Pietro will not move with the times, and I've given up being offended when neighbours mollycoddle me like this. Why bother, when everyone gets so much enjoyment out of your idiot foreigner persona?

Anna has turned her back pointedly on the house as she plucks. She has no time for Franco, who once got her husband Tonino embroiled in an unseemly bit of sharp practice over the purchase of a well, and she wants to make sure he remembers the fact. She is positively bristling as she crumples her handful of vine leaves and hurls them on to the mulch pile around the roots of the lemon tree on the next terrace down; glowering off down the valley to where the sea and the sky mingle in misty blue at the bottom of our steep hill. The well in question was, as it happens, the source of our home's only water supplies, yet my sister and I managed to get over the outrage and re-open diplomatic relations with Franco years ago. You'd think Anna might have forgiven and forgotten too. But not a bit of it. As I arrive at her side she nudges me rudely in the ribs and rolls her eyes skywards.

Surely, she says, you don't seriously believe Franco knows what he's about here? On horseflesh and cattle, fine, you can't fault him. He maybe knows a thing or two about olive-farming and basil-growing. Not to mention water supplies and their intricacies, she adds darkly. But bees? Don't make me laugh! What a pity your own man's not up here to take care of the situation, she adds, with a conspiratorial smile and a naughty lift of the eyebrow.

Yes, Anna knows I have a man of my own these days. She was the first to find it out; caught us together all alone up here in the middle of the night. And she's very much enjoying the knowledge. She's been doing the conspiratorial smile at every opportunity ever since, just to let me know that it doesn't bother *her*, whatever anyone else might think . . .

She's certainly right that Franco did not look his most confident and devil-may-care when I informed him breathlessly, as I dragged him away from his olive-pruning a few terraces downhill, that I urgently needed his help with an invasion of giant black bees in my kitchen. Still, I got the impression that this was more to do with his inability to name the creatures in proper Italian than with actual ignorance of them and their habits. He announced, doing his best to brazen the thing out, that they were called '*boumburumboum*'.

That doesn't sound like Italian, I said severely, having already had several bad experiences with vocabulary taught me by Franco. There was the time, for example – to name but one – when, thanks to his help, I made the entire staff of a sophisticated Riviera builders' merchants collapse in hysterical laughter by asking for a set of door hinges in what turned out to be deepest downhome Ligurian hillbilly dialect. After this embarrassing event I requested Franco in the strongest possible terms to own up like an honest man when he didn't know the name of something in Italian. This time my suspicions were confirmed when Franco, avoiding my eye and any more inconvenient linguistic debate, stepped down from the tree he was working on without more ado, picked up his ladder, hung it over his shoulder, and headed off up through his olive grove towards my house and lands.

I may have been exaggerating slightly when I called it an invasion, but we're talking monstrous bees as big as scarab beetles here, creatures with fat black shiny bodies and great stumpy iridescent blue-black wings. Even a mere handful of these things tumbling drunkenly out of the ceiling and on to the table unprovoked as you are taking a peaceful mid-morning coffee with a passing neighbour are a lot more than required. The outbreak began with just two of them, accompanied by a small shower of fine sawdust and backed up by a series of loud buzzings from somewhere on high, deep inside a roof beam; suggesting strongly that more of the creatures were lining up to join in the party. There being no fly spray to hand, I took Anna's advice – one kind of spray being, in her opinion, much like another when all's said and done – and nipped into the bathroom to grab a can of anti-perspirant deodorant; climbed nervously up on to the table and sprayed a powerful burst of the stuff right down into the suspicious hole in the beam.

Result: over the next several minutes three more of the monsters came plopping out, one after another, to bumble around among the cups and buzz about on their backs. Scary. Five bees down, and still a muffled buzzing in the beam. Was there a whole nest of the things in there? Time to go and get

4

help. And it was lucky for us that Franco was up here at all. I am the only person mad enough to live this far from the village. No local people can see anything at all attractive about such a lifestyle. In the past it was a sign of the most abject poverty to have to live in isolation on your land; you would only do such a thing if you had absolutely no choice left in the matter. Luckily for Diano San Pietro, such misery no longer exists round here, and even the poorest have managed to join their neighbours down in the village, where you get a good gossip of an evening and there's always someone around to lend you a cup of sugar (or, as it were, olive oil) in time of need. And you simply commute to your land to work the olive groves and vegetable gardens, as and when necessary. Everybody's happy except for Ministers of Agriculture, who have been totting up the nation's agricultural work-hours wasted in travelling back and forth like this, and disapproving loudly, for the last century or so. But who cares about them? Let us be thankful for Franco. There might easily have been nobody around at all. And who am I to cast the first stone, anyway, when it comes to naming varieties of bee? I happen to know that these big black bees don't have a name at all in my own language, unless you count a Latin one much too long to pronounce. I checked them out years ago in my *Insects of Europe* book, when I first bumped into one casually buzzing around the garden and found myself wondering if it was as dangerous as it looked. The entry concerning the species began, with what seemed to me quite unwarranted enthusiasm: 'This Handsome Bee . . .' so that's what I've ended up calling them. Handsome enough, maybe, outdoors in their proper place, but not a creature you'd want hanging about your home, joining in the morning coffee. Especially not if they make a habit of drilling holes as thick as your little finger in the roof beams. I don't recall hole-drilling being mentioned among the habits and lifestyle of the Handsome Bee, but I have not forgotten the remark that, 'though by no means aggressive', this Bee is armed, like all its kin, with a sting – a sting which presumably matches its vast size and strength. Wouldn't need to be very aggressive, would it?

A sudden loud cry of '*Porca Miseria!*' rends the air, accompanied by a small amount of buzzing, a positive storm of sawdust, and a large amount of clattering as Franco descends his ladder in a single leap to evade bee attack. He comes bursting out of the door wild-eyed, the clasp-knife he's been using to investigate bee-headquarters clutched in his fist. Not a reassuring sight. Now he leans against the wall to catch his breath, tips his straw trilby back on his head, unties his neckerchief and mops his brow with it. Another nest-tunnel, he says, two beams along from the original one. The whole roof is a wreck. Where is the spray?

I wave towards the can of expensively imported Sure on the kitchen table, being too cowardly to go in and get it myself. No point, I decide, in explaining that it isn't really insecticide. You can't buy anti-perspirant sprays here in Italy; only deodorant ones, because (according to our village chemist, at any rate) the Italian medical authorities have decided they're about as good for you as fly spray. And it certainly seemed to have the desired effect.

Franco goes boldly back in to face the enemy, arming himself with the spray *en route*, and climbs back up his ladder, nozzle at the ready.

Euh! says Anna scornfully. Did you ever see the state of him? So much drama over nothing! Next thing you know, she goes on, raising her voice provocatively, your friend in there will be telling you a few bees are about to bring the whole roof down. And offering to put it back up for you, too. At a bargain price, no doubt.

Franco returns some minutes later, stuffing the can of Sure casually into a trouser pocket as he comes. (He must be impressed with it, then.) He has overheard Anna, as he was meant to, and he is not amused.

Anna may think she's joking, he says, but she's not wrong for all that. And, he adds, he has got rid of the bees for us, but the problem has nothing do with them. Nothing at all. You can always trust a pair of women to get hold of the wrong end of the stick. The roof, as it happens, really will have to come down. Not right away, maybe, but I'll see when the autumn rains set in, if not this year then next, and the terracotta tiles double their weight with all the water they absorb, that I've hardly got a sound beam left. The roof will be drooping like an egg. He won't offer to do the work for me, he adds with an evil glint at Anna, since the *signora* obviously knows people who'll give me a much better deal than he ever could. And so saying he hangs the ladder over his shoulder, turns on his heel, and starts off down the steps towards his pruning. Hang on a moment, I say. What do you mean, the roof will have to come down?

2

I can hardly believe this casual attitude from the man who practically bludgeoned us into buying this place: the man who first spotted us from afar admiring it, cunningly put into our heads the notion that it could be ours, and then eliminated any last smidgeon of common sense we had left by inviting us to a seductively wine-laden bonfire dinner on its cobbled patio with its grizzled owner, Pompeo. Under the influence of a spectacular sunset framed by trailing olive fronds, of rather a lot of home-grown wine made with our hosts' own hands (and feet too, naturally), of yards of savoury sausage skewered with rosemary and thyme twigs from the herb-bed outside the door, of voluptuous home-grown tomatoes sprinkled with Franco's own olive oil and no end of fresh basil, we shook hands first with Franco and then with Pompeo; and our destiny was sealed.

I admit that all this was rather a long time ago; but still, Franco knows perfectly well that (a) I'm as strapped for cash as ever and (b) my sister has left for Bulgaria – the call of the East always having been strong in her blood, and Bulgaria having turned out, once the Iron Curtain had finished falling and the mental distance it engendered slowly dissolved away, to be so near here you can just drive there in a day. She's found herself a job there teaching English, and is so far showing no sign of returning to the bosom of her family, so I'll have to deal with this crisis, if crisis it be, all by myself.

Now I come to think of it, I say, one of your major selling points at the time was the soundness of the roof, wasn't it? I know it was a while ago, but still, surely the definition of a sound roof is that it will last a decade or two?

Not, says Franco sternly, if it isn't taken care of properly.

This is a new one on me. How do you take care of a roof, exactly?

Lime, says Franco. A good coat of limewash on the beams every couple of years. But as far as he can see, we haven't given them a lick of paint since the day we moved in. This is certainly true. Lucy and I decided, once we'd given them a good scrub down, that the beams looked lovely the way they were, with the remnants of past centuries of limewash rubbed well into the grain. Distressed, I believe the look is called in interior design circles back in old England. Now I see why. Still, it's hard to believe that a coat of paint could have any structural purpose. Is Franco just winding me up?

No, he isn't. If I cast my mind back, he says with a menacing twirl of the moustache, I will recall that on the very day we went to the lawyer's to buy the house, he brought us up a whole sack of lime. As a gift.

Ligurians being the Scots of Italy, renowned for their thrift, this fact has obviously stuck in Franco's mind. It has stuck in mine too, as it happens. Who could forget those thirty huge immovable kilos of an unknown substance that was probably highly dangerous – didn't murderers use it to dispose of unwanted bodies? Didn't it burn your skin off? – scary white powdery stuff that leaked slowly out of the sack sitting stubbornly under the lean-to tile roof outside the front door while we wondered what on earth to do with it. And the steep learning curve as various inhabitants of San Pietro showed us the light – with various degrees of amazement and scorn at our ignorance. (As any civilized person knows, of course, you mix it with a bucket of water and a kilo of glue to create a lovely thick paint that transforms your internal stone walls from dirty earthy spidery things you wouldn't care to lean on, into smooth domesticated wildlife-free zones; you sprinkle a spoonful of it dry down your earth closet after every use, where it keeps stinks at bay most impressively; and moreover, when the water in your well develops that hint of stagnant pond perfume in the late August heat, you just throw in a kilo of lime and magically a day or two later your mountain spring water is clear as a mountain spring once more. No end of uses.)

Well, say I with spirit, recalling the many humiliations of this period, you may have brought us the lime, but you didn't think to leave any roof maintenance instructions, did you? No one ever suggested that we ought to be coating our ceiling with the stuff as well as our walls.

Mah! says Franco, throwing up his hands in despair. He decides to explain anyway, even if this proves that I am, as he has often suspected, gravely intellectually challenged. The Handsome Bee, it seems, is an opportunist bee, a bee that loves nothing more than a nice crevice in any old dead wood to lay its eggs in. In this particular case, it is taking advantage of a system of tunnels already drilled into our beams by some species of wood-beetle that would never have thought of attacking a bit of wood nicely coated with lime. Franco can't believe we didn't hear the beetles – or their larvae, rather, which are the things that do the damage. They make such a loud noise, a kind of clicking, crunching sound, especially of an evening in hot weather.

I think this one over; and with dawning horror realize that, in fact, my sister and I have been bravely ignoring this very clicking, crunching sound from above for a good few years, in a devil-may-care, we're-not-scared-of-unusual-country-noises-any-more kind of a way. After a few fruitless hunts for the source of the clicking we decided it must be some sort of harmless house-cricket high in the beams, something so minute that it was invisible. I see now, perhaps too late alas, that studied nonchalance in the face of unusual Ligurian hillside sound-effects is not always the correct response. In this case, for example, panic might have been the best reaction.

Ah, si, si, says Franco. Yes indeed. If you'd caught them early enough, you could have solved the problem with a spot of diesel fuel, and that would have been the end of that.

Seeing at last the correct expression of despair and repentance upon my face, Franco relents, unhooks the ladder from his shoulder, and takes me in for a look. From the top of the very wobbly ladder – these three-legged things are designed for steadiness on the stony, uneven terrain of your olive terraces, and feel oddly precarious on flat tiles with nothing to dig their toes into – I see a truly awful sight. The beetles, if beetles they are, have cunningly left a paper-thin outside layer of beam completely intact. But where Franco has scraped away this veneer, instead of solid wood there is only a lacy network of sawdust-stuffed tunnels following the grain. Or what once was the grain. Tunnels almost as thick as my little finger. I prod gently at the exposed bit of wood: a cloud of sawdust and splintery tunnel-linings cascades on to the tiles below. Now I prod gently at the apparently sound surface a few inches away. Yes: squashy as a sponge. Doom.

They only eat the sapwood, though, and leave the heartwood, says Franco cheeringly, so it really just depends how much of the beam was heartwood in the first place. You still might be able to sort it out with a bit of diesel if you're lucky.

This is one of the most infuriating features of life around here: you can never tell how much of what you're getting is hard information, and how much is just a bit of drama being created by your neighbours for the entertainment value, part of some pre-television make-your-own-fun tradition still going strong among the older inhabitants of this valley. Is the roof seriously about to fall in? Or is it all right really, since the heartwood, which must (I suppose) be the strong bit that actually keeps roofs up, won't have been eaten? Another infuriating feature, of course, is having weird folk-remedies proposed to you all the time and having no idea whether they're a sensible thing to do or not. This is why I have been ignoring Franco's references to diesel fuel. Will the diesel remedy for beetles be some mad ancient superstition, something like a voodoo curse, that you (or the beetles) would have to believe in for it to work? Or will it be the wisdom of ages revealed, like, say, willow-bark tea as a remedy for headache? And even if it is the wisdom of ages, might it not have been superseded by some infinitely less smelly and dangerous modern invention? These days, for example, you no longer have to leap from your bed of pain, track down a willow tree, and boil up its bark. You have the aspirin tablet: salicylic acid. A *salice*, just to confirm this, is a willow tree in Italian.

Who knows, though? How would you find out except by trial and error? There is no escape. I brace myself and wade in. All right, I say, what do I do with the diesel fuel? The answer, predictably, is that I have to paint every beam liberally with the stuff. If, a week or two later, I can still hear clicking, then I must take matters further, get hold of a syringe and actually inject the stuff into the holes. Great idea. Living in a home that smells like a petrol station for however long it takes the fumes to wear off. With autumn on its way, too, and would you dare light a match, never mind the wood-stove or the open fire – the only forms of heating up here – when the merest spark might turn the whole place into a Towering Inferno?

Are you sure that's the only solution? I ask plaintively. Isn't there some kind of insecticide I could use instead? Franco is horrified; so is Anna, who has finished sorting out my agricultural shortcomings and come in to join the fun. Insecticides, they both agree, are poisonous. (Anna and Franco agreeing! Things must be really desperate.) A quick squirt may be all right when there's no other solution, but no one in their right mind would go filling their whole house with insecticide. No. Nice, healthy, natural diesel is the answer.

Fine, I say, diesel it is then. Still, I make a treacherous mental note to sneak off alone to somewhere more modern and forward-looking than Diano San Pietro – down to the cosmopolitan coast at the foot of our valley, perhaps, to the seaside resort of Diano Marina; or maybe even right over the perilous clifftop corniche road to our technologically advanced county town of Imperia, a whole six miles away – to seek some roof-beam equivalent of the aspirin.

With Franco away back to his pruning, Anna and I have moved out to the old marble table in the sunny centre of the patio, well away from the house and its fearful wildlife, for another try at that quiet cup of coffee. This is a first: I've never ever seen Anna sit down in full sunshine before. People from San Pietro don't sit in the sun; not people who are over forty, at any rate. As far as Old San Pietro is concerned, the sun is something you go out into when you have to work; then you find a nice bit of shade to relax in. Once upon a time I thought this was a terrible waste of all that lovely sunshine. Now, in these days of sunblocks and skin-cancer scares, we see how wrong I was. There you have it: wisdom of ages.

As soon as I've poured Anna's coffee out and she's added her sugar, though, she's off: shunting her chair right away from the table and into the shade of the vines. Only dappled shade left there now, since she's pulled off half the leaves, but that's her own lookout.

It's getting on for lunchtime, and down below we can hear Franco getting ready to leave; a series of clangs and crashes as he collects up his tools and chucks them into the open back of his three-wheeled truck, his *Ape*. Appropriately enough to the day's events, an *Ape* means a Bee: though the low-key buzzing of Franco's transport as its Vespa motor starts up and grinds into gear is nothing compared to that of a Handsome Bee under the influence of a good burst of anti-perspirant. Now a slam of the door to its tiny cockpit; and it bumps its way off along the dirt road below us. We glimpse it, off and on, through the olive trees on the lower terraces until, at the sharp bend where the asphalt starts, it takes off on the downhill run, making a dash for home and pasta.

As if on cue, the midday bells start to ring out from all the churches of all the many and various Diano villages dotted about the valley. First Diano Castello, then Diano San Pietro; now the nearest one to us as the crow flies, the onion-domed *campanile* of Diano Arentino. Anna rises obediently at their bidding and gets ready to leave too, giving another snort or two about That Franco as she tugs at her apron strings and reties them more firmly. What's he done now?

Isn't it obvious? He doesn't even wait for the Midday to sound before he stops work, that's what! Sign of a deep lack of commitment to home and family. Franco is not a serious person, says Anna. Thank goodness her own man, Tonino, would never dream of such degenerate behaviour. Or your Ciccio, for that matter, she adds magnanimously. We can only thank the Lord you've got someone reliable around to give you a hand with that roof! In the nick of time! She gives me the conspiratorial smile again and sets off for home, turning, as she reaches the bend in the path, to give me the eyebrow-lift for good measure.

3

Truth to tell, not just Anna but the whole of Diano San Pietro
has been rather relieved to know that there is a proper man in
my life these days – whatever they may think about him
staying the night, which hopefully they will know nothing
about. Unless Anna hasn't been able to resist spreading the
word. Till now, the only men-friends Lucy or I ever produced
were strange foreign creatures even more gormless than ourselves, whose extraordinary behaviour we would always defend quixotically, once the village had spotted their lazy,
unmanly ways, by claiming that they were on holiday. Absurd!
Do you stop being a man just because you're on holiday?

It was always a worry to the village, even when my sister
was still here, to have us living up here in the hills, two foolish
foreign women so far from civilization – a good ten minutes
by car up the twelve hairpin bends, or fifteen minutes on foot
up the steep cobbled mule-track that cuts straight across them.
And doing all that men's work by ourselves! Chopping firewood, lugging gas bottles up and down the long winding
path, pruning olive trees, fixing the drystone walls of the olive
terraces when the odd bit collapsed, as they so often do, under
the weight of gushing storm water – just two women all on
their own!

How hard it is, too, to be proud of your great success at
self-sufficiency – I am secretly very pleased with my ever-
improving skill at drystone walling – when everyone around
you takes it as some kind of personal reproach. You are giving
the village a *brutta figura*: making them cut an ugly figure,

showing them up, giving them a bad public image. In the past, well-wishers like Anna, or Franco's wife Iolanda, would even send us up their own menfolk every now and then, so that no one could say we weren't properly looked after: husbands armed with a chainsaw at olive-tree-pruning and winter-firewood-preparing times, or a giant petrol-driven brush-cutter in late summer when your terraces have to be stripped of ground cover before they dry out and become a forest-fire hazard. Just to check we had everything under control.

Things calmed down a couple of years ago, once it was known that Ciccio and his large workforce of friends-and-relations were often to be seen about our place, helping out with the heavy pruning and the olive harvest. Finally, a man to keep things in order! A sensible local man, too, with a respectable few hundred olive trees of his own. Not entirely local, of course – after all, his parents came up from the deep South of Italy a mere fifty years ago – but Ciccio was born and bred here in the valley, at least, so he knows what's what; even though (another small black mark against him) he doesn't devote himself entirely to the family olive groves, but runs a small restaurant up in the hills on the side.

Of course I kept claiming that he was just a friend: but I would, wouldn't I? Everyone knew how it would end up.

Was romance bubbling away under the surface all that time we were going around replying wearily that, no, there was nothing at all between us except friendship? Or were we brought together by the power of suggestion, a sort of arranged marriage with the whole valley conspiring at our downfall? The uniting of a pair of neighbouring olive groves is certainly something to warm any Ligurian's heart. Such economies to be made!

Whatever may truly underlie our change of heart, though,

the thing seemed to us to happen out of the blue. Let me rewind to the beginning.

Here I sit late one moonlit summer night on the patio of a certain restaurant up at the head of our valley, being plied with wine in the gloaming by an amorous German holidaymaker. I have suggested the place myself, telling my suitor, most truthfully, that it's the best place to eat for miles around. I have been proven right; the high point of the dinner, a dish of wild boar spiced with the pungent leaves and berries of wild mountain *mirto*, was positively spiritual. All created by a certain Ciccio, who is not only a genius of a chef but also an old friend of mine, my closest friend in all the valley. There he is, just visible through the archway in his brightly-lit kitchens, slamming oven doors, banging saucepans about: and laughing and joking, as he clears up for the night, with a young woman customer who has managed to penetrate his private domain.

I am keeping half an eye on Ciccio's scenario, as you do with a friend; and he is keeping half an eye on mine. My German has drunk far too much, and is beginning to caress my hand and gaze into my eyes in a maudlin manner. He keeps apologizing for speaking English to me, and promising earnestly that his Italian will soon be up to conversational scratch. I can't make out whether he's forgotten that I am English, or does he just feel that Italian would be more romantic?

Ciccio catches my eye and I roll my eyeballs: he grins, waves and does a throat-cutting gesture through his serving-hatch. I see now that his companion is that wildly flirtatious Milanese girl who has turned up for the third weekend in a row. She has not only made herself at home in his kitchens, but is now insisting on having a holiday snap taken with him in an intimate embrace. Ciccio's teenage nephew, Alberto, who is helping out up here in his school summer holidays, is holding the camera. Now (the scene is burnt indelibly into my soul) the woman stuffs a colander up her tee-shirt to represent an advanced state of pregnancy, for which Ciccio is to be, photographically at least, responsible.

My German's caresses are creeping farther and farther up my arm; his wine-flushed face looms ever closer to mine. We are the last two customers left, now; and we are all alone out here on the terrace. Unless, that is, you count Pierino, *éminence grise* of the restaurant, who is sitting as usual right down at the far end of the terrace, elbows on table, glass in work-grimed fist, hunched around his regular litre-and-a-half bottle of red wine; and dressed now, as always, in rags, a pullover more hole than stuff, unravellings dangling from elbows and hem. Pierino is not, however, a customer. He is the freeholder of this restaurant, and of the house next door to it, where he lives; and he is in fact sitting at his own table, in the grounds of his own home, though you'd never guess this unless you were told, there being no visible barrier between the two. (Pierino is also, extraordinarily, the proprietor of a whole apartment block in elegant downtown Milan, and a multi-storey car park across the road from it as well: an inheritance that must be bringing him in a fortune, but has made not a whit of difference to his lifestyle. He still spends every morning digging away in his vegetable patch up on the hillside, and of an evening he likes to sit out here, playing the odd game of cards with his cronies and keeping a firm eye on his property. Behaviour somewhat unnerving to the restaurant management, to whom he is known (though not to his face) as *il vero ligure* – the True Ligurian.)

Alberto's camera flashes again, capturing Ciccio voluptuously entwined in Milanese arms for the third time; the girl in the kitchens adjusts her colander and unleashes a stream of wild giggles; and now, as my eyes meet Ciccio's through the archway again, I find myself inexplicably seized with an intense desire to throttle the woman. I am dumbfounded by this surprising new emotion, and naturally make no attempt to act upon it. But Ciccio, as he tells it, discovers at that very same moment that he feels something startlingly similar about my looming German. And Ciccio, always a man of action, abandons his post at the stoves, storms out of his kitchens, and in the twinkling of an eye has appeared at my side and put a possessive arm around my shoulders.

Perhaps my suitor does not realize, he announces in a menacing eyeball-to-eyeball fake Mafioso style, most convincing to a half-cut foreigner who doesn't know him too well, that The Englishwoman is With Him? And he folds me in a passionate embrace. After a moment or two of shocked paralysis, I find that I'm embracing him back: and that the thing seems to have stopped being a joke.

We surface for air at last; and hear, from way off in the shadows at the far end of the terrace, an explosive cackle of laughter, a cry of '*Bravo! Finalmente!*' and a burst of loud hand-clapping. Pierino, it seems, approves.

A bit of mutual gazing and a few more embraces later, nothing remains but to give the German his bill, see the disappointed Milanese off to her lonely hotel room down in Diano Marina, close the restaurant for the night, and take our leave of Pierino, who actually comes right out of his domain in order to shake both our hands ceremoniously. Now, at last, we are free to spend what's left of the night canoodling on the deserted moonlit sands down in the bay of Diano.

The rest is history.

4

Well, not quite history, of course. This is small-town Italy, and there are many hurdles yet to be got over. The first one hits me the very next day: it is this. You hardly ever bother arranging to meet people round here because you bump into them anyway in the natural course of events. So we haven't arranged when we'll meet again. After a companionable break- fast out on the terrace up at my place (Ciccio does not fear the sun's rays, being a modern man) he has gone off to cook a few lunches. Now, as the day wears on and the warm glow wears off, I find myself beginning to wonder whether I've made a terrible mistake. Have I just ruined one of my best friendships for a tawdry night of passion, expended my spirit in a waste of shame, and so forth? It's dawned on me that I can't go and check out the situation, just pop in to the restaurant and hang around the kitchens, chatting and chop- ping the odd bunch of basil the way I've always done. Certainly not. The terrible suspicion that I might be thrusting myself, Milanese-style, upon a captive chef who couldn't escape if he were so minded, would be overwhelming. I wouldn't even be able to tell if I was welcome, never mind whether it was in the capacity of friend or lover.

Luckily tomorrow, Tuesday, is the restaurant's official weekly *giorno di riposo*, or Day of Repose. Every bar and restaurant in Italy has to have one of these, by law. I see now what an incredibly good and useful law it is. So a mere twenty-four hours of fretting later, I pull myself together and get on down the twelve hairpin bends, pausing to check out the bar at the crossroads – no, no Ciccio – and onward to the coast, to Diano Marina. And there he is, just parking his car in the piazza, accompanied (darn) by his cousin Paolo, ex-footballer hero of the valley, commonly known as Paletta. *Paletta* means shovel, and I'm told Paolo was awarded this nickname because of the immense size of his hands. They don't look at all out of proportion to the rest of him to me. As far as I can see, he is entirely larger-than-life, so strong-featured that he looks as though he was drawn by a cartoonist rather than born of womankind. Be that as it may, I sincerely wish he would scarper immediately. His presence is not required.

They have just got back from the fish market on the port at Imperia, they tell me, where they've been getting in supplies for the restaurant, and Ciccio (how can he be so annoyingly un-neurotic?) bounces cheerfully about, insisting on taking me round to the boot of the car to show me his haul. His huge enthusiasm for food overwhelms any embryonic notion he may have that inspecting a whiffy wooden crate full of tangled sea-creatures may not be high on the agenda of a woman in a state of emotional turmoil over her status, as of yesterday, in his life.

The sea bass look particularly good, he says, leaning into the boot to gaze right into their eyes, big square fingertips prodding lovingly at their firm flesh. Baked in a crust of sea salt, he thinks, for tomorrow's lunch.

And what, I ask, doing my best to rise to the occasion, are the small pinky-orange fish with the long thin bodies, all mixed up with the fat silvery bass?

They are called *ballerine*, says Ciccio, because that's how they move in the water; they dance. Fried in a light batter, for a *fritto misto*, I think, he adds dreamily. There are also a pile of squid-like creatures, *seppie*, which I believe are called cuttlefish in English. Strange how, in my own land, cuttlefish is a hard white brittle thing you give to budgerigars to sharpen their beaks on, whereas here in Liguria at this time of year you use it to make a fresh-pea-and-cuttlefish stew, all thick and voluptuous with onion melted in olive oil and plenty of white wine; a classic of local cuisine, and so delicious that even a culinary coward like myself, never at her best when confronted with squiggly tentacly bits, finds the thought of it making her mouth water.

Ciccio shuts the boot on his treasures. Would I like to come for a coffee? he asks. Ah, this is more like it! Certainly I would, I say, hoping against hope that his cousin wouldn't. Luckily for me, Paletta had two coffees this morning at breakfast, and thinks that perhaps he shouldn't have another.

Ah, no, I agree with deeply sincere concern. You don't want to go upsetting your digestion.

No, indeed, agrees Paletta, pressing a shovel to his stomach. Bad for the nerves, too, he says.

Yes, indeed, I reply. And once we've completed this ritual exchange, one being re-enacted all over Italy at this mid-morning will-I-won't-I coffee crisis point, off he goes like a lamb. How handy are all these Italian dietary rules and regulations once you've studied their intricacies and know how to manipulate them to your advantage!

Where shall we go? I ask happily, looking forward to a pleasant half-hour communing with Ciccio at a small intimate table under the palm trees of some seafront café, a bit of quality time alone to consolidate our new relationship, or re-establish the old one, or whatever it turns out we're going to do. Put an end to the angst, at any rate.

Fool that I am! What was I doing congratulating myself on my intimacy with local customs? Of course, having a coffee together at this time of day involves no communing at all.

It merely means ninety seconds of standing side by side at a crowded bar being elbowed by a milling throng while you knock back a couple of teaspoonfuls of scalding black homicidally-strong espresso, wait for the small earthquake in your central nervous system, and dash off again, fighting your way out through a head-high thicket of flapping pink sports newspapers. Why didn't I have the presence of mind to order a cappuccino? There is some small chance of being allowed to sit down at a table while you drink a cappuccino, especially if you order a brioche with it, making out you haven't had breakfast yet. Didn't think of that till too late, though.

And yes, here we are three minutes later, back out on the streets of Diano. They're nice spacious streets, at least, since the tourist season officially finished two days ago and they are no longer infested with the decking, frilly sun-umbrellas and swing-seats, the jumbled displays of plastic beach toys, swimwear, blown-up lilos and suntan lotions amongst which holidaymakers apparently love to nestle. Normal life has begun again. In fact, the streets seem a wee bit too empty just at the moment, with the pair of us standing awkwardly in the middle of them, not quite sure what's meant to happen next. We wander along the palm-lined promenade at the edge of the bay, dodging the struggling pairs of workmen busy dismantling the rows of stripy beach huts and loading them on to lorries for their winter rest.

What are you doing this afternoon? asks Ciccio, sounding, at last, faintly unsure of himself.

Nothing much, I say. (Ten out of ten for original dialogue.)

As it happens, Ciccio isn't working today (heh, heh! I knew that!). He is due for lunch *dalla mamma*, at his mother's, he says, but after that he's off for the afternoon, *in giro* – around and about. Do I fancy joining him?

I'd love to, I say, going all soggy with relief.

5

Some hours later, here we are *in giro* away up in the hills, a couple of miles above my house, where olive terraces end and wilderness begins. Ciccio, like so many of his countrymen, is constitutionally unable to gyrate aimlessly, simply enjoying the bounties of nature. Not that he doesn't enjoy them; he just likes to collect a few of them up while he's at it. He views these hillsides as a sort of vast larder, or possibly supermarket, with the added attraction that whatever you find, you don't have to pay for. True to form, after a quick inspection of the hunting and gathering possibilities of the moment, he has chosen today's booty. We are busily picking wild rocket, *rucola*, as we wander. No idle hands for us. And better still, no idle angst. Neither of us has shown the slightest tendency to revert to just being friends. Lovely. So is the rocket, whose leaves I've got quite good at recognizing by now, in spite of the constant distraction of the exciting not-just-friends situation. It's much more peppery and robust than the cultivated version. We collect a huge bunch: Ciccio will show me how to make rocket pesto when we get home, he says.

Is there such a thing as rocket pesto?

Of course there is. The word 'pesto' comes from the same root as *pestare*, to trample. Or squash. We establish that it's closely connected with the word 'pestle' in my own language, the thing that goes with a mortar, and is used for squashing stuff. Once upon a time, 'pesto' was probably just any old mixture you'd bashed up, with a pestle, in a mortar.

Not so much of the 'once upon a time', either. A pestle and mortar is still all you get at my place, even on the very cusp of the twenty-first century. No liquidizer, because my little solar panel, recycled off a camper van, can't make anything like enough electricity for kitchen gadgets. It can manage a few Christmas-tree-sized light bulbs, a couple in each room; and on a good day gives me the choice between a music machine, a couple of hours of telly, and the laptop computer upon which I am slowly writing the book that will enable me, if I strike lucky and everyone else finds my anecdotes of my early years in the Ligurian hills as entertaining as I do, to buy several huge big solar panels. Think of that! Listening to music with all the lights on at once . . . not having to worry about whether the electricity's going to run out before the end of the film . . . I could get myself an electric bedside lamp too, maybe, luxury of luxuries. Then I'd be able to read myself to sleep without moths flying into my candle and making the flame go all lopsided so I have to put the book down every five minutes to dig their half-cremated corpses out. And all sorts of other degenerate electrical knick-knacks that I shall think of later. If ever I manage to finish the book. And sell it, of course.

As we head back downhill, arms full of the rocket we've gathered, I find I'm having trouble resisting a powerful temptation to let Ciccio in to one of my own best kept secrets. Would it be a terrible mistake to give so much away on a first date? Probably: but I can't resist it. Taking him by the hand, I lead him off into the wilderness, on to the steep half-abandoned terraces up above my house, and show him where, half-hidden among the roots of the untended olive trees, the rare and delicious coral-shaped mushroom called a *manina*, a little hand, grows in abundance at this time of year. Soon we have laid our bundles of leaves carefully aside and are stuffing every pocket we have with mushrooms.

Back at the house, Ciccio rises to the challenge. Wild mushroom risotto! he announces from somewhere deep inside the larder, where he is already checking out my supplies. Rice! White wine? Delicious! Wait and see! Have you got any tomatoes? We'll make a big tomato salad and dress it with the rocket pesto. Dusk has already begun to fall, so I grab a torch and go off to the vegetable patch down by the well. Return proudly with half a dozen beautiful ox-heart tomatoes to find Ciccio outside the door with a large kitchen knife, decimating the parsley patch I've only just got established. Can he really need that much parsley? Oh well.

My contribution to the cuisine is the job I always get: chopping bunches of leaves. At least, for a change, it's rocket instead of basil. Does he not trust me to do anything else but chop leaves?

Of course he does, he says soothingly. In fact, I can start with the parsley. He'll be needing that first.

Bah! I chop away, doing my best to keep an eye on what he's doing. I thought I hated risotto – terrible way to cook rice, making it go all sticky and glutinous – till I tasted Ciccio's version; but he's hopeless at explaining recipes. You just have to watch. Olive oil into the frying pan. Slicing the mushrooms, peeling some garlic, chopping an onion very fine. Hiss-and-smoke as they go into the pan. Loads more olive oil and some garlic into the mortar – now, pass him the parmesan and the grater. Lots of that too. Put the chopped rocket in with it, please, when it's ready. Ah, nothing to do with the risotto then. Switches back to the frying pan and adds a dash of white wine, another of water. Don't I have any rock salt? The chopped rocket is battered into submission with the pestle; now he wants the parsley for the risotto pan. Pass the rice. Where's the wine gone?

It's hopeless. I've already lost track of the risotto. May as well go and chop the tomatoes instead. At least they're not leaves.

We have a bottle of Ciccio's father's *vino d'uva*, too, to go with our dinner. *Vino d'uva* is 'wine-made-of-grapes'; called this because you make it yourself without the help of chemicals or indeed of sophisticated equipment of any kind – unless you count the sort of giant wringer you use to squeeze the fermenting juice out of the grape skins – and is hence of a strength randomly determined by how good the weather has been and how sweet the grapes were when pressed. Last year's weather was particularly good; and this brew is most powerful and flavoursome. And the bottle contains a whole litre-and-a-half of it. His father, Ciccio tells me, refuses to bottle his wine in normal-sized bottles; the classic 75 centilitre bottle is, according to Salvatore, a foppish, pretentious waste of time, effort and space. Twice the corks, twice the bottling work, half the quantity. You know it makes sense.

Once the risotto is bubbling gently away, Ciccio insists on trying out an absurdly complicated romantic toast to celebrate our first dinner together as lovers. With a full glass of wine in our right hands, we link right arms as if we were about to start some kind of country dance. Now, says he, we both have to drink from our glasses at once. Very tricky. The thing must have been invented, we decide, by people with much longer arms than us. Positively ape-like arms, you'd say. And very wasteful people, too, to judge by how much wine has gone everywhere except down our gullets. We pour another glass and go for the more traditional, separate-armed drinking method. Much more satisfactory. Fortified, I go off to set the table out on the terrace and get some candles lit. There are a couple of those tiny light bulbs out here, running off the solar panel; but if you actually want to see what you're eating, rather than just find your plate, they need a bit of back-up.

Something tells me the meal will be worth the candle. And this way there'll be electricity to spare for music as we dine.

The finished risotto is the best ever (naturally, says Ciccio, who is not modest about his culinary skills), and I still don't know how he makes it. We have the rocket pesto, lovely summery stuff, on the salad of utterly delicious tomatoes. (I am not modest about my gardening skills, either.) We just need some raw olive oil to sprinkle on the risotto, says the chef, for absolute perfection. So off I go into the larder to refill the oil bottle from the lovely new olive-oil container where I keep my year's supplies for the household. (Solid stainless steel, fifty-five litres, utterly state-of-the-art: no more messy siphoning from greasy glass demijohns for me.) I turn on the stylish wee spigot, and as I watch the golden-green oil from this spring's last pressing stream out into the bottle, I recall an amazing fact. This is seriously symbolic stuff! I didn't have enough olives left for a whole run of my own at the San Pietro olive mill that day; and Ciccio came to the rescue with several *quarti* of his own harvest.

Ciccio! I squeak from the depths of the cupboard. Do you realize what oil we've been using to cook with tonight? It's my olives and yours combined! His and Hers Extra Virgin!

We try the country-dance toast again to celebrate this amazing fact. Surprisingly, even after several glasses of Salvatore's wine, we still haven't got any better at it.

Now, meal over, wine-bespattered, we sit stargazing out across the valley over coffee and *grappa*, marvelling at the unfathomable forces that sealed our kiss (or do we mean anointed our cup?) with oil from the communion of our olives. Before the thought of amalgamating had so much as crossed our minds. Positively mystical. All of a sudden Ciccio is struck by some inspiration. Wait a minute, he says, and dashes off into the kitchen. He returns a few minutes later looking very pleased with himself, the olive-oil bottle in one hand and a Magic Marker in the other. He has written something on the bottle. I squint at it in the candlelight. What does it say? I can hardly read it.

It says '*L'Olio dell'Amore*', he tells me, leaning over to give me a long, lingering kiss.

Beautiful, I say, giving him one back.

But look at it properly, he says once we've let go of one another. He moves a candle right up close so I can see. I've written it in English, he tells me. Especially for you. Finally I make it out. It says 'LOVE OIL'.

Yuk! I say. You can't call it that!

Why not? says he.

Because it sounds like some kind of repellent bodily fluid!

Ciccio does the what-on-earth-are-you-on-about gesture – the one where you turn your hand palm up, put all the fingertips together, and waggle it up and down from the wrist as if you were testing the weight of some particularly heavy fig.

But you just agreed it was a beautiful name! he says.

Not in English, I say. It does not translate well. Oil is not a word of beauty in my language, the way it is in yours. It's too closely related to 'oily'.

Ridiculous, says Ciccio. Your language is mad. Or you are. What's wrong with oily, anyway?

Well, I say, in Italian it would be something like '*unto*' – greasy, unctuous.

Yuk! says Ciccio.

See? say I.

Anyway, according to Ciccio, we're talking more unction than unctuousness. In this olive-obsessed part of the world there couldn't be a more perfect omen. No troubled waters for us: our future together will be *liscio come l'olio* – smooth like oil.

6

And indeed, life has proceeded very calmly for a fortnight or
so. Ciccio has stayed up here rather a lot, and so far the only
thing I don't find positively lovable about him is his alarm
clock. And that isn't an integral part of his personality, I
suppose; it's just that he has to go to market at crack of dawn
several times a week for his restaurant supplies. Today, though,
dawn has hardly begun to crack, there is only the faintest
glimmer of pale, thin light, and something loud has woken
me up. That darned alarm again? No. Not the alarm. Shouting.
And barking. Somebody is shouting their head off right above
the house, up among the oak trees, and they've brought a
pack of dogs with them. Unless it's an innocent passer-by
being attacked by a pack of dogs? No wonder nobody wants
to live in the countryside here. You never get a decent night's
sleep. I extricate myself crossly from the sheets. Ciccio mutters
something uncomplimentary and covers his head. I struggle
towards the garden door, grabbing a dressing-gown. But the
door won't budge more than a couple of inches. Some solid
yet shifting weight seems to be pressing against the outside of
it. Shoulder to the wood, I finally get a gap big enough to
poke my head out. Beyond the doorway, before the hillside
plunges down another terrace, the eye usually meets several
yards of grassy turf under the two big gnarled olive trees that
stand outlined against the sky. But now, here in the half-light,
there is only a pallid, white nothingness. Vertigo strikes. The
ground has vanished. I blink hard. Still nothing. A formless,
heaving type of nothing, at about waist height. No, wait a

minute: not just formless, I see now, but hairy too. The barking is still going on, but these things are not dogs. I begin to distinguish pairs of eyes amongst the heaving and the hairiness; eyes scarily unlike any of God's friendly and familiar creatures. Brain creaking into gear, I identify the problem. Their pupils are not round, but oblong. Some of them have horns. Goats. A milling herd of goats, filling the landscape as far as the eye can see.

A series of shouts and another hairy apparition, this time in bearded human form, comes bounding towards me from the hillside above, agitatedly waving a large stick, leaping down the terraces and sending stones flying off the tops of the walls. (Why do people do this all the time? Why can't they just walk down the path, for goodness' sake? Do they not know how much work it is to put a terrace wall back up?)

Buongiorno, I say politely; then find myself wondering whether it should have been '*Salve*'. Faced with the incomprehensible, my brain has gone on to automatic pilot and randomly focused on matters of protocol. '*Salve*', as well as having the appeal of a couple of thousand years of history behind it, being something the ancient Romans used to go around saying to one another, is still the preferred greeting of mountain folk round here. *Buongiorno*, on the other hand, is more for the jacket-and-tie brigade; to be used once you're past the level crossing that divides the tidy townsfolk of nice flat Diano Marina from the olive-farming hill-dwellers. This individual looks distinctly as if he may never have got that close to civilization.

The new arrival is too busy trying to get his goats in order to care for such niceties. He just goes on shouting and stick-waving. Suddenly I'm wide enough awake to realize that all my new geranium cuttings, the pretty ivy-leaved trailing ones, as well as a pair of avocado trees in pots that I was about to plant, and of which I have high hopes since I saw one actually fruiting in Imperia recently, are somewhere underneath these animals. I abandon etiquette and add my own cries of alarm and despair to the general pandemonium. Ciccio, apparently under the impression that all this racket is being produced by some electronic means, joins in from the bedroom, roaring at me to turn it down.

The tidal wave of goats is now gradually receding up the hill, half a dozen dogs barking to the rear of it, and the hairy being who is, notionally at least, in charge of the animals has descended to my level. He apologizes for the disturbance – I should think so – and introduces himself. He is Tommaso, and his goat sheds are over there (he waves the stick inland and uphill) above Roncagli. He was taking the goats up on to the steep scrubland above the oaks for the first time this autumn, he's just brought them back from their summer pasture up near France, and he can't understand what possessed his dogs. They suddenly swerved downhill and brought the flock here. Tommaso has a strange bony face, his beard a short frill round the edges of it. No hanky on his head, either: an odd bod, evidently. All respectable farming people around here wear a knotted hanky when working. And they have a moustache, not a beard. He is so desperate to placate me that I am certain he has broken some iron rule of mountain protocol. It really was his dogs that brought the flock down here, he keeps repeating. He couldn't stop them.

I am not impressed by his attempt to blame poor dumb dogs for his own herding failures. Perhaps it shows.

We must come up to his place, try some of his goat cheese, he says desperately. Or will he drop us a wee gift over later on?

Why all this unsolicited generosity in a person unknown? Probably people are supposed to pay you for grazing or something. I can't see why I should mind, in a general way, about the odd goat. In fact, if only he'd brought them earlier, and on to the lower terraces, we would have been saved all that hot noisy strimming to clear the ground ready for laying the olive nets. Should I propose a deal?

Not just now though. Too early in the day for speech. The only thing I find I can really take an interest in at this precise moment, now that the goats have receded and I've managed to see in the half-light that my geraniums haven't been either eaten or squashed and the avocados look more or less unscathed, is coffee. I ask your man if he'd like a coffee too; can't just stomp off and leave him, I suppose. He is clearly relieved that I'm not going to do whatever it was he thought I might do, and agrees to a coffee with alacrity.

I go inside: and I don't invite my beardy guest to follow me. Not from rudeness, but for his own good. Ask an unaccompanied Ligurian countryman into your home, and you'll be lucky if he doesn't faint from the terror and embarrassment. I know this from experience, having innocently tried it out on various of my neighbours when we first arrived in these parts. Our neighbour Nino was my first victim; a tall skinny serious man, very shy, who does twice as much work on his olive trees as the whole of the rest of the valley put together, which means that we see a lot of him up here. Ever since the side wall of his *rustico* fell down in an earth tremor – it did have an enormous crack in it already, though – he had nowhere of his own to hang out any more, and often took his coffee break with us. So on this particular day of blazing hot sun it seemed only polite to ask him indoors into the cool of the house. But in spite of the fact that we were on friendly enough terms to be receiving regular bulletins on how his wife was doing in hospital, on the outrageously high estimates he was being given for putting his *rustico* wall back up, on the outrageously low price he was expecting to get for his olives this year, and so forth, an awful hunted look came over his features at the very suggestion that he might cross our threshold alone and unchaperoned. I just managed to retrieve the situation, seeing him so pale and goggle-eyed with horror – he couldn't actually refuse to come in, could he, without being openly rude? – by pretending that I had never meant to suggest such a thing at all; it was a misunderstanding caused by my imperfect grasp of Italian. What I'd meant was, why didn't he come under the lean-to roof that makes a sort of porch outside the door, where there is a comfy bench out of the sun? Phew!

Nino happily colluded in fudging over the enormity of my *faux pas*, and all was well. Naturally, I tried the same thing out later on Ugo, who has the olive grove to the landward side of us, and is altogether a more robust type of character, just to check whether we were looking at a fixed rule of social behaviour or a simple personality problem of Nino's. Same hunted look. No, no, I'll just take it out here on the bench, thanks. The hills, as we know, are full of eyes, and they are not always of the square-pupilled variety. A single pair of San Pietro eyes, for example, could make a meal (as it were) of a lone male entering the house of two Foreign Females.

In I go, then, leaving Tommaso outside, and put the coffee on. The welcoming sounds of the espresso pot unscrewing, the tapping out of last night's coffee grounds, the water running, the gas going on, finally drag Ciccio from his bed. He neatly evades guest and goats by coming right round the house and up the back steps. (The sister and I have managed to build an extra set of steps on the inland side of the house, so you can do a whole circuit of the place these days; but we still haven't quite got round to the trickier question of an indoor staircase. If it's raining when you want to go to bed or bathroom, you still have to take an umbrella. Luckily, it hardly ever rains.) Ciccio creeps carefully into the kitchen. Who is it? Is it someone you know? he asks. Don't let on I'm here, for God's sake. It'll be all round the valley by lunchtime.

How sweet of Ciccio to be worried about my reputation! Not that I've got much of one to lose after all these years of eccentric behaviour. Never seen him before in my life, I say, pointing out our uninvited guest, who is now lurking under the lean-to roof. Funny: I thought I knew everyone up here by now. Anyway, I add, he must have heard you shouting, and it'll look a lot odder to be hiding a man in my bedroom than to be displaying him openly. Do you know him? Ciccio peers out through the glass. No, he doesn't think so. Thank the Lord. But what's he doing hanging about out there?

I'm making him some coffee, I say.

Why on earth haven't you invited him inside, then? says Ciccio. You can't offer someone a coffee and then leave them dangling about outside the door in the dark like that! Have you no manners? Ciccio goes out on to the terrace, handshaking and *salve*-ing (See? I knew it should be *salve*), and now Tommaso comes in and sits down at the kitchen table as if it were the most natural thing in the world. Well, really! You have a whole new set of rules and regulations to learn, evidently, when you've got a man in the house to protect you. Or to protect your guests, rather.

I lean on the marble sink-and-drainer arrangement, waiting for the espresso pot to finish its hissing business, while Ciccio and Tommaso catch up on one another's pedigrees. Tommaso's family land is up above Roncagli. Ah, did he and his father once have a fishing boat? Epifanio, yes! And Ciccio's land is above Diano Castello, near the pinewood. Ah, is he Giacomo's neighbour? And so on. The usual lightly abridged version of Genesis you get when two people meet round here. Oddly, though, Ciccio does not mention the restaurant. Is he trying to conceal his identity? The coffee gurgles through at last, and I take it off the stove. In the sudden silence we all hear a rather loud outbreak of clicking from somewhere high above the table, up in the beams.

What's that? says Tommaso in alarm, goggling at the ceiling.

Ciccio doesn't know, but it's nothing to worry about. It's been going on for ages.

Hasn't it? he says, turning to me.

Yes, I say. But there's nothing up there at all when you climb up to look.

As long as it's not something eating the beams, says Tommaso prophetically.

7

Two of the goats seem to have returned. I can see them through the doorway, over by the olive tree on the far side of the terrace. No, wrong shape for goats. A pair of large white shaggy dogs – dogs, now I come to look at them more closely, that I know rather well. Dogs that kept popping in to visit me, off and on, this spring; a matching pair, identical except for their noses, one pink, one black. I thought they were strays, and grew rather fond of them in spite of their being filthy and smelly, and in spite of (or was it because of?) their being utterly impervious to all my attempts to get rid of them. They would pretend to leave, shuffling forlornly off as far as the other end of the terrace, keeping on turning to gaze hopefully at me in case I'd changed my mind, and eventually settle down, hangdog, behind the first of Nino's olive trees, just over the invisible border between my terrain and his. (Amazing how a Ligurian dog has no trouble spotting these invisible frontiers; it took Lucy and me, a pair of mere English humans, months, if not years, to grasp exactly where our land finished and our neighbours' land began. In fact, yes, we'd already been here a good four years when we got into bad trouble for pinching Nino's very important pile of flat stones to pave the muddy bit outside our back door, having mistakenly thought (a) that they were on our land and (b) that since they had been lying there for years, overgrown with creepers, they must be a natural phenomenon. Wrong on both counts. They were on Nino's land; and they had once formed part of the roof of his *rustico*, before he re-did it with tiles. And if we'd only asked him first, he would have let us have them, no problem. Oh, the guilt.)

Half an hour later, here the dogs would be again, wiry fur full of dreadlocks and burrs, lying immovably, doggedly, right outside the door like a pair of great hairy draught-excluders. They had obviously been well trained, Italian style, never to come into the house. So they just got as close as they possibly could, wagging their tails ecstatically whenever they caught sight of me. Of course, I took pity on them and put them out a few scraps. Bad mistake. Now I would find them waiting for me when I came home, sitting on the bend of the road where I park the car, lolloping joyfully in and out of my legs as I lugged the shopping along the path, tripping me up irritatingly on the narrow bits. Still, it's undeniably heartwarming to have some living being, even a matted and hairy one, care whether you come home or not. This is what comes of sisters abandoning you all alone up a foreign hill. Maybe I would adopt them after all?

The dogs had definitely decided to adopt me, at any rate; they took to showing off their guarding skills whenever they popped over, baring their teeth and growling ferociously at visitors. In this case, Franco, who immediately spotted that they were working dogs. A breed called Maremmano, he said; great for herding except for one small defect. When they reach a certain age, they are prone to suddenly going off their heads, destroying everything around them, and having to be put down. Cheering news.

Somebody, said Franco, shooing them away with his stick in an authoritative Ligurian manner that made them cringe and slink off a good twenty yards – ah, a stick, that's what I was missing – somebody must be seriously put out by their periodic disappearances. I would not be thanked for keeping them away from their job. I was being irresponsible and unneighbourly, and should drive them away home. With a beating, if necessary.

I had always imagined, thoughtlessly, that working dogs must like their work. I saw now that they had even less luck than us humans in these matters. No changing career midstream; no downshifting. And certainly no spur-of-the-moment breaks away. At least humans don't get beaten with sticks into the bargain. Not in most parts of the world, that is. Luckily for my new nice-to-dogs self-image, something in Franco's manner, presence, smell, or perhaps just stick, reminded them of their duties, and they had vanished within the hour. I did wonder at this one small wave of a stick having been so effective that the pair of them never returned at all, ever; but here is the explanation. They've been away all summer, up where the grass grows green, keeping their flock in some alpine meadow.

I take my coffee out on to the terrace. Daylight has broken properly now, and I'm looking forward to being reunited with pink-nose dog, my favourite, and hoping that he hasn't yet become violently insane as predicted by Franco. No: he flops docilely over on to his back, as always, hoping for a belly-scratch.

Do I know his dogs, then? asks Tommaso through the doorway, surprised by this intimacy.

Yes, I say nonchalantly. I've met them quite a few times wandering about these parts. I thought they were strays.

Strays? says Tommaso. Not a bit of it! This spring they developed a terrible habit of vanishing every now and then, though, deeply inconveniencing their owner, who had to spend all day rounding up his abandoned goats every time they did it. He had to get those other dogs as back-up in the end. (Ah, I did think there seemed to be an excessive number of dogs about earlier. My fault, it turns out.) You must have been feeding them, he says accusingly, obviously feeling a lot better about his recent trespassing now. Didn't she, eh, Peppino? he shouts through the doorway.

Which one is Peppino? I ask, looking to create a diversion.

Both called Peppino, says Tommaso with great satisfaction. A stroke of genius. It occurred to him in an inspired moment what an enormous amount of wear and tear on the vocal chords he would save if he just used the one name for both dogs.

Che furbizia! says Ciccio: very cunning! Very Ligurian, too!

Ah, si, si! agrees Tommaso with a grin, doing the finger-under-the-eyeball gesture for *furbizia*. Waste not, want not!

Peppino! I say experimentally. And yes, both dogs rush back over to me. It dawns on me now that it really was their own idea to bring their herd down here. Bitter experience has taught them that there is nothing humans like so much as to have a load of goats brought to them; and in their doggy simplicity, they have brought me as many as they could manage. Poor dogs! Better show no sign of appreciating the gift, though, for fear of a repeat performance.

I go back indoors, wondering whether this is the right moment to offer to adopt a few goats for lawn-mowing purposes. But Ciccio and our guest are now in deep debate at the kitchen table. They seem to be discussing Tommaso's cheese enterprise; Tommaso is running through his wares, while Ciccio busily takes notes on the back of an envelope. Small fresh cheeses, large fresh ones, matured ones in various sizes, goats' milk ricotta; and their prices pre- and post-tax, for small orders and for bulk buys. In amongst this, they are lamenting the days when tax evasion was the norm in this country. What a bitter pill it is to swallow, they agree, bonding away like mad, when you've spent your youth apprenticed to highly accomplished tax-evaders, learnt your trade from men who've never paid a *lira* to the state in their lives; only to find, when it ought by rights to be your turn, that you can't get away with a thing any more! *Euh!* says Tommaso. The artisans of today are paying for the sins of their fathers. Or rather, they're paying for the sins of other people's fathers, because if it was your own father, you'd be rolling in money already and you wouldn't give a dry fig, would you? Still, Tommaso's mother, he says, made and sold cheese all her life, and nobody so much as mentioned tax to her!

Ciccio finishes writing, folds up his envelope, stuffs it into a back pocket, and turns to me triumphantly. Evidently he has given up his attempt to conceal his restaurant connection. Guess what? he says. Tommaso is ideally placed to supply cheeses for the restaurant! His headquarters are in the hills directly above Roncagli, which means that his stuff could be delivered by hand, or rather by foot, over the mule-tracks.

The pair of them look at me expectantly, Tommaso winking away, a big grin on his face; Ciccio giving me a conspiratorial gleam. But though I do notice the unusually geographical use of the phrase 'ideally placed', I don't get it.

I knew the Slow Food Movement was going from strength to strength in this country, I say, but I didn't realize the return to the good old ways included the delivery methods too.

What did she say? asks Tommaso. The what movement?

Slow Food Movement, I repeat. You know, movement against Fast Food?

The Italians have adopted the phrase 'fast food' in English; and have gone on to invent 'slow food' to describe their own traditional way of eating. The Slow Food Movement is pledged to defend Italy to the death against Mr McDonald and his ilk. But Italians have also adopted their own pronunciation of 'Slow Food'. Lots of emphasis on the first word, none on the second: and make 'food' rhyme with 'hood'. I try again, remedying these defects, and all becomes clear.

Ah, of course, says Tommaso, the Sloffood Movement! Ha, ha! Yes, maybe this way of transporting dairy products would be slower; but not by much, not when you think of how many hairpin bends you save by cutting straight across country.

And it would also, much more interestingly to both parties, avoid the eagle eye of the ubiquitous Finance Police, who hang about the roadsides, stopping and inspecting suppliers' vans and their VAT forms and their Bills of Lading and all the other pointless and troublesome documentation with which the Italian State delights in tormenting its innocent citizens whenever they try to turn an honest penny. The *Finanza* would certainly not be staking out mountain pathways, or stopping rucksack-laden hill-walkers. And, still chuckling, Tommaso goes off to round up his dogs and his goats for the trip home.

Yes indeed! Sloffood! Ha, ha!

Ciccio and I go back to bed to recover. It's not even seven o'clock yet. Funny, though, says Ciccio dreamily as he snuggles back under the sheets, that Tommaso should be at large up here in the hills. Last he heard, the man was supposed to be locked away in Genoa jail . . .

Prison? Tommaso? I am startled. What would a goat-herd be doing in prison? Fiddling the cheese-tax office on a massive scale?

No, no, says Ciccio. Marijuana. Three whole terraces of the stuff, I think it was. He'd planted them in among a load of tomato canes for camouflage.

I am gobsmacked. I found Tommaso completely convincing as a local goat person born and bred. But, I protest, he must be sixty if he's a day!

Yes, says Ciccio, and do I think marijuana was invented yesterday? It's been around for centuries. Millennia. I can take it from him: Tommaso's goat land of today was his grass land of yore. And that'll be why I haven't met him before: he wasn't here.

In his youth, Ciccio has heard, Tommaso worked as a fisherman beside his old dad; but when the fishing collapsed, leaving just the tiny fleet in Imperia, he sold the family boat and got a job as a sailor on the big Mediterranean cargo ships; ships that plied between Greece, Spain, North Africa, and were strongly suspected at the time of smuggling quantities of cheap foreign non-extra-virgin olive oil into the Ligurian ports of Genoa and Imperia, thus contributing to the ruin of many a poor local olive-farmer. In those days the big olive-oil packing plants could still get away with murder; and a lot of their foreign clients wouldn't have known the difference anyway. That's probably where Tommaso developed his interest in marijuana, says Ciccio, on his seafaring travels. Then he retired – or so he claimed – up to his family *campagna* in the hills; only to be caught growing the marijuana.

I am chastened; I should have learnt by now that peasant farming is not some hermetically sealed lifestyle cut off from the rest of the world. Especially in a land of migratory folk like this one. Several places round here claim to be the true birthplace of Christopher Columbus, one of the better-known Ligurian travellers. Among them is a small olive-farming town a couple of valleys along from here, quite remarkably similar to San Pietro . . .

Ciccio just hopes, he says, that Tommaso's equivocal position in the local community will cause him to keep his mouth firmly shut about catching us up here together.

Oh, don't worry about my reputation, I say. People in San Pietro don't do modern live-in relationships much themselves, but they've got used to them in the mass media. They don't find it too shocking any more.

But no. It's not my reputation, but his own, that Ciccio is worried about: and not Diano San Pietro, but Diano Castello, under whose jurisdiction his own family lives, that must be kept in the dark. His mother doesn't even know we're seeing one another, does she? That's why he didn't want to give Tommaso too many clues about his identity. But then the cheese opportunity came up and in the excitement he somehow forgot the need for dissembling. He just hopes he hasn't landed himself in it.

(Landed himself in what, I wonder? Why shouldn't his mother know? Is it our sleeping together she'd disapprove of, or me personally? I hope not: I've always liked her a lot.)

Well, I say, quelling the paranoia, Tommaso is in no position to point the finger, is he? And who would he be telling our business to, up here in the hills? No. His arrival at such a compromising moment was purest bad luck. Nobody's ever around up here normally, except during the daytime olive-farming hours, when Ciccio's presence, if spotted, has no special significance. No reason why anything like that should happen again.

And there we leave it – until the next outbreak of neighbours at antisocial hours, a mere week later.

8

We're tired, it's the middle of the night, we've eaten and drunk too much, and there's no moon at all. As we drive up the last stretch of road before Besta de Zago, I am rooting about desperately in my bag for a torch. No. Nothing. Why do I never remember to bring a torch unless it's already dark when I go out? We're going to have to feel our way step by step along the path to the house in pitch darkness, worrying all the way about whether we're past the narrow precipice bit yet, the bit where the path's only a couple of feet wide and there's a high terrace wall to the right and a horrible ten-foot drop into a bramble patch to the left.

Once we've parked the car and switched off the headlights, though, we are surprised to make out, ahead of us through the trees, a faint pool of light. Mysterious. Can it really be coming from the house? You can't tell from here. We're on the wrong side of the haystack-sized rock that looms over neighbour Nino's ruined *rustico*, and of rather a lot of olive trees. Still, where else would it be coming from? I must have left the bottom terrace light on. Idiot. The solar batteries will be flat as a pancake, and like as not the whole system will switch itself off as soon as we turn on the living-room light. Something urgently needs to be done about my electricity situation. Never mind, says Ciccio. At least we can see the path now.

But now I don't think the light's coming from the house at all. There seems to be something oddly wavery about the quality of it. It couldn't be a forest fire starting up, could it?

No, it's much too quiet . . . you get loud crackling and roaring from a forest fire. Could it be one far away behind the ridge, though . . . ? We head along the path in single file, breath bated. Past the precipice, and we see at last that there is no forest fire: nor is the light coming from my house. It is down on Anna and Tonino's land. There are voices down there, too. Very strange. What can they be doing up here at this time of night?

Never mind. Ours is not to reason why: not in this state. I for one am never going to eat or drink ever again. Only another twenty yards to go. Still can't see the house, though. It is a sad fact that you can never see the place at all unless you're practically standing outside the door. Invisible from here, to the seaward side: and from the front it's even worse – the terrace ends fifteen feet from the house, and from the next level down, you're too low down to see anything but a bit of roof and a chimneypot, veiled by a pair of stout olive trees. Enough privacy, you might think, to save you from being pestered by neighbours. Especially in the middle of the night, when neighbours ought to be tucked up in their beds down in the village, getting in a good night's rest before their wake-up call, six sonorous bongs and a breathless bing from the San Pietro *campanile*. Not tonight, though. We've just fallen gratefully through the front door and turned on the lights – the batteries not being flat after all – when an agitated squeaky-spring voice starts calling up through the trees.

Anna-a-a! Anna-a-a-a! *Venite!*

Yes. It's Anna. And there's no doubt about it: she means me. (I often get called Anna, too, here, because 'Anni' means 'Years', which is much too peculiar to be anybody's name.) She doesn't mean me alone, though. She must have heard us talking, because she didn't use the singular, '*vieni*'. She said

46

'*venite*': plural. Could we just pretend we haven't heard? The thought of trailing right down past the well and through the brambly bits by the bottom track to find out what she wants is very unappealing. Please let me go to bed!

But the screech is renewed.

Anna-a-a!

I give in. They've seen the lights go on, anyway, I say; we'll have to go. We can't be so un-neighbourly. Maybe it's an emergency?

We drag ourselves back out of the house, grabbing a couple of torches from the efficient drawerful I never remember to take out with me, and totter off through the groves, calling and responding as we go.

Anna-a-a! I reply. *Veniamooo!* We're coming!

Anna-a-a-a! calls Anna.

Anna-a-a-a-! I call back.

Anna-a-a-a! calls she.

You sound like a pair of screech owls looking for love, says Ciccio. He says it, moreover, in a distinctly grumpy tone of voice. Can he be blaming me? Yes, he can. They're not his neighbours. He doesn't even know them. He's tired. And it's the middle of the damned night.

Veniiiite! shouts Anna again.

Arriviamoooo! I shout back, dragging the reluctant Ciccio down the path in my wake. And it's a good job we went. There really is an emergency. The eerie flickering light of a low bonfire illuminates Anna sitting on a low bench under the spreading fig-tree outside her *rustico*, her eyes dark with exhaustion, surrounded by an unimaginably enormous quantity of tomatoes. A tomato landscape glowing in the firelight, overflowing from crates, from bowls, from buckets, from ancient tin baths, from oil drums. Tomatoes whole, tomatoes peeled, tomatoes puréed into *passata*.

You've got to help us, she says, waving desperately at the rampart of old screw-top jars piled to one side of her, a dim hurricane lamp planted among them. The mincer went wrong, Tonino had to go all the way to Imperia for a spare part. And she'd already blanched all the tomatoes in boiling water to get the skins off . . . They've sat in the heat of the sun all afternoon now, and if they aren't all got into their jars and brought to boiling point before morning, they'll have gone off in the heat, turned acid, and be fit for nothing. Look at it all! she says, almost in tears, going on ladling *passata* at breakneck speed from the bucket at her side into the set of jars at her feet, hardly pausing to glance up at us as she speaks. A whole year's tomato harvest about to go to waste, a whole year's *sugo* for the pasta lost . . . !

I do look: it's terrifying.

Yes, give us a hand, for the Love of God! shouts Tonino, who is standing inside the *rustico* battling with a great silver mincing machine, red in the face from his exertions, his bush of grey curls standing out from his head as though he'd been electrocuted, his knotted hanky cast aside. He is pouring peeled tomatoes into the maw of the machine one-handed from yet another bowl, winding away with the other like a man possessed, while an erratic stream of *passata*, blood-red in the light of the hurricane lamp, spurts from it into yet another bucket. The eerie light out here is coming not from just the one bonfire, I see now; there are three of them burning in pits in the ground a few yards apart. Each fire has a simmering oil drum balanced over it on a few small rocks; each drum is filled to the brim with jars of tomato *passata* that rattle gently against one another with the rolling boil. A kind of gigantic outdoor version of jam-making.

I'm quite desperate to lie down and have a nap. But it is not to be. *La terra e bassa*, the earth is low, as they say round here, miming the peasant farmer's backache for you in case you don't get it.

All right, I say, rising heroically to the occasion. What do we have to do?

Ciccio, even more heroically, doesn't need to be told. Without so much as an introduction, he's dashed in and taken over the pouring-bowl from Tonino. No more fits and starts now; a strong steady stream of puréed tomato pours from the mincer into the bucket. Something tells me he's done this before.

Till now Anna has been too panic-stricken to notice who or what my companion was. Now the thing sinks in at last. A man! It is the middle of the night! And she has caught me up at the house with a man! I get an extremely sharp sidewise look. Isn't he that lad that runs the restaurant? Ciccio, she thinks they call him?

I admit that he is.

Engaged to be married, are you, then? Anna heard a rumour that I was seeing him, she says, but she didn't know we'd got engaged.

Well, no, we're not exactly engaged, I say, wishing Ciccio would come back out and answer this one. What am I supposed to say? I just hope Anna doesn't know his mother. We've hardly been together any time at all, I add hopefully; then realize too late that that sounds even worse . . .

Inside the *rustico*, Tonino's minced-tomato bucket is almost full. Ciccio swings into greased-lightning action, swapping an empty bucket for the full one, which he whisks out here and dumps at Anna's feet ready for potting, then darts back in to carry on pouring, the whole move so nifty that Tonino's tomato-stream is hardly broken at all. Anna, registering the great competence of the Lad from the Restaurant, is clearly considering very carefully the correct moral position to take in this irregular situation. After all, a man who bears himself so nobly in the teeth of a major tomato crisis is not easily come by.

She withholds her verdict for now. Get that other ladle over there, she says to me, the one hanging off the door, look. Help me filling the jars. Right to the top, now: but not so close that the *passata* will be touching the lid. *Vabbene?*

Vabbene, I say, doing my best.

No, no! Too full! It'll taste of metal from the lid!

I try again.

No, no! Too much space at the top now, it'll go mouldy . . .

Well! How absurdly temperamental the stuff is. If it doesn't go acid outside the pot, it goes metallic or mouldy or whatever inside it at the drop of a hat. I can certainly see why so many people have given this *passata*-making tradition up. Especially when the stuff hardly costs anything in the shops. Though this, I'm told, is down to the underpaid work of poor migrant Senegalese folk on the tomato plantations down in the South of this country . . . Still, would even the evil exploiters of migrant labour sink so low as to drag exhausted people from their beds in the middle of the night to slave away over their hot tomatoes . . . ?

Maybe they would, come to think of it. Just as I'm getting rather competent at jar-filling, and telling myself that it's not so bad really, Anna bustles off into the *rustico* and reappears with another few hundred jars, which she starts busily cleaning out, leaving me alone at the filling station. Wail!

Ciccio and Tonino meanwhile, sweating and *porca-madonna*-ing, using a pair of rolled-up T-shirts to protect their hands, are grappling in the firelight with the great boiling oil-drums, heaving them off the heat. Us women will unpack them when they've cooled down a bit, says Anna. Now the men drag another three empty drums over and sit them over the fires; add a couple of hissing buckets of water to each. Ciccio is making horrible faces at me from behind Tonino's back as he works; miming a left hook to the jaw. My jaw, it seems. Outrageous! What have I got to do with it? It's his country, after all. Nothing like this would ever happen to you in Shepherd's Bush, mate.

Anna stops at last to make a pot of coffee, balancing a blackened espresso pot on the edge of one of the fire pits. Thank God! Maybe it'll give me the energy to see this thing through. After a longish period of silent sipping while she wrestles with the issue, and a series of sharp glances in Ciccio's direction – he and Tonino seem to be getting on very well back in the *rustico*, guffawing away over their mincer – Anna now faces up to the knotty moral question of Ciccio's presence up here. She begins by announcing that she knows his mother.

O Lord. What to make of this? On the one hand, to admit to knowing a person's mother is to admit them to the fold of acceptable humanity. But on the other, it is exactly what Ciccio won't be wanting to hear.

At least, Anna goes on, she and Francesca always say hello when they bump into one another on market day in Diano Marina. A nice woman. Very proud of her son. Rightly so, as we see now. Just the man you've always needed about the place. He certainly is, I agree, trying not to sound too enthusiastic. Don't want to give the impression that passion, not agricultural prowess, is my bottom line.

She's not bothered, herself, she goes on, about what people get up to in private, but you know what men are like. So conservative about these things. We'd best tell her husband that Ciccio and I are already *affidanzati*, engaged, but just haven't quite got round to announcing it yet. Better for my reputation too, anyway. Word gets out in no time in a place like San Pietro.

It surely does. I can't help feeling, though, that it might have got out quite a lot slower if only I hadn't kindly come down here to help a neighbour in need.

Anna goes to empty the hot jars from their oil drums now, and I'm given a new job. A nice easy one. All I have to do is to wrap every single jar in newspaper before we pack them into the new drums to boil. Every single one? Yes, say the experts. Otherwise they'll bang against one another when the water starts to bubble, and they might crack.

Some three hundred jars later, Anna produces a huge round fresh *focaccia* dimpled with onion, olive oil and sea salt crystals – a thing that used to be one of my favourite local snacks until I resolved never to eat again – and starts toasting it over the fire. Its perfume is soon filling the air, and I find that against all odds my appetite has unexpectedly returned. Tonino and Ciccio come out to join us, bringing a couple of bottles of Tonino's *vino d'uva* from his store in the *rustico*. Now my resolve never to drink again evaporates too.

Feeling much better now, I energetically wrap untold quantities of newsprint round untold numbers of jars: pile them into drums over face-scorching fires: help heave the drums off again to cool once they've boiled, scalding myself several times: unload more hot jars: load up more cold ones. Now Tonino joins me in the jar-wrapping zone for a rest and another glass of wine. Anna is out of earshot stoking a fire. Tonino leans confidentially over my hillock of jars-in-paper.

Anna's putting a brave face on it, he says, but she's an old-fashioned woman at heart. It doesn't bother him, of course, but his wife will have been very perturbed to find us up here together, all alone in the middle of the night. So he and Ciccio have agreed on the quiet that it would be best if we told Anna that we've just got engaged, and haven't quite got round to announcing it publicly yet.

Good plan, I say. Why not?

Next time Ciccio and I are out of earshot, we congratulate one another *sotto voce* on our phantom engagement. Ciccio can't believe he ever thought my house was a quiet, isolated retreat, he says. And now do I see why he didn't want his mother to know? He's not even related to Anna and Tonino, hardly knows them at all, and look at the performance!

Not a shotgun wedding, I say, giggling inanely, but a Sloffood engagement. Goats' cheese brought us Tommaso; and *passata* brought us Anna and Tonino. A cheese-and-tomato engagement.

Ciccio just looks at me quizzically. There's no particular affinity between generic cheese and tomato in the Italian worldview; only between specific cheeses and specific tomato dishes. Probably due to the serious shortage of generic cheese here. A mozzarella and tomato salad, yes. A pizza with stracchino and tomato, fine. Parmesan on your pasta *al pomodoro*, certainly. But what recipe would combine goats' cheese and tomato *passata*? The *passata* would overwhelm the delicate goat flavour . . .

By the time the night begins to lighten and the bongs from the various *campanili* dotted around the hillsides amount to something worth counting, we have forgotten sleep and are suffering no more. There has been more *focaccia*; more wine; more coffee. We've almost stripped the tree bare of figs. And by now we're partying away as if we'd never done anything else all our lives but bottle and boil *sugo*.

When we finally finish the job, dawn is in the sky and cockerels have begun to crow up and down the valley. As we leave, Anna and Tonino both insist on shaking our hands and congratulating us on our engagement. They're so pleased to be the first to know! And we needn't worry – they won't be letting our secret out of the bag! Not until we want it made public! Meanwhile, as our engagement gift, we must take as much *sugo* as we can carry.

Ciccio and I trail off up the hill carrying a fine haul of hot jars, but otherwise utterly perplexed. All four of us know that this engagement doesn't exist. Correct. But then if all four of us are claiming that it does exist, for the benefit of at least one other person . . . and we've even got the engagement presents to prove it . . . Except that none of us is going to tell anybody, anyway, so does that mean . . . ? It's like some labyrinthine conundrum from a Borges tale. Best just to cross our fingers and go to bed. Sufficient unto the day is the evil thereof.

9

So, forward to my ailing roof. With one last conspiratorial smile from the bottom of the steps, Anna has left me up here with my deodorized bees and my putative beetles, and followed Franco down to San Pietro and lunch. All alone now, I slink nervously back into the house – no buzzing in the beams at the moment, praise the Lord – and edge round the room towards the bookcase, keeping my back to the wall. Yes: *Insects of Europe*. Here it is. I make a dash for open air and safety with my prize, riffling wildly through its pages. Where is that Handsome Bee? Knowledge, as they say, is Power.

The book reveals that the creature definitely doesn't bore holes in beams; and – here's a mercy! – it doesn't build vast colonies like its cousin the honey-bee either. It is an opportunist that just lays a few eggs in any nook or cranny in any dead wood it finds about the place. I suppose there's no denying that my roof beams are, from a certain short-sighted point of view, nothing but dead wood.

Franco is right, then: if the bees are just opportunists, the tunnels that gave them the opportunity must have been there already. Depressing. Beetles it is. I flick on through the book. Thousands upon thousands of beetles, their lifestyles alternately fascinating and repellent: but not one wood-tunnelling variety. By now I'm thirsting for action, any action, to protect my home. Keep a roof over my head, as they say. The words 'drooping like an egg' echo menacingly through my brain. Odd how powerful this image is, though, since there is nothing particularly droopy about an egg, is there?

I urgently need a Product. No chance of buying anything, even diesel, at this time of day, though. Diano Marina will be a ghost town, all shuttered up for the lunchtime break; nothing to be done till four o'clock when siesta time finishes and the shops open again. Still, I'm due to join the staff lunch up at the restaurant as soon as Ciccio's finished lunch service. Time, I think, to adopt the San Pietro view of the problem and get my man on the job. Collapsing beams, roofs destined to droop like eggs at the first sign of rain, may be a mere bagatelle to Ciccio. I set off down the path to my waiting *motorino*.

Except that now I discover that the *motorino*'s sitting here, just outside the house, at the bottom of the steps. Ciccio! Why on earth can't he leave the darned bike along the path, where I've always kept it? How right I was, I say crossly to myself, giving the nearest olive tree a violent kick and hurting my toe rather badly, when I decided years ago that it would be a very bad idea ever to get romantically involved with a local. Look what happens when you do. I'm just nipping down to the shop, he says, I'll take the *motorino*, it'll be quicker – and then he rides it right back, cross-country style, along the footpath to the house. He won't believe that I am seriously terrified of the return trip. Not all of it: just that narrow bit with the ten-foot drop to the right. It broadens out again after a couple of yards, of course: but this is immaterial. I panic anyway. And I can't get off and push the bike past the precipice, can I? Because you're rather a lot wider standing next to a bike pushing it than you are sitting on it, aren't you, so you don't fit. One or both of you will surely go tumbling into the bramble patch below.

I solved this problem very elegantly years ago by simply keeping my *motorino* on the far side of the pit of terror, by Nino's *rustico*-with-a-crack, and walking the twenty-odd yards between house and bike. But no Italian has ever agreed that riding a bike across a foot-wide precipice might be a problem at all. They just laugh. Not, probably, because they're cruel and heartless – though this may well be the case with Ciccio – but because Italians all learn to ride a *motorino* when they're about two years old, and by the time they've reached adolescence they've lost the ability to distinguish between a pair of wheels and a pair of feet. Unlike us nit-picking English.

Still, if I don't go on the bike, I've got to get into a car that's been sitting in the sun all morning baking to a nice, oven-like temperature; and then I'll be stuck with heaving a great hot metal box pointlessly around twelve hairpin bends. How much more appealing to waft peacefully on two wheels through a cool breeze down a nice straight mule-track. Go for it, girl. I grit teeth, stamp on pedal, rev handlebar accelerator wildly, zoom off. Manage, just, not to shut my eyes at the scary place. There. Heart thundering, but I've done it. On my way, and still alive. No thanks at all to that Ciccio.

I putter on down the mule-path, bursting with pride and adrenalin. Once you're out of the olive groves and you've met and crossed the zig-zagging asphalt road for the third (or is it fourth?) time, you're riding down the steep central alley that is still the heart of the village, squeezing under low archways with the houses crowding in on either side of you, their green slatted blinds firmly closed at this time of day against the sun. This alley used to be the main drag in the days before motor vehicles: it is cobbled and has shallow steps in it most of the way, steps being no more problem to a mule than they are to a human. The resourceful citizens of San Pietro have solved the slight problem the steps might present in these wheel-obsessed times by simply adding a small dollop of cement at the centre of each, and another dollop at either side, creating a set of bike-and-*Ape*-friendly miniature ramps. No car bigger than a Fiat 500 could fit down here anyway, so we don't worry about cars. I weave on through the jungles of potted plants that flank every doorstep, dodging the *nespolo* trees and grapevine arbours trained overhead for shade and snacks, while half-wild hill-cats, wiry skulking creatures whose job is to protect the stores in the cool ground-floor *cantina* beneath each home, the year's worth of wine, of olive oil, of firewood, of the many potted and bottled products of the vegetable garden, glare suspiciously from the shade of the side alleys as I roll elegantly past.

The last stretch before the bar-and-inn by the river is terrifyingly steep, with a hair-raisingly crooked double bend half-way down it under a narrow vaulted arch; and since I suffer from a superstitious fear that my brakes will surely fail as soon as I set my wheels on it, I always turn off on to the asphalt road here. It may be three times longer, but there's no risk of hurtling to sudden death. Surprisingly, seeing this is lunchtime and the place ought to be deserted, when I reach the crossroads I find the official Oldest Inhabitant of San Pietro, Umberto, sitting glumly on one of the wide slate steps where mule-track meets road, chin resting on knobbly stick, snow-white mustachios flowing. This crossroads is the perfect place for watching the world go by when you can't be bothered going all the way down to the bottom of the village to the church steps and the bar, and is often surprisingly busy. It has various nice high doorsteps and low walls for sitting on, with slate-slab tops worn smooth by centuries of resting bottoms. Also some good shady olive trees, a wooden bench, and a shrine with a Madonna. A Madonna seems to have been essential here in olden days for marking any and every crossroads, even on the tiniest of hillside paths, though nobody's ever been able to tell me why. I've heard that crossroads are very dangerous places in Irish folk tradition, though, places where supernatural beings of evil intent love to lurk. Maybe this was once a Europe-wide problem, and the Madonnas were the Italian solution to it? (It's a handy thing to know, anyway, if you're ever lost in the hills and wondering whether the path you've come across, the one that seems to lead off in the right direction, really is a path. Or is it just a goat-track that's going to peter out for good once you've got even more lost? If there's a Madonna at the crossing point, they are both definitely intentional human paths and hence must both lead somewhere. Where exactly is another matter; but wherever it may be, you will find people there. People who know where they are, too, which is bound to be of some help.)

Will I stop to say hello to Umberto? I'm sure he'd have a thing or two to tell me about beams and beetles. But then, how long might we take to get round to the question? He's a nice man, but a bit hard to get off his pet topics, which are (a) how old he is, (b) mules, and (c) his heroic days with the partisans when these hills were under occupation by the *Nazi-fascisti*. He raises his stick as I draw level. An order to stop, or just a friendly greeting? I dither for a second, squeak to a halt, and soon find myself sitting on the wall catching up with Umberto's latest news. Hot topic of the moment: how he came to eat his lunch early by accident today.

This is a surprising departure from the usual course of conversation with Umberto, which normally begins with both of us focusing on whether I remember what year he was born in. He's guessed, of course, that I'm even keener to know what he's doing out of doors at this time of day, when he ought to be at home eating, than I am to get my regular century-check. His lunch was left for him by one of his nieces this morning, he explains, but she didn't have time to stay and keep him company while he ate. (Most tragic and accusing tone here. Naughty, uncaring niece.) All alone like that, he somehow mistook the eleven bongs and a bing from the San Pietro church bell – which signify, of course, half-past eleven – for the twelve bongs of midday.

I commiserate, although I'm not quite sure why this would have stopped him taking his after-lunch nap – maybe he can't start napping till the one o'clock bong? Or did he just feel the need to publicize his desperate situation first? Soon we move on to birth dates; and thence, by a natural progression, to mules. How many of them Umberto used to own, how many of them there once were going up and down this mule-track, day and night, when it was one of the main highways along which essential salt supplies for the hinterland travelled, all the way up to Lombardy and the Piedmont (I'm not sure how authentic this one is: I'm told the salt trade petered out somewhere in the late Middle Ages, and I don't think even Umberto can be quite that old). We also cover the horribly unjust law, introduced perhaps a tad more recently than the late Middle Ages, which obliged you to attach an expensive tax disc to each mule, just like cars have today, as well as to waste money on a special bit of extra harness to hang it from; the last nail, according to Umberto, in the coffin of the mule transport industry round here . . .

Still, today I get two new items of information to add to my treasury: the first crops up when I suggest solicitously that there is rather a lot of *aria* blowing down the mule-track today, and hope it is not harming Umberto's health. The dangerousness of too much *aria*, air, is a matter that greatly preoccupies Ligurians. You can easily get a *colpo d'aria* from it. A *colpo di stato* is a *coup d'état*, practically a revolution, so you can see how serious a matter is the *colpo d'aria*. But Umberto explains to me in a most patronizing manner (hey, I'm meant to be doing the patronizing here) that on this particular crossroads you get a special type of *aria* that never harms you, however draughty it may seem. Really! Do you? This confirms, at last, my long-standing suspicion that the *aria* problem is all in the mind. When it comes to a good, central gossiping spot like this one, no amount of air can hold you back.

Now we move on to a feature of Umberto's life that I've not heard of before; the tax on bachelorhood, brought in by the fascists, which Umberto heroically resisted. Resisted, that is, in the sense of paying up rather than marrying to avoid it. And what a good move that was, he says. If he has lived longer than anyone else in the village, you can put it down to the lack of chattering women in his life. Well! This from a man who survives on the goodwill of an army of nieces, who never stops chattering, and who, moreover, happens to be talking to a woman at this very moment!

When I finally manage to slip in the matter of beam-eating beetles, though, neatly sidestepping the partisan period, Umberto comes up trumps. Of course he knows the things I mean, he says. They are called *tarli*, you come across them all the time, they're nothing to worry about. Of course my roof's not going to fall in! I should take no notice of Franco; he is nothing but a drama queen. (Or words to that effect.) Has Franco, perhaps, offered to do the job for me? he asks. Not yet? Ah. It's just that Umberto thought he might have done. And yes, a dose of diesel is the correct way to get rid of *tarli*; though there's some kind of new-fangled German poison these days, too, that he's heard you can get down in Diano Marina. Or was it Imperia? Anyway, no problem.

Very cheering. I leap back on to the *motorino* much reassured, and roll on down towards my tryst with Ciccio. Foolish of me to let Franco get me into a state about a bit of munching in the ceiling that's been going on for years with no ill effects. The bees are gone, *tarli* are nothing to worry about, and all is well.

I wonder, as I swirl round the next bend, whether I ought to stop and put my helmet on now I'm on the public road. There is actually a law these days that says you have to wear one, even on a tiny put-put *motorino* like mine. Fortunately local opinion has it that this law is only to be obeyed – especially on a hot day like today – once you are beyond the level crossing, gateway to Diano Marina, and has no force up here in the higher reaches of the valley. And who am I, after all, to quibble with local opinion? Especially in sweltering heat like this, when putting a miniature Turkish bath over the head is the last thing anyone in their right mind would be doing. I press on regardless through downtown San Pietro and cross the bridge over the Torrente San Pietro. At last I can get some speed up. Off I roar, a lovely cooling wind in my hair at last, along the deliciously hairpin-bend and pothole-free stretch of tarmac that leads back up the other side of the valley towards Diano Borganzo, lunch and beloved.

10

Up here the river is sunk deep between tall narrow banks; Ciccio's restaurant sits at the roadside end of an ancient row of houses perched along its edge. At the far end of the row, with its toes right down in the gully, stands a tall narrow water-mill, half derelict, with its great rusty mill-wheel still in place; another of Pierino-the-True-Ligurian's properties, I'm told. His grandfather was once the village olive-miller. Outside the restaurant, on the wide terrace perched above the rushing water, the usual few tables of foreign holidaymakers sit basking happily in the sunshine as they eat. Through the French windows, the usual few tables of Italians are sitting inside in the cool, doing the same. At the far end of the terrace nearest Pierino's house, shaded by the vines whose tangled trunks form a barrier between this level and the river below, stand another half-dozen tables. Here, outdoors yet in the shade, the races can occasionally be found intermingling. Only one Italian couple with a small child down there today, though – and Pierino, of course, sitting at his own table, identical to the restaurant ones. The table, and the daily lunch required to be placed upon it by Ciccio, are part of the terms of the restaurant lease. Pierino raises his fork in salutation and gives me a knowing wink. Waving back, resolutely ignoring the wink, I head for the kitchens, dodging Ciccio's partner Franchino who is dashing about serving, helped by young Alberto and Cousin Paletta, who often pops in to lend a hand when the removals-and-lorry-transport business is a bit slow.

Indoors, I skirt a few more tables of diners. Through the

kitchen hatch, Ciccio is going about his work over the great stainless steel pans, slicing, chopping, flipping and stirring. Yet I detect, from something oddly emphatic about his movements, that all is not well. No indeed. I enter the kitchens to find him positively sizzling with rage. He is at his wits' end, he says. It's the cats again. They're driving him mad. And a table of fifteen has just rung up to book for tonight, and he's only just finished making the *antipasti* for the twenty-four clients he knew he had, so now he's got to start all over again and he's not even going to be able to sit down to lunch with me . . . What ever possessed him to take up running a restaurant, when there are so many other careers in the world?

What does he mean, the cats are driving him mad? I ask.

Do I see that group of Italian diners sitting over by the window? I do: a very well-heeled-looking bunch, tucking into a large platter of golden-roasted quails with shallots, today's special. They're locals, Ciccio says, and influential people whose custom you would not want to lose, even if, at this precise moment, you might want to murder them. They began their meal outdoors on the patio, down at the shady end. Then half-way through their *antipasti* they suddenly called Franchino over and insisted on being moved indoors. They were unable to eat, Ciccio says, mimicking their tones of disgust, with all those nasty dirty kittens mewling around their feet.

What is to be done? Several feral cats have recently made their homes about the place, down by the river banks: very useful, too, with all those clients dropping tasty morsels of potential mouse-and-rat fodder about the terrace. The restaurant has just the one official cat, Oliver, a fine figure of a ginger tom who stays upstairs in Ciccio's tiny flat above the restaurant, hidden from the eyes of diners, during mealtimes. This is because, as far as most Italian customers are concerned, cats are merely a kind of higher vermin; dirty, unsavoury creatures that may be useful for keeping other, smaller vermin at bay, but should only get on with the job after the last client has left the restaurant, and not before.

Now, though, thanks no doubt to Oliver's extra-curricular activities, there are a dozen-odd tiny ginger feral kittens roaming about the place. And Germans and other such foreign folk (me, for example, until I was shown the error of my ways) dote upon the creatures, encourage them to hang around by feeding them scraps from their tables. Not good. In fact, Ciccio strongly suspects that it was the behaviour of the German family sitting near them, as much as the actual kittens, that the Italians found so revolting. The Germans were picking a kitten up and putting it on their laps; even – O horror! – letting their children touch it and then go straight on eating without washing their hands!

Paletta comes in to collect the pasta for table two. Look out there! says Ciccio, absently passing the plates to his cousin. There they go again! They've got three of them sitting up on their laps now.

So they have: and a few feet away from them in the shade, the young Italian couple, who would certainly slap the wrist of their own child if he so much as thought of touching a cat while eating, is casting them appalled glances.

I'll go out with a broom and shoo them away, will I? says Paletta helpfully.

No, certainly not, no brooms, says Ciccio, gazing hopelessly past his cousin, in the manner of one who has decided it's not worth trying to explain. The whole thing has given him a terrible pain in the side of his neck, he adds. His neck is *inchiodato*: nailed up. (Or nailed through, would it be?) A sort of permanent crick, anyway, he says plaintively, which is showing no sign of going away.

Ah. I did wonder why he was holding his head at that peculiar angle.

It's a nightmare, he goes on. If the foreign visitors see their hosts chasing hungry skinny cats away, they become upset and agitated. The poor little creatures are starving! How can Italians be so cruel to animals? Maltreating them in front of innocent children, to boot! Likely as not, they will now threaten never to return to the restaurant. But then, if Italians decide that this is a filthy unhygienic place and spread the bad word, local custom could vanish at a stroke. If only the races would stick to their preferred spheres – Germans outside, Italians indoors – the problem would be just about manageable. But everything is dry as a bone at the moment, Italians have lost their fear of the damp miasma that may attack them from the riverbed, and they want to sit outside too.

Shouldn't you just go with the Italians, then? I ask. They spend a lot more, don't they? And they're here all year round, too.

No, says Ciccio gloomily. He needs both lots. Italians may come in groups of ten or twelve, they may eat, drink and socialize for the traditional two or three hours over the proper four- or five-course meal; but they'll only do it once a week, if that. Foreign tourists may hardly ever eat a proper meal as conceived by local tradition and the Sloffood movement, true, but they'll come every day for the whole of their stay in some hillside holiday house, bringing all those hungry children who just love the sweet little kittens. And be back year after year as well. Until the cat problem is resolved, if it ever is, he and Franchino are just checking which nationality is in the majority, then ad-libbing their cat strategy. Ciccio demonstrates.

Here, nice pussy, pussy! he says in saccharin sweet tones, holding out a hand to an imaginary kitten lurking on his cooking range; then snaps to an expression of ferocious hatred and leans in to hiss horribly at it: *Te! Via!*: You! Get out!

Franchino, who has popped in to deposit a pile of used dishes on the counter, laughs sepulchrally. Poor cats! he says. They don't know if they're coming or going. One day, one of them's going to lose its rag completely and go for some innocent client's jugular.

That's what you think, says Ciccio passionately to Franchino's back, as he leaves the kitchens with another armful of plates. But you're wrong. It won't be a cat that goes for some customer's jugular. It will be the chef himself, driven beyond the reach of reason.

So before the chef really does crack up, he adds, please would I *motorino* off to the next village and see if I can get him something for his pain in the neck? He thinks they have sulphur sticks in the shop there – yes, he knows it will be shut but Giuseppe in the bar next door has a key for emergencies, and if I tell him it's a matter of life and death . . .

Paletta, as it happens, is just off to the bar to buy a lottery ticket for tonight: he'll give me a lift, he says. Does Ciccio want a lottery ticket too? Ciccio certainly does. He wants anything that might save him from this infernal restaurant. Winning the lottery would be fine.

Paletta gazes thoughtfully at his distraught cousin, awaiting inspiration. He feels in his bones, he says after a few moments, that the numbers he should play on Ciccio's behalf will be his date of birth, plus whatever figures correspond to quails and shallots. This combination will be the one to win Ciccio his escape from the tooth-and-claw world of catering.

Quails and shallots? Not Germans and kittens? I ask.

Certainly not! You should never, ever play the negative elements of life. And have I tasted the quails today? A triumph! . . .

Fine, says Ciccio. Do it. Anything. Just get back quickly with the pain relief.

Giuseppe is very understanding about the neck emergency, and we have the sulphur stick in a trice. Sulphur may sound an odd medication for a pain in the neck, even for this Frankenstein version: but here in Italy you buy sticks of the stuff, like giant pieces of yellow blackboard chalk a good inch in diameter, which you roll to and fro across the pain. If you're lucky the sulphur stick will make a loud cracking noise and fall apart in your hand. This means that the pain has been drawn out; and now you feel much better. Peculiar, but there it is. It works on Italians.

But the lottery numbers are another matter. First we have to find the number for a quail and a shallot respectively in the bar's *cabbala*, the book that translates any object or situation you care to name into a number. (I've only known it used to interpret dreams till now; but Paletta says it works just as well on reality.) Decoding the quail is simplicity itself: it stands for the number 43. (I would very much like to speak to the author of one of these *cabbalas*: how do they *know* that a quail is a number 43? How do you go about establishing such a thing?) But alas, the shallot is nowhere to be found. You can have an onion, red or white; you can have a spring onion or chive; you can have a clove of garlic, or even a whole head. But there is nary a shallot to be found. Could we go down to the Bar Marabotto in Diano Marina, where they have a much bigger and better *cabbala*?

But what about Ciccio's neck emergency? I ask. Paletta isn't sure: it might be worth his while to suffer a bit longer if it improves his chances of winning . . . No?

No. We settle for a white onion, number 12. But we'll be very lucky if the ticket wins. Couldn't be expected to, could it, says Paletta, with no way to play the correct type of vegetable? He would very much like to speak to the authors of that *cabbala* . . . !

Fortunately, the sulphur stick does work. After just a couple of passes it explodes to smithereens in my loving hand, and the chef is able to face his imminent lottery loss, and consequent obligation to cook all those extra dinners for the evening service, with something approaching equanimity.

Ciccio and Paletta now devise a brilliant scheme that should get rid of the cat problem, for the rest of the afternoon at least, without causing any upsets. Hopefully the disgruntled Italian table will be mollified when it meets a feline-free terrace on its way out after lunch. Ciccio will simply fill a carrier bag with delicious meaty leftovers, and perforate it carefully round the bottom so the aroma will seep out. Carrying this item, I am to wander casually over to pass the time of day with Pierino, walking exceedingly slowly, especially as I pass the Germans-and-cats table. Once I am sure our furry friends have detected the tasty snacks, I am to return through the garden, still trailing my bag, wander nonchalantly down to the river-bank, and, once I'm absolutely certain I'm out of sight of all clients of any nationality, deposit my cats' dinner down there.

The plan works brilliantly, except for the part involving Pierino, which we hadn't thought through properly. Pierino clearly thinks I've taken leave of my senses when I go over to his table, say hello, and then leave immediately without so much as joining him in a glass of wine. I can't sit down, though, can I? I am already being tracked by several kittens, their mother following close behind. We'd be inundated in cats within seconds.

Mission accomplished, I take another look at the rushing restaurateurs within and decide that this is not the atmosphere I wish to be hanging about in until the shops open at four.

There's no hurry for beetle-killing substances, is there, now Umberto's put the problem in perspective? It's horribly hot, too, which makes another cooling *motorino*-ride most appealing. I think I'll go for a quick swim in the Roncagli pools by the cool green ferny waterfall up the hill; then, once things have cooled down a bit, go home and get on with stacking the firewood Ciccio kindly chainsawed up for me the other day, which is still lying about all over the back terrace amid piles of sawdust.

Ciccio sees me off with my own personal lunch-bag of delicious leftovers, human grade, which we strap on to the back of the *motorino* – stuffed *zucchini* flowers, lovely, and stripy-grilled aubergine slices to put in a fresh roll from the mayor's shop – and promises to make up for the missed lunch today by taking me on a proper date tomorrow. He's got a surprise lined up, he says. If he can't make it up to my place tonight, we'll meet after lunch tomorrow, down in the piazza, Pepe's bar, okay?

11

Visiting the family land isn't the first thing that comes to mind when someone suggests a proper date: not to my mind, at any rate. So I'm a tiny bit surprised to discover, when I meet him in the piazza, that Ciccio is planning to take me up to his *campagna* for the afternoon. I'm not sure I'm dressed entirely appropriately for the outing, either. I rather primped and painted before coming out, imagining some slightly more glamorous engagement.

It's a beautiful spot, he says hopefully, the place he's often pointed out to me from the terrace at my place, high up on the ridge opposite, behind the pine trees above Diano Castello. You can see for miles from up there, right out as far as Corsica and Capraia even, if the weather's right.

By the time we've zoomed up half-a-dozen of the ferocious hairpin bends involved in almost any trip in these parts, and have come out of the villages and into high olive terrain again, I'm reconciled to the idea. Being introduced to the family land must be the stuff of true intimacy to Ciccio – next best thing to being introduced to the family. And there wouldn't be much point in that, would there, seeing I've met them all already. Though in my new role as his partner, I am still being kept, for inscrutable Italian reasons, firmly under wraps. He still hasn't told his mother: and I still don't get what the big problem is. He just can't face it, he says.

Ours is not to reason why. Off to inspect my suitor's lands, I tell myself, with a view to deeper understanding of his true character. Just like some Jane Austen heroine. Or am I inspecting the family-maintaining and food-producing potential of the *campagna*, perhaps, like some peasant bride of yore?

It is not long before I find myself distracted from these airy ruminations by a rather peculiar smell in the car. It seems to be getting stronger and stronger. I wind down my window. He hasn't got fish in the boot again, has he?

No, no, says Ciccio. That will be the three sacks of cow manure he's just collected from the Giacomassi boys' farm at the top of the hill. We'll be needing them up at his father's. He's promised to do a couple of jobs up there this afternoon.

(I should probably explain that in local parlance 'my mother's' means the family home, while 'my father's' means the family land. This will save others from mistakenly thinking, as I did for some time, that a surprisingly large number of parents round here seemed to be divorced, or at any rate living in separate establishments.)

So we're going to be spreading manure up there, are we? I ask, wondering how much more ethnic this date can get.

Don't be daft, says Ciccio. Of course not! At this time of year? No, we're going to use it to mend the oven, which urgently needs to be working before the tomatoes are ready to harvest in a week or two. Because then the whole of his clan will be going up there to pick them and turn them into a zillion pots and bottles of tomato *sugo*, the way we did at Anna and Tonino's, and it'll take a couple of days at least. And while they work they need to be able to feed themselves in the style to which they're accustomed.

Oven? Dung? Not only incomprehensible, but sounds distinctly unpromising as a prelude to romance. Best to probe no further.

Ah, yes, says Ciccio. That reminds him. There's a canister in the boot, too. Five litres of diesel for me.

Diesel? For me? How did he know? I didn't even get round to telling him about the *tarli* . . .

He does that Italian mind-your-own-business gesture, laying his finger along the side of his nose. I answer with a fine ferocious English glower. He gives in.

He knew, he says, because the entire Province of Imperia spent the whole of yesterday afternoon pestering him about my urgent need for diesel. First Anna-the-neighbour turned up on a *motorino* loaded down with shopping, telling a dramatic tale of ferocious giant bees set to demolish my home. She wasn't sure I'd quite understood, what with That Franco confusing the issue, how urgent it was to apply some diesel to the problem. So she thought she'd make sure my fiancé (knowing smile) was put in the picture.

Next, who should turn up but That Franco himself, looking for the money the restaurant owed him on the ten kilos of horsemeat steak he delivered last month. (Ciccio is very resentful about this – he only asked for five kilos, hoping there might be some call for it as a speciality item, but Franco, finding young Alberto momentarily alone in charge, left ten. And then, adding insult to injury, in spite of horsemeat's age-old reputation as an ideal pick-me-up for anyone who needs to raise their energy levels, it turned out that tradition has decayed so rapidly in this country, *pace* the Sloffood movement, that hardly anybody wanted to eat it except Ciccio himself. Which explains, I dare say, why he is so extremely lively these days. The rest is still lying in the freezer, taking up an unconscionable amount of room.) Horsemeat-trading over, Franco too decided to share his concerns over my welfare with Ciccio – though in his version, my problem was not rampaging bees but rampaging beetles. Franco feared, he said, that I hadn't understood that diesel was my only hope of stopping the roof falling in on my head.

Naturally, with public opinion so strong in its favour, Ciccio thought he'd better pick up a few litres of diesel for me. Which is it, then, he asks, bees or beetles? Is the roof really about to fall in? And why didn't I tell him yesterday, when I was up at the restaurant?

Beetles, I think, I say. But it's probably nothing serious. Everyone seems to think Franco's exaggerating wildly. And as for not telling Ciccio, well, I didn't need to, did I? Why deprive my neighbours of their entertainment?

Ciccio can't believe I even considered believing Franco, who is known locally, for well-founded reasons, as *il coltello*: Frank the Knife. But then, Ciccio admits that he himself has no expertise when it comes to wooden beams and their problems. In fact, he can't imagine why anyone would rely on wood as a building material at all. His mother's house, down on the coastal plain between here and Diano Marina, has, he says, good solid ceilings of vaulted brick and stone, floors of brick tile laid over them, no structural wood involved. Wooden-beam houses are a backward hillside hinterland tradition, of which he knows nothing.

What does he mean, backward? Practically every house in my entire country is built on wooden beams, I say. Not just the roof, either, but the storeys below as well; and there are many proud examples of them lasting for centuries. I get a most disbelieving look for this: a look to which I will become accustomed over the next few months. People in this part of the world seem, some time in the last half-century, to have lost all faith in wood as a building material, to the point where they can hardly believe they ever used it themselves. And come to think of it, where in England you touch wood for luck, Italians touch iron. Maybe they never did think wood was up to much?

What, I ask, does Ciccio think about popping in to the

paint and hardware shop in Diano Marina on the way back, or better still driving over to Imperia, to see if they can give me some up-to-date DIY roof-preserving advice?

Why? he says. What's wrong with the diesel?

Smelly, I say. And highly flammable. Does it really kill insects?

Of course it does, says Ciccio. His father always uses it in the vegetable garden. You just go round with a cupful of diesel, pick off the insects, drop them into it. And they're dead in seconds. *Morti stecchiti*! Moreover, he has little faith in the Diano hardware shop; and Imperia's a long detour to make. Why don't we just stop at the bar in San Pietro? The afternoon card-playing session should be in full swing by now, we'll be passing the place anyway, and it will be packed with wooden-beam pundits from up in the hills, old-timers ready and waiting to share their wisdom with any passing ignoramus.

Good plan, I say. And I say it in spite of being certain that the San Pietro bar will be one hundred per cent in agreement with the diesel prognosis. Why do I do this? Because I am pleased as Punch that Ciccio's suggested going to my local bar at all, that's why. Since we've been together, he has developed a strange reluctance to enter the place. He's in too much of a hurry, or he's arranged to meet somebody-or-other in his own local bar, down by the Diano crossroads; or he doesn't want anything to drink anyway . . .

Why has he developed this allergy to Luigi's bar, the hub of San Pietro social life? I have no idea. The clients at Luigi's tend to be San Pietro born and bred; while Ciccio's own local bar, the pleasingly named BarLady, is a whole mile closer to the coast, and a lot more cosmopolitan, frequented not just by Ligurians but by people whose origins lie as far afield as Rome, Naples, Calabria and the Abruzzo – even, on occasion, Morocco, Albania or Senegal. Still, that doesn't seem much of a reason for cutting me off from my roots. This bar, or rather a room in the Pensione above it, was my, and my sister's, first ever home in San Pietro, arranged for us by our boss, Signor Patrucco, King of the Rose Nurseries; and without the guidance doled out to us by the serious Luigi, self-taught intellectual, and his statuesque wife Maria – not to mention the vast quantities of succulent supplies they provided us with – I doubt whether we would have survived that first hard-living month up at our new residence in the hills. Or, indeed, learned how not to make a fool of ourselves in a Ligurian restaurant. Since then, hardly a day can have gone by without my popping in for a quick cappuccino or *aperitivo*, a dose of good village gossip, or a handy hint or two from Luigi, Maria, or their assembled olive-farming folk. So I'm extremely glad that Ciccio has seen the error of his ways.

In we go, then, pushing aside the multicoloured strands of the anti-fly curtain over the door, and ordering ourselves an espresso from Luigi's son Stefano at the bar. (I'd prefer a cappuccino, as it happens, but if you ask for such a thing in here at this time of day, you have to put up with a bar-load of humorous sallies about whether you've only just got out of bed.) After the long lethargy of summer, you can sense as soon as you walk in here – though perhaps you need some training in these matters to do so? – the buzz of energy slowly building as everyone gears up for autumn and the outbreak of hard work to come. Not much rest from September to February in San Pietro; first the *vendemmia* and the wine-making, the harvesting, potting and bottling of all the products of the vegetable gardens; then the last clearing of the olive terraces, the preparing of the winter firewood from the olive prunings, the laying of the olive nets; all to culminate triumphantly, after a few weeks' break for the Christmas festivities, in the olive harvest, the lugging of great heavy sacks on to your *Ape* and down to the mill: and, at long last, the pressing of the year's oil and a nice big dollop of hard-earned cash.

Within minutes all the assembled knotted-hankied heads are telling us that a simple coat of limewash every couple of years is enough to keep the *tarli* at bay.

Has she not been doing that, then? they ask, turning to Ciccio.

Another irritating feature of life round here; if you're a woman accompanied by any sort of man at all, relative, friend or passer-by, the custom of local men is to address their remarks to him, not to you. To speak to the woman in preference to the man is to imply (I gather) that he's an idiot or a child or an incompetent; or at any rate, a man undeserving of the respect of other men. It took me a decade or so of randomly mystifying occurrences – had my Italian suddenly become incomprehensible? Had I become invisible, maybe? – to deduce the existence of this ridiculous rule. I was almost always in here with my sister, of course, and as long as you haven't brought a man with you, you can have a perfectly normal conversation. Today, adding insult to injury, I find myself in the absurd position of actually being pleased to be spoken to, or rather not spoken to, in this manner. Because I wouldn't want my Ciccio disrespected, would I?

I am soon admitting, humbly, even though the question was not addressed to me, that I haven't limewashed my beams at all, no, not in all these years. The brows of San Pietro darken at my foreign negligence. It is beyond all understanding. And there's no point in my saying that where I come from there aren't any monstrous beam-munching insects, and nobody ever paints their beams with lime, because I will just get a volley of even more disapproving looks if I do. No need to make up absurd excuses, young woman!

I notice now, right over in the corner by the window, the ancient Pompeo, grizzled ex-owner of my home and direct descendant of the man who built it. Pompeo usually loves nothing better than doling out advice and information; at the moment, though, he is ostentatiously reading the bar's newspaper, participating not one whit in the debate. Extraordinary! Pompeo, a tiny wiry personage with piercing eyes and a serious pair of eyebrows, always takes a strong proprietorial interest in my every doing, especially where it concerns the house that was once his own; in fact, without his sterling services during the well drama some years ago, when I found that some unknown person had inexplicably pumped our well dry just as it had begun to fill up after a long and droughty summer, the sister and I might easily have decamped for good and all, in utter despair.

Luckily, Ciccio doesn't know Pompeo well enough to spot this unusual behaviour; and I'm certainly not going to mention it. Is this what Ciccio feared? Being weighed and found wanting in his new role as my official partner? Pierino won't have wasted any time spreading the good news down the valley, naturally.

Yes, just a bit of paint, says everyone except Pompeo. I get several serves-you-right-for-your-laziness looks; while Ciccio gets a selection of wise nods and winks that absolve him from any guilt in the matter of my female foolishness. Not, though, from Pompeo.

And would there be any point in our lime-washing the beams now? asks Ciccio. He hasn't mentioned Franco's prediction that the roof was about to fall in: and I think I'll follow his lead. I can already see the finger-under-eyeball comments on The Knife's craftiness, hear the delighted guffaws at my gullibility.

Luigi is behind the bar, giving it a pensive wipe over with

78

a large blue-and-white dishcloth. The years are beginning to tell on him, especially since the sad loss of Maria last year. He and Stefano, who is now busy piling clean espresso cups neatly on top of the coffee machine, have both got a good half-a-stone thinner without her cooking skills to keep their figures up to scratch. But Luigi is as sharp as ever in the brain department, and his son has been brought up to match. You can always rely on them to get to the heart of the matter: and thanks, no doubt, to the combative Communist tradition from which they spring, they are able to speak to members of either or both sexes without any difficulty.

The point is this, says Luigi once he's given the matter thorough consideration and brought up a good shine on the bar. People paint their beams with lime so that wood-eating insects won't recognize them as wood: and therefore won't lay their eggs in them. Once the things are already in there, though, the limewash treatment would be pointless.

Now I've spotted saturnine Nino-the-neighbour, who is always, in spite of my various assaults on his property over the years, a great help in an hour of need. He is not joining in the conversation either. He is just leaning on the bar and looking Ciccio up and down in the most unsubtle manner. Unnerving. I've known all the denizens of Luigi's bar a lot longer than I've known Ciccio, though, and I suppose they're the closest thing I've got to family round here. And very possessive father-substitutes they are turning out to be.

It might be worth giving your wood a coat of paint anyway, though, contributes Stefano. It would discourage the *tarli* offspring from following in their parents' footsteps, at least, and keep the invasion down to a generation or two.

Some hope! I hate to imagine how many generations are in there already. And all for the want of a couple of buckets of that magical solution to all life's little problems: lime. But now things have gone this far, the only option open to me, everyone advises Ciccio on my behalf (except for Pompeo and Nino, who remain sternly aloof in the face of the interloper) is this: we should coat every bit of wood in the house liberally with diesel.

Now there's a surprise.

12

Half-a-dozen bends back up the other side of the valley, we
park behind the string of Mediterranean pines on the top of
the ridge opposite my home. Ciccio puts a rock-solid arm
through mine, making up for my unsuitable official-date footwear, and we scramble off down a narrow footpath. Round
the brow of the hill, and here we are, in a south-facing suntrap
sitting snugly between two high shoulders of wild broom-
clad mountainside. Two broad silvery phalanxes of olive trees
march on down a couple of dozen wide shoulder-high terraces; and between the two groves of olives lie the *orti*, the
vegetable gardens (think of h*orti*culture). Level upon voluptuous level of aubergines, tomatoes, peppers, peas, beans; of
salad plants, basil and spinach lie basking in the sun, all perfectly
hoed and weeded. Just above us is a whole terrace devoted to
nothing but flat-leaf parsley. No wonder Ciccio has such
profligate habits with the stuff.

Down below us to seaward, Diano Castello sits atop its own
private hillock, a pretty jumble of terracotta roofs snug inside
the remnants of its ruined castle walls. And beyond Castello,
nothing at all: just a spectacular quantity of wide, cobalt blue
sea and an intense, cloudless sky. Ciccio's father Salvatore's
olives stand tall and wide on either side of us. No sign here of
the lazy modern pruning techniques already adopted by so
many less stoical olive growers. Not too surprising: I've never
forgotten Salvatore's erratic and irascible presence at the series
of classes laid on for us by the Olive Board of Liguria, or some
such body, whose aim was to get us all to prune our trees low

and dangly for maximum olive harvest with the minimum of hard labour: the *Taglio Drastico*, or Drastic Cut. An outrageous suggestion, according to Salvatore, who had spent fifty years nurturing his trees' every centimetre, and was certainly not going to be wasting his time with acts of folly like cutting the top fifteen feet off them.

I may have adopted the Drastic Pruning myself, not being much of a work ethic girl, but I can see now why Salvatore felt like that about his trees. Or I should say his Plants, *piante*, as they call them round here, without bothering to specify what kind of plant they mean, because it's so obvious. Every one of them is a work of art, a model of perfection in the old-fashioned candelabra style. Your father, I say admiringly, is clearly a man who does not fear a bit of hard labour.

No he doesn't, says Ciccio, because he just makes me come up and do it. And all the rest of the family, when he can swing it. Osvaldo and Giovanni must rue the day they ever married my sisters. And Beppe, the elegant third brother-in-law, always makes sure to have very important business that keeps him in Milan from September until well after the olive harvest.

Salvatore's *orti* put my own efforts to shame. We've pushed our way through a six-foot-high leafy alleyway of ox-heart tomatoes now, out into an orchard of apple and pear, fig and apricot, peach and nectarine trees. The path starts to curve back uphill through plots of artichokes, of potatoes, of *zucchini*, taking us towards a level area at the top of the ridge, where an old stone *rustico* stands: the family storehouse. Above us now are two entire terraces devoted to some low bushy plant covered in bright red buds. Miniature roses, are they? Does Salvatore grow flowers too? Seems unlikely, but then floral terraces do pop up in all sorts of unlikely places these days – you can get good EEC subsidies for floriculture, which come in handy for subsidizing other things you can't get help with, such as growing olives in less-than-industrial quantities.

Ciccio laughs at the thought. Certainly not! These are a special strain of extra-hot chilli peppers that his father has created himself by saving the seeds from the hottest of the year's harvest and replanting them. After a decade or so of this inbreeding, they've ended up like that, with all the chillies concentrated in a bunch at the top of the plant. And ferociously hot. Try this! he says, plucking one casually and aiming it at my lips.

No, no! Take it away! I yelp, shrinking back in terror.

His father, Ciccio tells me, is completely addicted to chilli, the hotter the better. He can't even eat a plate of pasta without it.

Well, there you are. Another very good reason for not trying the things. One addiction, at least, that I've so far managed to avoid.

In his father's youth, Ciccio says, down in the poverty-stricken deep South of Italy, people used chilli peppers the way South American peasant farmers use the coca leaf – a sort of combined appetite suppressant and energizer. That's how Salvatore got hooked on them. The less food there was, the more chilli you added. When there was nothing but bread, which in the 1930s was rather often, you hollowed out your share of the family loaf and filled it with a handful of chillies – and added a slice of onion and a drop of olive oil, if you could get them. The jolt this recipe gave your system would get you through a hard day's work just as well as if your stomach was full. Agh! Thank the Lord I wasn't born a poor Southern Italian. I would certainly have starved if the only alternative was to live on chilli sandwiches. Salvatore has certainly made up for the hungry years of his youth now, though, I say wonderingly. There are enough vegetables growing up here to feed an army. What on earth does he do with it all? Does he sell it? Is it for the restaurant?

I get a look from Ciccio. Of course. If you count up Salvatore's son, his five daughters, the three husbands, the five grandchildren, as well as his own household, he does have an army to feed. Round here, although children may get jobs, get married, move out into homes of their own, they don't seem ever to become a separate unit. Some combination or other of them will always be eating round at Salvatore and Francesca's. That gives Salvatore sixteen mouths to contribute to. No wonder he needs so much chilli. As an insurance policy. If by some mischance all his other crops fail, the family will still survive the winter, and when spring comes he'll find the energy to replant all this land.

When at last we have climbed, breathless, up off the last terrace and arrived at the *rustico* on the level ridge-top, I stand amazed. Forget Jane Austen. Doctor Jekyll and Mister Hyde take up landscape design, more like. With the deranged Hyde in total control of the area around the *rustico*. There is a small neatly paved bit with a wooden bench just outside the house; but otherwise the Garden of Eden has vanished at a stroke. On the flat triangle of hilltop all around us, as far as the eye can see, a wilderness of chaos lies baking in the sun. A small hillock of twisted Venetian blinds here, another of rusting buckets and bent sheets of corrugated iron there, overgrown with Morning Glory; a mouldering sofa, a shoulder-high pile of broken slabs of marble; a heap of old bricks, a mound of prehistoric iron bedsteads tangled in burgeoning old man's beard, another of disintegrating cardboard boxes full of floor tiles, of rusting iron bars, of rolls of chickenwire. Right to the end of the ridge, the whole landscape is dotted about with the stuff.

I can't believe that the state of this place doesn't bother

Ciccio; that he even describes it as beautiful! The contrast between the ordered perfection below and the senseless chaos up here is positively alarming. Elizabeth Bennet would be taking to her heels right now, convinced that a dangerously unbalanced mind was at work here.

What on earth is it all for? I ask feebly.

Ciccio looks around him vaguely. All what? he says.

All this . . . stuff, I say, at a loss for the right word to describe it. These piles . . .

Ah. Well, he says, his father never throws anything away. It always comes in handy for something.

OK. Abandon the Jane Austen angle. The peasant bride wins. No fear of my offspring going hungry once I've allied myself with this place, and plenty of thrift in evidence. Moreover, certain areas of this junk wilderness turn out to have actual nameable functions. What appeared at first sight to be a mere tangle of wooden laths, bricks and wire netting now resolves itself, with a bit of help from Ciccio, into a chicken run full of fat brown chickens that squawk happily as we draw near.

See? says Ciccio, opening, or rather untangling, the gate. The hens rush out, skidding over one another in their excitement, to cluck and scrabble in the dust. It may not look much, he adds, but it provides the family with a good dozen eggs a day. And I would never guess how much this chicken run is worth. Would I like to make a bet on it?

I refuse to gamble, suspecting trickery. And I am right to suspect. The correct answer, according to Ciccio, is four million lire: over a thousand pounds.

And how can a pile of sticks, bricks and chicken wire be worth four million lire?

Easily, apparently: if you have evil neighbours who denounce you to the *comune* for not having planning permission for it. An official came up from the town hall and pronounced it *abusivo*. The alternative to the thousand-pound fine was to knock the thing down. But Salvatore loves those chickens. They don't just keep the family supplied with eggs: they come when he calls them, they follow him about lovingly while he works on the vegetables, and he says they protect his crops, pecking up pests before they can get on to the plants. It would have broken his heart to lose them. So Ciccio paid up.

Terrible. I certainly haven't got myself in with the rich and influential of Diano here, then. Some people, people with friends in the right places, manage to surround their new homes on the outskirts of the villages in these hills with acres of shiny tiles and pre-cast balustrading, and get away with it scot-free; while Ciccio's family can't get so much as a chicken run nodded through. Hearts of gold, though, as we see. And, of course, very strong on recycling.

13

Why don't I come and sit down, says Ciccio, and we'll have a drink before we get started.

Sit down? Drink? Where?

We go down a set of crumbling stone steps, past a particularly large and ramshackle pile of something completely overgrown with ivy; and unexpectedly take a sharp right into the heart of the pile. Which turns out not to be a pile at all, but a thick ivy pergola extending its cool green shade from the high stone wall of the terrace behind, out over a great square oak table that could seat a good fifteen people, no trouble. Exactly what it's here for, of course. A beautiful table, too, which I would very much like to take home with me. Fancy leaving that sitting about a hillside! I can't believe some roaming antique dealer hasn't passed by and made off with it. Though I suppose they'd have to find it first.

Once you've settled down at the lovely table on one of the (also rather attractive) big long benches that surround it, chickens clucking contentedly about between your feet, strings of those ferocious chilli peppers hanging above to dry, it is surprisingly easy to forget the rubble without. All you can see are enormous amounts of blue sky and even bluer sea, cascading tendrils of dark green ivy and bright red *peperoncino*, with the occasional glimpse of perfect *orti* below when a welcome breeze stirs the leaves. Nailed lopsidedly to one of the set of old green slatted wooden shutters that serve as a side wall to this bower is a light switch. Watch this! says Ciccio, pressing it: and a light bulb blazes out amongst the ivy. Proper electricity! I'm impressed. Even more so when I realize that the rusty old freezer standing picturesquely amongst the grass and weeds under its own separate pergola of grapevines is not only in working order, but full of lovely cool bottles of fizzy water and white wine. All is not mere senseless chaos after all.

Over in the corner formed by the steps Ciccio points out a tap set into an upright stone slab, with an oval stone basin below it like the ones you get at village springs. Eat your heart out, he says, turning it on with a flourish.

Proper piped water too! I watch it splashing the dry earth for yards around. No wonder Salvatore's vegetables put mine to shame. Cut the shame.

No need to gloat over those less fortunate than you, I say petulantly. As Ciccio knows to his cost, up at my place the water has to be pumped up to my tank once a fortnight from a well several steep terraces below the house, with a horrible erratic old petrol-driven pump sold to me a decade or so ago by a certain Franco the Knife. The thing conks out on me, as often as not, half-way through the operation; whereupon Ciccio, for whom the internal combustion engine holds no mysteries, is called in to save the household from death by drought. As for freezers, some hope! I have a minute fridge, no bigger than a couple of generous family-size breakfast cereal packets, which runs off a gas bottle.

While Ciccio roots about in the freezer for refreshments, I spot a small and comparatively tame pile of discarded household objects lying beside me, between the two benches. Idly sorting through it, I come up with a little old wooden coffee grinder with a curly cast-iron windlass on top and a tiny drawer at the bottom for the ground coffee. I'm sitting winding it happily round and round when Ciccio brings the glasses. Do you like that? he says. Take it. Nobody's used it for years. *La mamma* buys the coffee ready ground these days. Stick it in your bag.

I'd rather have the table, I say hopefully. Or the water supply.

Later, says the Man Who Has Everything.

Once I've actually met the oven, which lies at the far end of this more domesticated terrace, a cow-manure cure for its ailments seems somewhat less unlikely. It's an outdoor one, for a start. It is also, as you'd expect under the circumstances, lightly disguised as a pile of rubble; in this case a domed heap of rather beautiful mellow old bricks. It is one of those simple beehive-shaped ovens that have been around since before written history began: you light a wood fire inside them, then once it's good and hot and the flames have died down you just shove the embers to one side, add your dough – your loaf, pizza, *focaccia* or whatever – and block off the entrance. This one has developed hairline cracks all down one side, it seems; cracks that, according to *la mamma*, are stopping the thing getting up to heat properly, and wasting a lot of firewood.

I've been chosen, I now discover, to participate in a bold scientific experiment. According to local wisdom in general, and Salvatore in particular, the only way to fix the defect is to knock the oven down and start again from scratch. But an old man in the town of Pieve di Teco, twenty miles away up in the hills, described this cow-manure repair technique to Ciccio; a technique that was rubbished by Salvatore and his cronies when Ciccio suggested trying it. The same bunch of Luddites who walked out on the Olive Improvement Course with him, naturally. They don't realize, says Salvatore's son, his eyes lighting up with evangelical zeal, that the cow-manure cure won't just fix the cracks, but will double the insulation. Keeping the oven hotter longer, and greatly gladdening his mother's heart. His father's too, once he gets over the insubordination involved, and discovers how much less wood he needs to chop for it.

I can imagine that nothing about Pieve di Teco would inspire Salvatore to trust the place. Instead of these steep sun-baked coastal terraces that are so like Salvatore's homeland in the South, up there in Pieve they have cool chestnut forests and smooth green mountain pastures; instead of growing olives and keeping the odd goat, they farm cows and sheep in vast numbers. Travellers from our Diano valley, if they make it that far, comment on the distressing fact that olive trees will hardly grow up there at all, except in the odd sheltered nook, because the winters are too cold; also on the ghastly mountain food they have to eat up there. Butter where there ought by rights to be olive oil, and too much polenta. Poor things! How can they stand it?

Exactly, says my beloved; this is why I'm the ideal helpmate for today's job. As a rank outsider I don't suffer from the idiotic village chauvinism that suffocates Progress. And better still, I have no opinions at all about how to repair pizza ovens. But he had better find me something proper to wear, he says, giving my hitherto unnoticed slinky outfit a disparaging look. He vanishes into the *rustico*, rustles about a bit, and reappears with two voluminous floral aprons, Anna-style, and a pair of down-at-heel ladies' house slippers. His mother's stuff, he says, but it's more sensible than what I've got on. I can choose which of the aprons I like best.

Thank you, Ciccio. Progress, here I come. Swallowing my pride I replace my stylish footwear with the floppy foam-soled slippers and wrap myself about with the larger and flowerier of the aprons. Where are these neighbours who complained about the chicken run, anyway? I ask, fearing that they may pop up unexpectedly and catch me in this ludicrous disguise.

Come and look, says Ciccio: and he takes me off through

Salvatore's devastation zone, almost back to where we left the car. There below us, just over the brow of the hill, sits a pair of brand-new snazzy little villas. Balustrades, yes, but no acres of tiling. Yet.

Two families who have risen above the peasant life and rebuilt their *rustico*, says Ciccio. They were going to rent them out as holiday lets, but then they discovered they could live in them instead, and rent their old homes, even closer to the sea, for even more money.

But they can't even see your chicken run from here, I say.

Of course not, says Ciccio. They wanted to buy us out, that's all, and when we wouldn't sell, they took to sneaking about looking for things to denounce to the *comune*. They were hoping for a fine so big we'd be forced to sell up to pay it; but all they could come up with was the chicken run. The bigger house, he says, the one with the pointless brick gateway, belongs to the devils who called in the *comune*.

I see at a glance that he is right. That gateway is a certain sign of devilry. Why would you want a huge car-width gate that was unconnected to a wall or some such barrier, a gate you can just walk, or drive, around, in the first place? With a two-foot-wide tiled roof over it that wouldn't keep the rain off a matchstick? San Pietro villagers are not mistaken: isolated country living is not good for the mental health. I'm pleased to hear from Ciccio that the abominable gateway has never been used, not even once. Nowadays with no hoeing and planting to be done, the inhabitants of both houses devote themselves to feuding over parking spaces and driveways and who is spoiling whose view. The folk next door disputed their right to use the bit of land on the other side of the gate before it was even finished. The court case will run for years. Most outrageous of all, adds Ciccio, that bunch with the gateway have even tried claiming that his father's land is an eyesore that lowers the value of their property! An eyesore! Have I ever heard anything so absurd?

I'm saved from answering this by one of the neighbours popping out of her house: the one without the appalling gateway. She is in her slippers and dressing-gown, but she doesn't seem to be bothered. Why should she be? Look at my own outfit. Her slippers are high-heeled mules with little floaty bits of ostrich feather on the uppers. The dressing-gown is of clinging apricot satin. Hard to know whether you'd say she was overdressed or underdressed for the occasion. Or, indeed, whether we were both participating in some hillside fancy dress competition.

Buongiorno! says the lady, looking at us with myopic suspicion.

Buongiorno! we reply in unison.

Ah! Ciccio! It's you! she says, in tones of relief. How are you? How is your mother?

Fine, says he. And yourself?

As this conversation follows the usual time-honoured lines, I find myself staring in fascination at the householder. She has a sweet little dolly face, a face you'd say was in its mid-forties so long as she keeps looking at you straight on; but when her head turns slightly in either direction, she suddenly ages twenty years. And of course, since she's talking, her head is in constant movement. Old, young, old, young . . . old again . . . it's like some kind of filmic special effect. I am still gaping rudely when I realize that I'm being addressed.

You must be Ciccio's English fiancée, then, are you? she says. The one I've heard all about from Francesca?

Ah, um, I murmur, unsure of the correct response. I feel horribly self-conscious. What must this woman be making of my jaunting about the countryside heavily disguised as Ciccio's mother?

Ah, um, echoes Ciccio, pausing for thought. Well, he adds . . .

Capisco, says our interlocutor menacingly: I understand. And she goes on gazing at us as if her understanding knew no bounds.

Well, *buongiorno* again, says Ciccio, and we scuttle off to the shelter of the pine trees on the ridge, where I collapse on to the bed of pine needles at our feet and giggle. Nothing like Italian rural morality for making you feel as if you were a delinquent fourteen-year-old again. Ciccio stays standing, though, muttering horribly to himself about nosiness and neighbours and his mother and his English fiancée and the Gestapo.

What on earth's happened to your neighbour's face, anyway? I ask once he's calmed down a bit. Is that a facelift?

Ciccio doesn't know for sure. But rumour says it is, yes. Frightening, isn't it? But his heart is not in this conversation. He is a worried man. Has the news about us already leaked all over the valley? Could it really be his mother who's mentioned me to the neighbour?

Surely, I say, if these people are sworn enemies of your family, that isn't too likely?

Wrong. Apparently this kind of war is played out among men only, and there is nothing to stop their womenfolk stopping for a friendly chat if they happen to bump into one another.

We're going to have to get down to see his mother pretty sharpish, Ciccio says worriedly. She'll be mortified if somebody else has really told her the news before we have.

What, I say, do I have to come too? Can't you just tell her yourself?

No, he can't. I have to come too, or it doesn't look respect-ful. Or respectable. It looks as if I've got something to hide.

Does it? What sort of thing would I be hiding? I ask curiously.

Ciccio is exasperated by my foreign idiocy. Nothing spe-cific, he says. An honest woman wouldn't be afraid to look her man's mother in the eye, that's all.

But I've met her loads of times, I say, she knows perfectly well I can look her in the eye.

I've missed the point: it's a matter of protocol. We both have to go round to dinner with the family one evening, that's all.

Strange. I've been to his house before; I even had a Boxing Day lunch with the whole family once. I've always enjoyed their company, too. Why is he looking so doomladen about it?

These pine trees we're under, I say, doing my best to distract him from the ghastly prospect of possibly being thought to be engaged to me, are the very ones you can see on top of the ridge from my terrace at home, look; so logically we ought to be able to see my house from here.

Ciccio stares hopefully out across the valley, hunting for some sign of Besta de Zago; he is amazed, some five minutes later, to have discovered no sign of it.

I, on the other hand, am not amazed. Logic doesn't come into it. Whenever you spot a hint of terracotta tile beneath the sea of olives, a building that might be my house, you will soon find some proof that it isn't – a pine tree in the wrong place, or an outcrop of rock, or a vineyard, or a stretch of broom-covered scrub. You can't see my house from close by; and you can't see it from afar either. I may be used to it, but it's not fair. Mine is a beautiful house, and I'd very much enjoy gloating over it, if only I ever got the chance.

Mah! says Ciccio, frustrated. Let's go and sort out this oven, then. And off we trek back through Salvatore's rubble-storage area, which may be slightly untidy but is certainly not an eyesore. What is a slight shortage of landscaping skills, after all, compared to a Rancho Gateway Monstroso? Faced with that, I'd choose Salvatore's aesthetics any day.

Now for the cow-manure repair mission. The cracks are hardly visible now, with the oven cold: but once we've heaved a few olive logs inside it and got them lit, smoke comes trickling, then pouring, out. Ciccio wheelbarrows the cow manure over from the car, and we're off. The Old Man of Pieve's recipe is certainly revolting enough; you mix the manure up with water into a thick slurry and keep applying layer after layer to the oven as it heats up, until it is a good foot thick. Once he's got a couple of buckets mixed, Ciccio kindly produces a pair of thick pink rubber gloves for me. Just the finishing touch my outfit lacked. No excuse left now for not participating fully, darn it, in this daring experiment with new technology.

So there you have it. This, it seems, is what my true love thinks of as a proper date: an afternoon of smoky oven-stoking and pink-rubber-gloved manure-slapping, your *figura* ruined by floppy slippers and mountainous aprons, chickens clucking about your ankles. I slop another dollop of slurry on to the warm oven, and meld it into its neighbours with the side of my glove. Another thread of smoke bites the dust. Quick, another handful just above it . . . Yes! There we are!

Is this some sort of suitability test for the peasant life, I wonder? Or should I just reconcile myself to the fact that the man doesn't have a shred of romance in his soul?

Do you not have a shred of romance in your soul? I ask as I dip my glove back into the slurry bucket, on the principle that it's best not to keep this sort of thought to yourself. What sort of proper date do you call this? I add for good measure.

Ciccio looks startled. No, this wasn't meant to be the date! Here, he says, fishing about in the back pocket of his jeans and producing a couple of squares of card, smearing them lightly with manure as he goes. Tickets for the Afro-Jazz concert tonight in Genoa, he says.

Just two tickets, as well. Very flattering. This must be the first time I've ever known Ciccio go out for the evening without at least half a dozen friends and relations in tow. Honour satisfied, I throw myself into the work with a will. Soon I've forgotten all about glamour and become a slurry-consistencies connoisseur. A genuine grown-up excuse for playing mud-pies. By the time we have the oven thoroughly covered in dung and nicely smoothed off – the rubber gloves turn out to be the perfect tool for this, you just pat gently and a layer of water rises to the surface – our repair is undeniably a triumph; smoke has completely stopped leaking from the cracks. Ciccio is dancing around me delightedly – Look at that! So much for the sceptics! Wait till they see this! – and doing his best to hug me while I'm busy trying to stuff another few logs into the oven, wanting to be sure its new covering is thoroughly baked on and won't wash off in the next rainstorm. What is it about women being busy trying to do something that makes men have to hug them? Or does this only happen to me?

As we're getting ready to leave, Ciccio dashes into the *rustico* again and returns with a whole armful of potted and bottled delights, jars of olives and aubergine slices and pickled mushrooms and pointy green peppers *sott'aceto*, pickled in wine vinegar, and little round red peppers stuffed with anchovies and tiny cheeses marinating in olive oil . . . We might as well take some up to your place, he says, stock up the larder a bit.

Might we? But won't they mind? It doesn't seem fair after all his parents' hard work . . . !

Ciccio fixes me with a pitying look. Who do I think they do it all for? I should see the expression on his mother's face if she ever catches him with a supermarket carrier bag! On the contrary, his parents will be happy as Larry to know we're making use of the stuff. They hate the idea of their offspring wasting their hard-earned cash in food-shops. And secondly, how many hours of his life do I think he puts in up here himself? Where do I think he comes at crack of dawn on his Days of Repose? And where do I think he'll be working almost every morning, starting next week, when he stops doing weekday lunches till next summer season? Why do I think his restaurant is closed for the whole month of February while the olive harvest's on?

Sorry! I keep forgetting that 'my father's land' is only a courtesy title. And I only ever see Ciccio working at the restaurant, not up here.

I am forgiven. To celebrate my new-found understanding of Ciccio's life and times, we take a pair of baskets down and decimate a few yards of *orto* into the bargain. Now we stuff our booty into the car, take a quick swill under the tap in the stone, a half-hearted wipe at the ash-and-mud-spattered clothing, and off we set, with a strong hint of smoked cow-dung still clinging to us. Good job the concert's outdoors.

I turn for a last admiring look at our oven repairs. Fantastic! I see now that by cleverly concealing its original elegant domed lines under a mountainous straw-spiky blob of manure, we have succeeded in making it blend in much better with the surrounding décor. Yes, now that we have finished with it, although it is perhaps a touch more organic-looking than its companion pieces, it does look quite remarkably like a pile of rubble.

14

It rained almost all day yesterday. Great. No need to go down to the well-terrace to water the vegetables. The landscape is looking green and refreshed. Soon the well will start to fill up again. I'm dying for proper autumn to arrive. What a luxury not to be hot at all! To be able to wear sleeves again! Roll on the day. The fierce August heat here burns all green ground cover to pale straw and brushwood; everything else hangs on by the skin of its teeth. Only an isolated lemon tree here and there, leaves still bright and green, is left to remind you of how things once were. But autumn in this valley, protected by its ring of mountains to the North and East, brings a second spring. No more eyeball-searing heat-haze and pallid dry dustbowl earth. Crocuses, violets and roses are often fooled into flower again, and new green shoots will soon burst out over the hillsides, to counterpoint the golds and rusts of autumn oak and vine-leaf and the silver of the evergreen olive trees.

My neighbours have an added reason to rejoice over the rain. A good big rainstorm brings hordes of snails in its wake. And a horde of snails, in this country, brings in its train a horde of hungry snail-hunters. Yesterday afternoon I met Franco's wife Iolanda coming down on her *motorino* empty-handed after an unsuccessful hunt for the creatures – she hadn't been able to wait till the morning after the rain, as you ought to really, because she had to take some cows to market today with her husband. So since I live in the middle of the game reserve, as it were, I promised that I would bring her some down if I found any worth having. Iole, even though she has personally witnessed my inability to eat snails at her own table on more than one occasion, could hardly conceal the fact that this offer seemed to her more of a mad eccentricity than a kind favour. Any sane person would guzzle the lot themselves, not give them away.

Still, at crack of dawn I leap from my bed and go hunting. What a pleasure to be nosing about in cool damp grassy corners after the sun-shrivelling last couple of months. I'm not quite sure whether to collect the smaller snails with cream-coloured stripy shells as well as the big fat brown ones. Luckily, I decide not. Only desperate starving folk, I hear later, would bother to eat such miserable creatures: they are so bitter that they have to be fed on sweet leaves and bran for weeks before they're edible.

I manage to collect a good carrier bag full of the correct type of snail, and get them back to the house; but it's lunch-and-siesta time by now, and it's not done to pay calls at this hour. I settle down to tell a few anecdotes to my laptop instead. When I resurface, it turns out to be nearly eight o'clock in the evening. Bother: suppertime. Followed by bedtime. Strange to relate, it's not done to drop in at this hour, either; not unless you've arranged it earlier.

Faced with the prospect of spending the night with my snails, I empty the wee beasties into a large pressure cooker so they won't asphyxiate in the plastic overnight, and give them a bunch of nice damp leaves to hang out on, so they won't dry out or slim down too much in the meantime. I rest the pressure-cooker lid, upside down, on top, to stop them wandering off whilst leaving them plenty of oxygen. Not, you'd think, that they'd bother trying to leave, nestling in the lap of such luxury. Then I shove the pressure cooker under the sink, where Ciccio won't spot it if he makes it up here after work. Not too likely, it being Friday, one of the days when, as he will tell you, his customers refuse ever to go home to bed; but if he does turn up, I have a strong suspicion that he won't be able to resist cooking them. Worse still, once he's cooked them, he won't be able to resist exerting all his powers of persuasion to make me overcome my prejudices and eat them. Pointless: I've tried, loads of times. And I know they taste perfectly fine. But after I've chewed through two or three, my upbringing wins out over my taste buds, and I can't go on.

Little do I know that the snail, small, slow and shy though it may appear, is not only a creature with a powerful wanderlust, but also one to whom a great heavy pressure cooker lid is a mere joke. Next morning I come upstairs to find snails everywhere. Snails clambering damply about in mid-air, up curtains and walls, across doors and windows; snails crunching underfoot as I go for the coffeepot to refresh the grey cells while I consider the problem; snails all over the draining-board, in the sink and the washing-up bowl, snails creeping all over the plates I didn't quite get round to doing last night. They are also making some headway on the sofa and armchairs, and having a party in the basket of freshly picked spinach I forgot by the garden door. It is rather a lot harder to gather them up from all the nooks and crannies around the house than it was to collect them from the hillsides in the first place. By now, what with escapees and accidental deaths, there are quite a lot less than there were yesterday. Still, it being eleven o'clock and a perfectly fine time to drop in on people at last, I dutifully stick my half-a-carrier of snails on to the back of the *motorino* and head off downhill to Iole's big airy kitchen half-way down the hairpin bends of San Pietro. I find her dusty with flour from the ravioli she's just finished rolling, and about to take a cup of mid-morning *caffè latte*. Would I like some?

Unusually for me, I refuse the coffee. I have a powerful motive. Last time I was here, drinking a breakfast cup of *caffè latte* with her husband Franco, Iole suddenly appeared carrying a large frothing pail of milk and, announcing that my coffee looked almost cold and that her husband was a useless host, beamed conspiratorially at me as if about to give me a great treat, raised her bucket and poured a great dollop of this steaming animal's-body-temperature stuff straight into my cup. It was all I could do to get it down without gagging: not the milk itself, but the warmth – or rather, the thought of why it was warm.

Today I can't actually see any lurking frothy buckets, but still, better safe than sorry. Naturally the milk comes, today, out of a nice cold bottle in the fridge. Damn. Iole takes a look at my snail bag at last, and, as is the wont of Ligurians, doesn't bother with any polite dissembling. She can't believe I've bothered bringing her such a tiny quantity. What would she do with that? Snails, I now learn, are gathered by the sackful or not at all. My half-a-carrier isn't even enough for an *antipasto*, says Iole; I may as well take them away again, they'll be more use as breeding stock in the wild than they would be in her kitchen.

Well! The quantity may be paltry, but they were gathered at great expense of spirit. I stomp off vowing never to do anyone a favour ever again, especially not raw-milk-assault-prone wives of cut-throat horse-dealers who wander the hills getting people into a state about their roofs for no reason. Should I just let my poor rejected snails out in the river-bed by the church at San Pietro? Seems a terrible waste. But the gods are with me. Just as I'm climbing off my *motorino* at the bridge, a small sky-blue *Ape* appears beetling down the road towards me. Drawing closer, it sprouts waving arms and shouting heads. Ciccio's friend Marco; with Ciccio squeezed in at his side. They pull over: they've just been to check out a drystone walling job Marco's been offered, up near the monastery in Diano Arentino. Ciccio's going to give him a hand on the job for a couple of mornings, seeing he's not doing lunches any more from next week, and Marco can't find anyone to assist him. (Silly idea, says Marco, he can manage perfectly well by himself. But Ciccio's got a head on him like a mule, so he may as well come along.)

Is there a monastery at Arentino? Strange: I've been gazing at Arentino across the valley every morning for years, but I didn't know there was a monastery up there. Certainly there is, says Marco, who lives up there these days. House prices down here by the sea have risen so high, thanks to the tourism, that a lot of locals have been moving back into the half-abandoned hill villages – all the more worthwhile these days, now the family olive groves nearby are no longer a millstone round your neck, but a profitable enterprise once more. Marco has just finished refurbishing a house up there for himself, his wife Laura, and their little son Michele. Her granny's old place. We'll have to come up and see it soon, says Marco. And the monastery too.

I show the boys my snails and tell my tale of woe. There you are! Marco tells Ciccio. Just the opportunity you needed! Take them round to your mother's!

Brilliant! says Ciccio. His mother Francesca, not being a Ligurian, will happily accept even a ludicrously small offering of snails. And it gives us an excuse to present ourselves at the house together, which will forewarn her of the state of affairs between us if she doesn't know. While, if she does, it will count as a formal introduction, and stop her being offended. She'll give us some lunch too, if we're lucky.

But you should take her a bunch of flowers as well, Marco says to me. A proper, respectful gift she can show off to the neighbours; or you'll get yourself a *brutta figura*.

Ciccio huffs and puffs. His mother doesn't care about such niceties, he says.

Wrong, says Marco in the special quelling tone of voice he uses for keeping Ciccio's wild enthusiasms in check. She's just learnt not to expect them from you. That's no reason to make your girlfriend look as if she has no manners. She can't go with nothing more ceremonious than a carrier bag of snails!

I, for one, am sure that if Marco thinks you have to take flowers to a mother, then that is what you have to do. Lunchtime is almost upon us, though, and the shops will be closing in no time. I leap back on to the *motorino*, and minutes later squeal to a halt outside Diano Marina's only flower shop. The roller blind is already pulled half-way down. Ducking in, I grab the first respectable-looking bouquet I see: a large bunch of golden chrysanthemums. The assistant, glowering, makes a performance of wrapping them in yards of cellophane. She ties the bunch with ribbon, runs a knife along it to twirl it up. Black ribbon, I now notice. Do I look as if I'm going to a funeral or something?

Could I have something a bit more cheerful-looking, please? I say. The woman, giving me a homicidal look, re-does it in red. Much better. Thank you.

Now she stamps out of her shop after me, clatters her shutter loudly to the ground, and padlocks it emphatically. She certainly doesn't need to padlock it against me. I've never been to a florist's here before – never had any call to, living as I do among vast amounts of spectacular wild flowers – and I shan't be doing it again any time soon, never fear.

Ciccio and Marco are hanging out on the terrace of the nearby Bar Marabotto, catching up on Cousin Paletta's latest news. Made it! I say, waving my chrysanthemums in triumph.

All three of them stand and stare open-mouthed at me. A deathly silence falls.

What on earth's the matter now?

Simple. In Italy, chrysanthemums are flowers for the dead, for cemeteries and funerals, not for the living. That's why you get black ribbon with them. And that's why I'd better chuck them straight into the nearest bin.

Never mind, says Ciccio, giving Marco one of his widest and most irresponsible grins. *La mamma* will love the snails.

15

Ciccio's mother's house sits in a small grove of orange and lemon trees in a hidden backwater behind Diano Marina, on the San Pietro side of the level crossing: an area that counts, oddly, as part of Diano Castello. Must have been one of its feudal domains, I suppose. I've only ever been here for the Christmas and New Year celebrations, so I'm surprised to find the place almost invisible under a jungle of trailing vines, bougainvillea, sweet peas and clematis, any gaps between them filled with clambering vegetable marrows, six-foot-high sunflowers, and a small forest of Jerusalem artichokes. As if Francesca's husband didn't grow enough food already! Plant-life seems to have taken over most of the patio too, stuffed into every size and variety of container. In the middle of it all, under the spreading tangerine tree outside the main door, we find Francesca standing among the spring onions in a small kitchen garden of pot-herb essentials, picking some bay-leaves.

Francesca is a tiny person, only up to my shoulder, with a mop of short curls streaked with silver and a look of smiling puzzlement, as if she is expecting not to understand something at any moment. And to be entertained by it anyway. Today, though, as she greets me, she looks even more puzzled than usual. She holds me at arm's length to inspect me, pinches hard at the flesh of my upper arms as though she was checking me for the oven, looks sharply at her son, and announces sternly that I am looking very skinny since the last time she saw me.

I'm not, of course – how could I be, with Ciccio around to fill my life with tasty snacks? Francesca, I deduce, knows all about my changed relationship with her son. It is not my physique that is different, but its significance. What a disappointment to find that when, at last, someone finally pronounces me skinny it is certainly not intended as a point in my favour. I am being weighed up as daughter-in-law material and found wanting.

Still, on to business: I present the bag of snails, readying myself for ridicule. Not a bit of it. Francesca is delighted. How sensible these Calabrians are! And how pleasingly avant-garde their notions of the ideal human physique!

Francesca takes me and my snails over to the tangerine tree, which not only provides essential shade for the table and chairs below, but has also been turned into a handy outdoor storage unit. A profusion of shelves are propped and jammed amongst its various limbs, some bearing yet more flowering plants in pots, others useful items like candle-holders and containers full of clothes-pegs. An old wooden bird-cage is perched high in its branches. We'll just pop them in there, she says. Looking closer, I see that the cage already contains a couple of dozen snails. Odd: you'd think, if you were going to have a snail-cage at all, that you'd keep it in some shady damp corner on the ground rather than high in the branches of a tree. And yet, so far as you can tell with such outwardly unemotional creatures, the snails seem happy enough in their aerial abode. Surreal. I can't help giggling as my offering joins the rest. Francesca giggles along with me. They have to be kept up there, though, she says, to stop them eating Dirt. Whenever she catches one in her garden, she just sticks it in there with the others, until she has enough for a feast. She feeds them on sweet herbs and dampened oats, so by the time she gets round to cooking them they have a delicious stuffing too. As predicted by Ciccio, we are invited to stay for lunch. Not, fortunately, snails, since even this superior kind must be put on a diet for a few days first. Salad for starters, says Francesca, then pasta with *sugo*, and spare ribs with meatballs.

Is she sure she's got enough? I ask.

Of course she has! She always makes enough for half-a-dozen. In this house, you never know how many might be going to turn up for a meal. Somebody will always eat it later, if there's anything left over. The table's set in the kitchen, though – will I be offended if we eat in there?

Of course I won't, I say.

Francesca is most impressed by this response. What a good girl she is! Isn't that great that she doesn't mind eating in the kitchen at all? she says approvingly to her son.

Strange. Can there be many Italian women who refuse point-blank to eat in kitchens? I have no idea. Still, I'm glad to be such a hit.

Indoors, we find Salvatore reading the paper at the kitchen table. He rises from his seat to shake my hand.

Drinka wine! he announces enthusiastically, slapping me on the back. Salvatore learnt quite a few English phrases during a short stay as an immigrant in Australia some twenty years ago, and he enjoys trying them out on me, whenever we bump into one another, to check if they still work. No sooner said than done, he nips off to his wine shed round the back of the house, to return with one of those giant bottles of *vino d'uva*. I sip at my glass carefully and slowly, remembering what ferociously strong stuff it is, while Salvatore necks his in one long draught and is on to a second straight away. A pile of those ferociously inbred red chillies is lying amongst the condiments in the middle of the table; and before Francesca's even got his food in front of him, Salvatore has one ready, pressed with his knife-blade against the ball of his thumb, poised for action. We get straight down to eating a fabulous salad whose main ingredient, unpromisingly you might think, is chunks of brown bread double-baked into a kind of crisp rusk. Once it's been dressed, though, with finely chopped tomatoes, garlic, olive oil, a few sprigs from the thyme bush outside the door and a sliced mozzarella – and in Salvatore's case, several *peperoncini* – it is deliciously moist-yet-crunchy. It is vital, Francesca says, to use the long oval type of tomato for this dish. If you use the round ones, *tondo liscio*, or the big beefy *cuore di bue*, the salad's no good at all: much too watery. Recipe-break here while I fend off the perilous chillies that Salvatore keeps trying to chop-and-sprinkle over my plate whenever my attention wanders. I win that battle; but he starts another one over my wine-glass, which he has been refilling to the brim every time I take a mouthful. I solve the problem by placing my hand firmly over it.

Where does the lovely bread come from, though? I ask.

Not from here at all, says Francesca: she gets it from a man who makes a living driving back and forth between Calabria and Liguria, carrying soul food for exiled Southerners. Her family used to make it themselves when she was a girl. You couldn't afford to be wasting wood lighting the bread-oven too often, so you would tear up a fresh loaf or two on baking day and double-bake the pieces to crispness before the oven had cooled down again. That way it couldn't turn stale or go mouldy on you. Of course, she could still do it herself, but it wouldn't come out right in an ordinary oven, and the pizza-oven's all the way up on their land.

She knows that, says Ciccio, she came up and helped me fix it.

Did she really? says Francesca. What a good girl she is! she adds, giving me another of those thoughtful weighing-and-measuring looks.

Mah! comments his father rudely. Call that fixing? Covering it with a load of muck? What nonsense!

Wait till you've tried it, says Ciccio even more rudely, before you say it's nonsense.

So could I place an order for some of this bread stuff, too? I put in quickly, before the situation escalates.

Francesca is most impressed by this sign of good sense – or sign of an intention to feed her only son in the style to which he's accustomed? – and announces approvingly that she will get hold of some for me. *E così semplice!* she says, turning to Ciccio. How simple she is!

I carry on munching my way through my gourmet rusks regardless. I'm not quite sure what to make of this backhanded-sounding compliment; I hope she means my tastes, though. Yes, it turns out, she does. There is my astonishing ability to eat in kitchens, to start with. And the way I've brought a useful bag of snails instead of a silly bunch of flowers or some such foolishness (smug nudge under the table from Ciccio). And the fact that I'm not too proud to get myself dirty helping up in the *campagna*. And my interest in good, plain food. Moreover, Francesca adds, I've got a fine, healthy appetite, too: and now that she comes to look at me properly, maybe I'm not as skinny as she first thought.

Ah, well.

As Francesca serves the pasta course, Salvatore insists that I remove my hand from my glass. He has to fill it, he says, so that we can drink a toast to Betty. You can't refuse that, now, can you?

Can't I? Who on earth is this Betty? Francesca, through an attack of the giggles, explains that he means the Queen of England.

I gather from Salvatore's devilish grin that he isn't all that keen on our Betty; but she'll do well enough as an excuse for a refill. Have I never been to Australia, then? he asks. They're dead keen on her down there!

No, I say, but I'd like to go.

No you wouldn't, says Salvatore, take it from me!

Have I not travelled very much, then? asks Francesca. Have I ever been to Rome, for example? Because if I haven't, her youngest daughter Annetta is looking for someone to keep her company next week, when she has to go there to sit some exams. Why don't I go too? It would only be for the one night, and one of the exams is English, as well, so I could help Annetta revise on the train . . .

Ciccio prods me under the table again. Fancy *la mamma* offering me such a responsible family position so soon!

Help. Hours and hours of train to spend just the one evening in Rome; and with the wayward Annetta, baby of the family, in a tense pre-exam state to boot. Do I really have to go though this ordeal to win Francesca's favour?

Salvatore saves me from answering by suddenly going ballistic. I have no idea what it's about – he's shouting his head off, mostly in Calabrian dialect, and I will never be as multilingual as your average Italian peasant farmer. Francesca is alternately remonstrating with him, apologizing to me, saying it's all down to too much wine, and laughing helplessly at the impossibility of getting him to shut up. Ciccio joins in, shouting almost as loudly as his father, telling him to calm down. Bad move. Salvatore's voice rises another few decibels, and he waves his fruit-knife wildly at his son.

The outbreak, I discover once things have calmed down, has been triggered by Ciccio giving me bits of apple. The meat course over, we have been munching our way through the various nuts and toasted pumpkin seeds and bits of fruit and cheese with which, it seems, you finish off a Southern Italian meal; Ciccio has been quietly peeling an apple and passing me the odd slice. Appalling behaviour. Peeling apples for women is the final proof of the depths to which Salvatore's son has sunk. He will never be a real man. Francesca joins us in laughing at her husband from her strategic post by the kitchen sink. But, she says, it is true, he's never peeled an apple in all the years of their marriage. She's always done it for him.

Luckily, Salvatore's rages die down as suddenly as they flare up. As his wife starts clearing the table, while his son mutters about reactionaries and lunatics, another Australian expression comes to him.

Come inna backa yardi, says Salvatore, *for-a coffee*!

I help Francesca bring out the espresso pot and one of those herb-based super-alcoholic *digestivo* drinks without which the Italian digestive system is unable to complete its operations. We take our seats in the vine-laden *backa yardi* under the tangerine tree with its precious cargo of snails and sip away, while Francesca points out all her varieties of salad leaf growing in neat rows around us. Now a small controversy starts up about whose rocket is doing better, hers down here in the kitchen garden or his up there in the *campagna*. Just as war seems inevitable, Salvatore's last sip of coffee reminds him of a topical Australian story, also concerning coffee. It is the tale of the time he went to the doctor's to give moral support to a friend with a bad chest-pain. Not that he spoke English any better than his friend, but still, as Salvatore says, two is better than one. The doctor, with his stethoscope applied to the friend's back, suddenly asked them if they wanted a coffee.

No thank you, they replied politely, looking askance at the doctor. Odd moment to be offering people coffee, they both agreed. But the eccentric doctor would not take no for an answer; he kept on repeating his offer, looking at them expectantly. They were becoming indignant about the man's lack of serious interest in the medical problem when it came to them that of course he was not *offering* coffee, but trying to find out *how many* coffees the sick man took a day. Obvious! The sort of thing a doctor would be bound to want to know.

Four or five, they said once they'd worked it out, showing the number on their fingers to avoid any more misunderstandings. But the doctor only became more and more agitated, finally resorting to mime. Salvatore laughs uproariously at the memory. English being an extraordinarily peculiar language, cough-i and coffee are the same word! *Caffè* means *tossire*! How could you guess that? Ridiculous! That's why he never managed to learn much English.

No it isn't, says Francesca, it's because neither of us had time to get to the classes, what with the children and working all the hours God sent. *Che ridere!* she adds. What a laugh! But she still has that puzzled expression on her face. And once the family photo album comes out (we still have another couple of hours of the traditional four-hour Italian lunch break to go, so there's no hurry) I see that Francesca has led a life that would leave anybody puzzled. We start with a shy barefoot girl amongst the mule carts and cobblestones of her hometown down South, posing with a bucket by a rococo stone fountain: an image, you'd say, out of the nineteenth century. Four years later and five hundred miles to the north, suddenly we're among the bright modern streetlights and shiny tarmac of the nineteen-fifties Italian Riviera; Francesca with shoes on now, fashionably winkle-picker, posing delightedly by the marble balustrade along the bay, her two small daughters all prettied up for the photo; she is pregnant again, and full of hopes of a prosperous new life. Hopes soon dashed, she says, when she found herself with Salvatore and the two little ones in two tiny rooms up in the hills in Diano Castello. One bedroom for all four of them, in a place without so much as a bathroom.

Nobody would let a decent home to Southerners in those days. Worse still, most people round here hardly spoke Italian then, only Ligurian dialect; and she'd been brought up speaking Calabrian, so her own Italian wasn't too hot anyway. I should have seen her trying to do the family shopping. There were no supermarkets, you couldn't just pick things up and stick them in a basket the way you do today – you had to know what things were called, stand right there in front of everybody and make a fool of yourself asking the shopkeeper for them by name. (I know just what she means – suffered the same thing myself when I first arrived in these parts.)

The only photo of this black period is on the steps of the Castello church at her third daughter's baptism; the puzzled look is already there. Now, cutting their losses, off to Australia; four children now, posing against the rails of the great white liner, the big sisters in trendy sixties gear holding on tightly to a small Ciccio in shorts and ankle socks, bright-eyed with mischief.

Salvatore went alone, first, he says, to prepare the ground for the family. Thanks to our Betty he found a horrible job in a sewage plant and a decent house at last, and Francesca and the kids set sail after him.

But, says Francesca, suddenly the Suez Canal got closed down, and their ship had to change course and go right around Africa. So she and her children stopped in all sorts of exciting exotic places on the way.

Ciccio has a vague memory, he says, of a fabulous port somewhere in Africa, monkeys and parrots and shouting street vendors with wonderfully desirable trinkets to sell. Too expensive, though – till his resourceful *mamma* collected up all the spare bread rolls from the ship's restaurant tables after lunch, sneaked them off the ship, and bartered them for toys for all her children. Francesca denies this hotly. Ciccio was just a toddler, she says. How could he remember such a thing? But she's laughing, and there's a certain thrifty twinkle in her eye. Australia was a terrible let-down after the thrilling trip, anyway. The house was huge, bursting with bedrooms and bathrooms and lavatories and taps. But there was no street life, no small shops or piazzas where you'd get to know people, no evening *passeggiata*. People just shut themselves in their houses of an evening.

Or, puts in Salvatore, if they were men they'd go to the bar. But they didn't do anything civilized in there, like play cards or read papers or chat. There weren't even any seats in the place. Just stood at the bar and poured drink down their necks till they fell over. Or were sick. Or both, he adds, disgustedly, raising the bottle and doing his best to top up all our glasses yet again, while his wife slaps ineffectually at his wrist. The land was flat as a pancake, too, dry dustiness for miles and miles, a long string of houses on an endless road. When it rained, though, there were masses of snails – and Australians acted as if you were mad to go collecting them! Didn't eat them at all! Like you, he adds, after a moment's thought. He quickly selects something less controversial. Artichokes, too, he says, wild artichokes all over the place and they never touched them. Feasts of artichokes wherever you looked! Salvatore reckons Australians couldn't stomach anything that was free. They thought it couldn't be any good if you didn't have to pay for it.

I have to admit that I've never eaten, or even knowingly seen, a wild artichoke; not due to any prejudice against free food, but to ignorance. I make a mental note to get Ciccio to introduce me to them as soon as possible.

Next photo: here is Francesca outside the gates of the first and only paid job in her life, a gloomy hangar of a meat-packing factory, where she stands smiling bravely alongside a bevy of other women – all from Yugoslavia, she says, so communication wasn't too simple there either.

Call that a job!! interrupts Salvatore. Five hours a day!

She was terrified, she goes on, pointedly ignoring her husband. And somebody stole her favourite cardigan from the cloakroom on her first day. Her big sister in Calabria had crocheted it for her. She was so homesick that day that she cried and cried.

Four years later, and back to Liguria again; a great relief, even to a mere spectator like me. The Odyssey is over, the photos now of familiar faces and places.

The best thing about the whole experience, says Francesca proudly, was that on their way back from Australia the ship went east, up through the Panama Canal. Which meant that by the time they got back to Italy, she and her children had been right the way around the world. Think of that! She gives her son's shoulders a big squeeze. Now there's a fine start in life for you!

16

This is Romeo, says Anna. He has been sent by Destiny to answer my prayers.

Oh, good, I say tentatively, coming out of my front door and accepting the outstretched hand of a short, spry, bustling individual I've never seen before in my life. Does Anna, in spite of his valiant service during her *passata* emergency, secretly disapprove of Ciccio? Is this some more acceptable replacement she's come up with? What, in fact, does Destiny have in store for me now?

Romeo is a cousin of Tonino's, up here in Liguria by chance, says Anna. He's come to take in some good sea air while he convalesces after a work accident.

Romeo brandishes a hugely bandaged thumb for my inspection.

And I'll never guess what he does for a living! says Anna. This will show That Franco! Roofs! He is a genuine roofer!

Light dawns. Not romance, then, but house repairs.

The doctors say he shouldn't start work for a month or so, says Romeo. But he can do me an estimate right away, at least.

Romeo is from Sicily originally, he tells me, but he left his island home a decade ago to take up earthquake repair work on the Continent. (This, I deduce after a moment's confusion, means mainland Italy.) And he's never made it back home. There's always another catastrophe somewhere that requires his services.

Is my roof in the catastrophe category already? I'm not too

surprised, to be honest. I've prodded deep into those chewed bits with a screwdriver and found no resistance worth mentioning. Just sawdust held together with splinters. So much for Umberto's diagnosis. In spite of all appearances to the contrary, he must be an inveterate optimist. Maybe that's why he's lived so long?

The Man of Destiny goes indoors and clambers up on to my table to have a look at the beams, taking my vegetable knife with him for security. Anna remains prudently outside. Romeo prods at the bits Franco has revealed; then he prods around them. He's never seen anything like it, he says, horrified. What on earth are these monstrous things that have been reducing my beams to dust?

I think they're called *tarli*, I say. Romeo gives me a strange look. *Tarli*? he says. Are you sure? Very ferocious *tarli* they have up here in Liguria.

So does he think the roof needs to come off? He tests another few beams. Put it this way, he says: he wouldn't want to be in here under this roof on a winter's night with a storm going on outside. It might be okay: but then again it might not.

I knew it. Frank the Knife is innocent. My roof is dead. I brace myself. Drooping like an egg? I ask.

Like two eggs, says Romeo with a grin.

He bustles off to inspect the problem from the outside, wielding a huge tape-measure. Anna's eagle eyes, following him, note one of Ciccio's white work-jackets hanging outside on my line. Has the lad from the restaurant moved up here and left his mother's already, then? She won't be too happy about that, will she!

What is the correct answer? In spite of our visit to Francesca and Salvatore, which at least means I'm now the official girlfriend, as far as I know we're still in conundrum land when it comes to our nocturnal arrangements. And I don't really know myself if Ciccio's moved in or not. Over the last few weeks rather a lot of his belongings have been winging their way, carrier bag by carrier bag, across the valley from his home to mine; and hardly any of them have made the return journey. But we haven't discussed the significance of this. Too early for commitments. And what about my sister? She may want to come back. I answer the only part of the question I know the answer to. Don't worry, I say, Ciccio hasn't lived at his mother's for years. He has a flat of his own. Like a normal person, I add, rather rudely perhaps. But I have never been able to get my head round the way men in Italy go on living at home with their parents into their mid-thirties. Or all their lives, if they don't get round to marrying, till they end up with a home of their own by default, when their parents finally leave the place feet first. Try asking Italians about the custom – which they will tell you began to die out in the sixties and seventies, but then rose again vampire-like from the grave – and most of them will say that its resurgence is due to selfishness: *egoismo*. Grown up children stay at home, the argument goes, because *la mamma* cooks for them, does their laundry and ironing and whatnot, while papa pays the bills. They are too *egoista* to strike out on their own. However hard I try to think myself into this mindset, it makes no sense to me. I can't help feeling (Englishly, no doubt) that selfishness, if that was what it was, would pull children away from their parents' embrace to seek their independence – even if it did involve crumpled clothes, piles of dishes in the sink, grey rings round the bath, takeaway pizza diet and all the rest.

An abiding mystery – but luckily not one I have to get to grips with in Ciccio's case. And there's not a lot of scope for the Italian version of egoism up here in the olive groves. No electricity bills, not with a solar panel. Free olive-wood prunings for the stove. Nothing to buy but candles and the occasional gas bottle for the fridge; and a mobile phone top-up when required. There aren't even any rates to pay, because this place has never been classified as possessing 'abitabilita' – habitability. (I don't know who does this classifying, or how, and I have no wish to find out, in case I accidentally got reclassified in the process: but sometimes, when it's raining at bedtime, I suspect they may be right.) Laundry goes to the laundrette in Diano Marina to save water; and ironing is impossible because I have nowhere near enough watts to heat an iron. Ciccio has brought up an old flat-iron *la mamma* was using as a doorstop, a lovely simple thing that you just sit on the hotplate of the woodstove until it gets hot, so he can do a collar and cuffs in an emergency. And since he loves cooking, he's doing most of that, whether we eat together up at the restaurant or here; while I stick to my leaf-chopping and the washing up. He swears that this arrangement has nothing at all to do with any lingering hint of Englishness about my cooking. Honestly.

Anna surprises me by being far from horrified to hear that Ciccio flew the maternal nest some years ago. What a nice woman she is. A good, independent boy! she says. Just what you needed – a man who knows how to take care of himself!

Romeo now returns, struggling with the tape-measure and the bandaged thumb, from his tour of the roof.

There's one that certainly doesn't know how to take care of himself! says Anna. Would I believe that Romeo's injury was engineered, on purpose, by an ill-tempered priest?

Hardly: but I am prepared to try. Romeo takes a seat and tells me how.

He had been commissioned to do the earthquake repairs on the roof of a certain church near Assisi. With the vast numbers of fallen roofs about the place, there was a bad shortage of skilled roofing workers, and Romeo couldn't put together a squad of trained men. The parish priest agreed, rather than wait, to accept a roofing gang of trainees under Romeo's supervision. The job might go a bit slower, but at least it would get done. Plus, of course, your man's church would notch up a few beauty points for Christian Charity into the bargain.

So Romeo finally presented the squad he had scraped together. He had chosen them from a list of young men recommended by a Naples de-tox centre; a much more charitable act altogether than the priest had in mind, it turned out. He stared transfixed at the long hair, the earrings, the tattoos; he noted the pronounced Southern accents. What would his respectable parishioners say when they saw this gang of *drogati* – druggies – infesting the holy roof of their holy church? And, taking Romeo aside, he refused point blank to have them on the job. Romeo could come back with a different bunch of workers, or not at all.

Romeo, a man with a pronounced Southern accent himself, stood by his gang. They were good strong boys, keen to learn an honest trade and start a new life, doing their level best to mend their ways. Well, most of them anyway (a pause here – I guess there was a black sheep amongst Romeo's flock, but he decides not to share this one).

And if the priest didn't accept them, he wouldn't get Romeo either. That's what Romeo told him. It was a ten to one gamble that he would come round. The man should have had sense enough to know that all clean-living, short-haired roofing workers with Northern accents, blameless pasts and no earrings were already working flat out. And yes, a couple of days later along he came, swallowing his pride. But not being much of a Christian to start with, not in Romeo's opinion, he had not forgiven and forgotten the *brutta figura* he'd got. Not him! Far from turning the other cheek, he lay low and waited for the *chiusura*, the closing of the roof, when tradition in this land dictates that the incumbent priest should climb up and ceremonially nail the last tile in place. Romeo, as master-roofer, had to be up there too, of course, holding the nail steady while the holy man hammered it in. And, surprise! Unaccountably the priest's hand slipped: the hammer landed, with the force of the Madonna, on Romeo's thumb. He wiggles the product of the massacre at us, wrapped in its voluminous bandage. Here it is, he says, the priest's revenge!

Romeo goes off to circle the outside of the house once again, returns hum-ing and ha-ing. He'd say that once I was doing the job, I should do the whole thing in reinforced concrete.

Surely not? Why?

That's the sort of roof most people want on their homes these days. Wood is only for historic buildings. Restoration and stuff. But concrete is cleaner; and better for protection against earth tremors.

Is it? I have no opinion about cleanliness in the matter of roofs; but I'm certain that I've heard from some convincing source, can't remember where, that the less rigid your building is, the better it withstands earthquakes. Look at all the villages round here. They have drystone walls, and roofs on wooden beams; and many of them have been standing since the eleven-hundreds, when the terracing and olive-planting first started on these hillsides. They have withstood the occasional click-and-jolt, which is as close to a proper earthquake as we get round here, all this time. (Sometimes a few cups will rattle; or you'll be woken by your bed doing a little lurch in the night; later you will hear that there was an underwater tremor whose epicentre was somewhere beyond Genoa, sixty-odd miles away. Nothing much to worry about, unless the place is already half-collapsed from neglect, like Nino's *rustico*. Or unless you have a great block of concrete dangling above your head, as proposed by Romeo.)

Romeo is not sure, he adds, whether modern building regulations would allow me to simply put my roof back up the way it was. But then, on the other hand, now he comes to think about it, getting all the sand and gravel and cement for the concrete version along our awful narrow path by wheelbarrow would take a couple of men several days and cost a fortune. He might overlook this putative regulation after all, if I wanted him to do the job. But, he adds, either way, if any officious bodies from the *comune* came to enquire, my best plan would be to deny that I'd ever had a new roof at all.

Would it? Why? Surely the *comune* wouldn't mind if I just put the roof back on the way it already is? I'd much rather do the thing above board, I say. If they fine you a thousand pounds for not having permission for a tiny chicken run, how much might they not want for a whole roof?

Don't be foolhardy, says Anna. You don't know what the bureaucracy in this country's like. Much more sensible to do the job first, and maybe pay a fine later, than to ask and be told not to do it at all.

Doesn't seem very sensible to me; but then I am an innocent stranger in the land of Macchiavelli.

I've only had a few hours to suffer the new sense of insecurity this information, or lack of it, brings – and I've been asleep for most of them – when another catastrophe strikes that makes the roof pale into insignificance. I am awoken, not long after dawn, by – is it possible? No, it can't be! – a faint sound of munching from the ceiling above me. Electrified, I jump out of bed, drag the chest of drawers across the room, and clamber up on to it. Ciccio mumbles and rolls over in the bed. Shhh! I hiss from my perch among the beams. I'm trying to listen!

He lets out a disobliging snore and turns over loudly again. For goodness' sake! Can't he keep quiet for a second? Now I hear it again. Yes. Faint, but definitely there. How could I not have noticed this before? I climb down and stretch out on the bed again, paralysed with shock. Ciccio! I whisper, once I've recovered the ability to speak. No response. I lie and gaze at the glowing terracotta-tiled ceiling above me; a beautiful ceiling that usually gives me much pleasure. Not now, though. There are several tons of lime mortar resting above those tiles. Tiles which rest on rafters; rafters which rest on the beams in question, where the munching is. Above the cement-stuff is another set of tiles, facing upward instead of down: the floor of the kitchen and living-room. Imagine demolishing and rebuilding that! You might as well knock the house down and start over. Changing the roof, which is only a load of wood and a pile of slotted-on red clay tiles when you get down to it, would be a joke in comparison.

Action. Diesel. Syringes. Quick. There are only a few munchers down here, by the sound of it: and these beams are easy to reach. My ceiling will be saved yet, even if the roof has to go. I throw on some clothes, grab my purse, and dash off down the path. No point waking Ciccio. I'll only be twenty minutes. The *motorino*'s in the right place, for once; but I begin to fear, as it carries me bounding from cobblestone to cobblestone down the hill, that getting hold of a syringe will be a tricky business. I will have to convince a chemist of the rather unlikely-sounding story that I am not a drug-addict, but simply a perfectly ordinary Do-It-Yourselfer who happens to want to inject her ceiling with diesel. Hopefully the chemist in San Pietro, on this more diesel-oriented side of the level crossing, will be open. Otherwise word could soon be all around the valley that I have become an addict, a *drogata*; one, moreover, who tries to cover up her sins by telling insultingly absurd lies.

None of the above comes to pass. Syringe-buying here turns out to be a piece of cake. I've never noticed this before, not being much of a habitual syringe-purchaser, but there are packs of the things just hanging casually on racks at the chemist's among the corn-plasters and the wrist-braces. You don't even have to ask for them. How come? It's perfectly normal here, says Ms Chemist, for people to use the things at home. Loving mothers will often give their kids a monthly injection of vitamins, for example. She went on holiday to London herself once, she tells me sympathetically, and was horrified at the way nobody there would sell her a syringe, even though she explained to them that she was a chemist herself, had a terrible headache, and badly needed to give herself a painkilling injection.

I wonder, as I zoom back up the hill, whether this lack of a mental barrier against using the needle could account for the ease with which many Italians, apparently perfectly sensible people, seem to have gone about injecting themselves with heroin in their youths. Resulting in the terrible national epidemic of Aids to which Anna and Tonino lost their eldest son a few years ago – to name but one local victim – and whose consequences we're all still living with. If the needle is a familiar homely item just like *la mamma* used to use, and not part of a scary doctor-and-hospital or desperate-junkie type scenario the way it is in my own land, I suppose giving the stuff a try would be hardly any different from taking your first sip of alcohol, or puff of nicotine.

I arrive home, bristling with syringes, to find Ciccio still fast asleep. I suppose I'd better wait till he wakes up before I start banging about injecting diesel above his head. It's the first time he's had a lie-in in ages. I'll go upstairs and make some breakfast first. Good Lord! I haven't even had a coffee yet. And I've only just noticed. That's how bad the situation is. The very fabric of my life is disintegrating.

I desperately want Ciccio to get up. I need to share this with him. But he's always vile if you wake him up. How to create the illusion that he's awoken under his own steam? I get out the rest of the coffee trappings as loudly as I possibly can without being actively offensive. No sign of life. I walk back and forth above the bedroom ceiling a few times; then remember the munching and withdraw hastily. What if it falls on his head?

Back downstairs, I waft his cup of coffee carefully under his nose before leaving it on his bedside table. Yes. A flutter of the eyelids. I wait till he's heaved himself sleepily up on to one elbow and taken a swig before making my announcement.

We've got beetles down here, too, I say, in a soothing, just-waking-up tone of voice.

Ah, um, says Ciccio, taking another large sip. Too early, he adds. What?

Beetles down here too, I say again.

Are you sure? he says. Shush a minute, then, let me listen, he adds, leaning back into his pillows. Nothing but a cunning ploy to get back to sleep. He reacts not at all to the next, extremely audible munch-and-click. I'll just get on with the job then. At least he can't say he wasn't expecting it.

By the time I return with my syringes and the diesel canister, Ciccio has disappeared into the bathroom. He had to get up anyway, he says, he has to go and prune the four palm trees outside the Hotel Paradiso down in Diano Marina.

Does he? How many jobs does he have? Since he's supposedly had his mornings free, his life seems to have got even more hectic than usual. Helping Paletta with an old lady's removals, packing away the summer street furniture for the Bar Marabotto, hoeing with his father, delivering vegetables at crack of dawn for his friend Gianni who couldn't make it; not to mention rendering a wall for his sister Giusi up at Civezza, taking his mother to the Imperia market, and two whole days fixing the motor on the small fishing boat he and Paletta keep down at the port.

I didn't know people did prune palm trees, I say.

Well, they do, or the last season's leaves just dangle there all brown and ugly for months. Ciccio used to do a lot of it, but he gave it up. Nasty dangerous job, miles up in the air sculpting away with a machete. He said no, but then the hotel woman turned up at the restaurant and went on and on about how she couldn't find anybody else. He used to have the maintenance contract for their gardens, so he feels kind of responsible. Still, he's game for a squirt of diesel before he goes. We share out the syringes, and twenty minutes later we have every crack and crevice in every beam positively overflowing with diesel. I even remembered to cover the bed with stuff out of the laundry basket, so hardly a dribble has touched it. Well, only at the foot end. Suppose I'd better change the sheets. Ciccio is off with his machete. He'll be at the Tropical for a sandwich at lunchtime, he says, if I fancy coming down.

I spend the rest of the morning sitting in front of my laptop pretending to write, but really nipping obsessively downstairs every ten minutes to my newly garage-flavoured bedroom to listen for death throes in the ceiling. At least there are no open fires down here. There don't need to be. The bedroom is dug back into the hillside and maintains its own pleasant temperature, never too hot, never too cold, all year round. This is because it's actually supposed to be a *cantina*: but the sister and I decided, many years ago, that it would be a lot more sensible to store ourselves down there during the hours of sleep than to waste such a temperate treasure on mere dry goods. By lunchtime I've been up and down so many times that my thigh muscles feel as if I've done a week of step-exercise classes. So far the death throes, if death throes they are, sound remarkably similar to the usual clicking and munching. Still, the diesel wouldn't work instantly, I suppose. Sometimes I'm sure the munching is slower and more lethargic. Sometimes I'm sure it's more manic. Either might be a symptom of approaching death, though, mightn't it? I can't tell any longer. I've never given my bedroom ceiling this much attention. I know I should stop doing this. A watched beetle never expires. I'm sure I've heard that somewhere. The only solution is to set off for the Bar Tropical, and distract myself with one of the walnut-bread rolls with the Gorgonzola filling that they do so well there.

17

Until now the village of Diano Arentino hasn't meant a lot more to me than an attractive view across the valley from my windows, a jumble of tiled roofs and an onion-domed stone *campanile*. And a fine *festa* venue. Arentino's annual party, coming soon, is a great evening of mass eating and dancing to loud accordion-and-saxophone music in the piazza at the bottom of the village. What a different perspective you do get on a place, though, when you've taken up with a local! Today, thanks to Ciccio, I discover that Arentino is also a place of last resort for the mentally ill, famous throughout Italy for its miracle cures.

We're paying a quick visit to Marco and Laura before Ciccio has to go to work, on our way back from an extremely hair-raising trip up into the mountains. This morning Ciccio suddenly whisked me off in his new four-wheel drive to explore the high pastures up near Nava, *Le Navette*, where the cows live in summer. Exhilarating at first to find yourself at the top of the world, higher even than the occasional drifting white cloud outlined against dark hills blurred with oak and ash. Two chamois bounded down towards us, turned tail and ran when they spotted the car. Along the side of a smooth green valley sweeping steep down to a scarily distant chasm way below, silvery threads of river shrouded in mist. Across a rocky moonscape plateau, the border with France. Piercing calls, hillside to hillside, from a family of mountain marmots. The track was impossibly narrow now, cut into the side of almost-perpendicular mountain. Unbearably beautiful, and unbearably scary. What if we met someone coming the other way? Adrenalin overdose. Too frightening. I wanted to get off. Now.

But nothing doing. Another hour of this, said Ciccio, before we got to some slightly less insane roads, near Limone. We could turn round if I liked. We'd driven three-quarters of an hour already, though. I thought it over. Try to turn the car here, and I couldn't see how we could avoid plunging off into the chasm. And going the opposite way, if by any chance we met another car, we'd have to take the crumbling abyss side of the road to pass it. No thanks. Onward! I boldly cried.

If you're scared, said Ciccio, not fooled for a moment, just watch the back wheels in the side mirror and you'll feel better. You'll see how far away they are from the precipice. I did see. About four inches, at a guess. Not comforting. Now a hairpin bend so tight that to get round it we had to reverse towards the abyss, skidding gently backwards as we braked on the loose crumbling rock. I am not one of those people who shut their eyes when they're afraid. But that's what I did, for the whole last half hour of the trip.

I have often been rude about owners of off-road vehicles who never get off the road in them. I will never mention it again. Especially not to Ciccio. And how I appreciate nice, sweet little Diano Arentino after all that rugged terror. Rugged splendour, I mean, of course.

Ciccio wants to pop in just to make sure, he says, that Marco doesn't sneak off and start his drystone walling job alone. Marco has not been well recently, and he shouldn't have taken the job on. He hasn't properly got his strength back. But he's spent a fortune doing up the house and he needs the money badly.

The house, once Laura's granny's place, turns out to be a

tall, narrow building leaning into a labyrinth of alleys. Its ancient stone walls look no different from the huddle of neighbouring houses: but we step into a wide airy ultra-modern kitchen-living room with an open circular staircase at its centre like some seventies James Bond set. Off up the staircase, to find big Laura and little Michele on a white-walled top-floor terrace, snug among the red-tiled roofs of the neighbours, and collapse into a deckchair. Useful washing-lines criss-cross the terrace at the back, and at the front, for frivolity, there's a huge wide view across the valley, clear down to the sea. Treetops rustle below us: a few tall palm trees for style, and below them, for prosperity, an ocean of olives. We congratulate Marco. Great job.

Marco and his father took the old sloping roof right off, says Laura, to make this terrace.

Took the roof off? Even my post-adrenalin-overdose exhaustion can't stop me investigating that one. Did they by any chance, I ask tentatively, get any sort of planning permission?

Am I mad? Of course not. They're waiting till the next *condono*, a sort of government amnesty for home improvers, usually declared when a Pope dies. Not too long to go, judging by the state of the present incumbent, says Marco cheerfully. Once the *condono* is announced, you confess to any building sins you have committed; and they are simply washed away, for a small consideration.

Ciccio is laughing at me. He's already said, in an annoyingly carefree manner, that I only worry about the town hall bureaucracy because I'm English; and I probably love standing in queues, too. And the roof doesn't need taking off anyway. We'll solve the beetle problem, easy as pie, with those few litres of diesel, when he gets round to bringing up a couple of ladders up to make a painting platform. I didn't feel much reassured. Lovely though he may be in many ways, Ciccio is an incurable optimist, and his forte is certainly more inspired improvisation than sound judgement. And when is he ever going to bring these ladders, anyway? Still, if the trustworthy Marco doesn't bother with the *comune*, either, I suppose that's okay, however barmy it may sound to me.

What you need, says Marco, is some serious, knowledgeable person to give you a definitive diagnosis about your roof.

Yes! Exactly! What a joy to hear this said aloud! Enough of living in a blur of guesswork and unknowing! But is there any such person? I ask, fearing that this lifeline may be snatched away as soon as it's been proffered.

Of course there is, says Marco. Ulisse the roofer, from Diano Borello. Ulisse has all the local expertise I could need, and no truck with concrete roofs, what's more, only terracotta ones. He will be tracked down immediately, and his great brain brought to bear upon the problem.

What intriguing names roofers do seem to have round here. This is a most confidence-inspiring one, too. Ulysses. Sounds like my kind of expert.

Ciccio, bored to death with roofs, is over at the edge of the terrace playing with Michele and a toy telescope. But the game is not as innocent as it looks. Ciccio is trying, yet again, to spot my house from across the valley. It has become an obsession with him. Having suffered from this fixation myself for some years until I managed to break the habit, I try to distract him by suggesting some more healthy pursuit, such as going for a walk to look at this monastery. But Ciccio is determined to find me the view I've dreamed of. We must be able to see Besta de Zago from up here! Look how clearly you can see Arentino's *campanile* from my windows!

No sign of the place, of course. Not even with the telescope.

Laura fancies a walk, she says. She'll take me to see the monastery, and Marco can catch up with us once Ciccio's left for work. So off we set, bouncing little Michele over the cobblestones in his pushchair. Within yards we've bumped into Laura's mother, Maria Chiara, who may as well come too. Here we are: the piazza outside the church. There's the *campanile*, and look, hidden round the back of it, the monastery. It straggles down the hillside away from the village, which will be why I've never seen it. Small, but perfectly formed. Laura points me to the edge of the high terrace below us. I look over, and see a scene from a medieval woodcut come to life. Think of that: you could have come here any time in the last eight hundred years – the church was built in 1120 or something – and seen just this. A row of monks in long habits and sandals, hoeing their vegetables down below on the monastery *orti*. I'm not sure if this is a scary or a pleasing thought. It's giving me goosebumps, anyway. Laura goes and spoils it by telling me that they aren't monks, but priests. Haven't I noticed that their heads aren't tonsured? The monastery is a seminary these days, she says: but it still owns a good half of the village land, olives, and housing stock.

Leaning right over the piazza wall to inspect the live-action-woodcut-scene more closely, I see now that a rather large proportion of the monks, I mean priests, are Black African priests. What on earth are they doing here?

Why wouldn't they be here? says Laura's mother. They're Christians, aren't they?

She has a point. Still, on the other hand, the black residents of this valley are hardly numerous.

Not only, says Laura, is there no shortage of black priests up here, but there is also a black Bishop closely connected with the place: Padre Milingo. He is a famous exorcist, she adds with nonchalant pride. Have I not heard of him?

No, I haven't. As luck would have it, I don't believe I know even one single exorcist by name.

If I ever happen to need one, Maria Chiara tells me, Padre Milingo is my man. He can cast out evil spirits like nobody's business. Arentino is the best place in Italy to bring your mad relatives to for a miracle cure. Padre Milingo will work on a one-to-one basis when there is an especially tricky case, but he does a twice-yearly mass exorcizing ceremony right here in Diano Arentino.

Does he? Extraordinary.

(Even more extraordinary is the build-up to the casting-out, which I will witness a few months on. Parked cars jam-packed along the narrow winding roads, just the way they are when there's a *festa* on. But a more un-festive atmosphere I have never seen. A wailing and a gnashing of teeth fills the air. The streets are full of small knots of people groaning and praying, clutching one another for support, working themselves and their poor mentally-challenged relations up into a state of hysteria. Some of the supplicants are making their way from car to church on their knees, muttering Hail Marys as they go. No possible way to tell which are the possessed, which the sane.) Padre Milingo will soon become a lot more famous when he runs off and gets married, while refusing to give up his post in the church hierarchy: which the Pope – still going strong, alas for Marco's *condono* – finds most annoying. But for now, not only have I never heard of this Padre, but I had no idea that these days anybody still believed that mental illness was a product of infestation by evil spirits. Talk about going back to the good old ways!

Still, I gather from the conversation that Marco and Laura have gladdened the hearts of a whole clan of relatives by abandoning the fleshpots of Diano Marina, a whole four miles away, and coming back home to bring up their son in this firmly pre-Freudian ambience.

In fact, Laura's father is so gladdened, says Laura's mother, that – amazingly – it seems that he may be joining his wife, daughter and son-in-law at the *festa* next week. How wonderful it would be if he would acknowledge Marco publicly at last, for the first time in the eight years of his and Laura's marriage, before the assembled eyes of all the village!

It certainly would. As far as Laura's father is concerned, Marco's sins are many and various: but there have always been two main ones. Firstly, Marco is a good foot shorter than the statuesque Laura. And round here, the smaller man with the larger wife is presumed by all comers to have done something heroic to deserve such a trophy of a woman. Laura's father has always taken exception to the way Marco was getting the impressive *figura* of possessing a beautiful big wife like his Laura, without any worthwhile claim to merit her. All done on pure charisma, not one concrete achievement to back it up. Secondly, Marco may have been born and bred here, but like Ciccio he's not a proper local boy. Till Laura announced her intention of marrying Marco, her father Carlo's worst nightmare had been that she might end up with someone from the Faraldi valley next door. Or from Diano Castello. But a Son of Calabresi? Of people who came up here with the dastardly intention, as Laura's papa sees it, of extending Mafia control over the whole country; and of stealing Our Jobs, Our Land and Our Women while they were at it? Unthinkable!

None of this bothered Maria Chiara, she says – perhaps because she worked at home, and didn't own any land or women? – but her husband Carlo refused, for months, even to meet Marco. It was worse still when he discovered that

Marco had nothing to his name but a job collecting waste paper and cardboard boxes in that *Ape* of his, and his father's couple of hundred Plants. Useless at the time, with the market for local olive oil at rock bottom: and in any case, clear evidence of those Southern Italian land-stealing proclivities.

Now, though, Marco has atoned for everything. He has brought their daughter back to the good old ways. Or almost brought her back: Laura has so far refused to give up her part-time job in a bar in Diano Marina. But nobody could blame Marco for that; he keeps telling her to give it up too. Anyway, says her mother, now she's back in Arentino where she belongs, those four full miles away from the pernicious influence of the seaside resort, she'll soon see sense.

Oh, will I just? says Laura.

Better still, Marco's olives are worth something after all, now that the well-heeled of the world have at last seen the folly of feeding themselves on cheap seed oils and nasty, acid olive oils from overheated climes. Ligurian Extra Virgin has prevailed, and Marco has restored his despised groves to their former productive glory, taking Laura's family's abandoned terraces in hand too: while her father, in his dotage, seems to be slowly coming round to his Southern son-in-law. To the point of believing that the resurgence of the market for local olive oil is a feat achieved single-handedly by Marco himself.

I am relieved to discover, once he catches up with us, that the heroic Marco does not take the same sanguine view of Padre Milingo as his wife and mother-in-law. Milingo is a dangerous man, Marco maintains, whose sinister activities should be halted immediately on grounds of public health and safety.

Good. I'm glad somebody round here has their doubts about exorcism as a treatment for the mentally ill.

Yes, the man's a menace to the community, Marco says.

Because what is to stop all those spirits of insanity – spirits doomed, once Milingo has dislodged them, to wander homeless and unstable around Diano Arentino – from invading the minds and bodies of innocent local people who happen to be *in giro*? Marco's own father, to name but one. He was perfectly fine till he came up here to help with the building work on the new house – in the very week of the castings-out. And look at him now! Can it be mere coincidence? Marco doesn't believe so for a second.

Why? I say nervously. What's the matter with him?

The thing began, he says, with his father refusing to eat at family meals; at first they thought he was just sulking at their mother. But he'd been getting the girl in the village shop to make up sandwiches for him every day – telling her that his wife was trying to poison him! The whole family went round to reason with him, but it was a waste of time. He refuses to see a doctor; and Marco's mother refuses to go on living with a man who thinks she's trying to bump him off every time she puts a plate of pasta down in front of him. Now he's gone and thrown a whole saucepan of chickpeas through the window, nearly hit the widow woman next door, and Marco's mother is threatening to throw him out. And who do we think has got a nice big house, just done up, with plenty of room? It looks as though their lovely refurbished *cantina* is going to have to become a bedroom for a mad father. Then he and Laura can be driven mad too. All down to Padre Milingo! The man's a curse on the village.

18

I'm just stepping off my bike in the piazza by the restaurant when, with a squeal of brakes, an ancient grey Renault zooms up to park beside me. Out of it clambers Salvatore, who chuckles at my startled expression, lifts a hand in greeting, stops to drag something out of his boot, and heads jauntily off through the diners on the garden patio. In one sinewy hand he's dangling a pair of plucked chickens tied together at the feet with a length of orange nylon rope; in the other he's dragging a large lumpy sack. I follow him as he fights his way, chickens swinging, sack bumping, through the indoor tables, oblivious to the stir he's causing among the customers. I wait respectfully while he lays down the chickens, heaves the sack on to the kitchen counter, and plants a pair of ceremonious kisses on the chef's cheeks; then I take my turn.

First lot of potatoes, says Salvatore to his son. I've taken a load each to your sisters; this is your share. Great, says Ciccio, opening the mouth of the sack, putting his face to it, and inhaling a good deep breath of damp earth and potato. *Gnocchi!* he says, returning to the light of day inspired. We'll make ourselves a banquet of potato *gnocchi.* Autumn is setting in, and *gnocchi* are a perfect protection against the cold. And yet, on the other hand, summer isn't entirely over, and there's still plenty of basil about, so we can have *gnocchi al pesto.*

Good: we've got that covered all ways round, then. Will he teach me how to make them? Because the only time I ever tried, following a recipe book, my *gnocchi* all melted together as the water boiled up, and I ended up with one enormous blob, a single gigantic *gnoccho*, I suppose you'd call it, floating on the surface of my pan like a revolting gluey pancake.

We'll make them together, he says, up at your place, then. Tonight after work, if he finishes early enough, so they'll have a nice long time to rest before we cook them.

Salvatore is giving me a bit of an odd look. Perhaps he hasn't met too many full-grown women who don't know how to make *gnocchi*? Or is it something worse? Does he object to the intimacy suggested by his son's casual decision to make the *gnocchi* at my house? Two of Ciccio's sisters, Marisa and Annetta, have told me that when they tried to get the gossip on my lunchtime visit from *la mamma*, Salvatore refused point-blank to have our relationship discussed in his presence. The sisters seemed to think it was hilarious, their father doing the old Southern Italian Patriarch act, and couldn't see why I might find it at all unnerving. I do, though. Very unnerving. Mystifying, too, since I've always got on well with Salvatore. What does he have against me all of a sudden? Can he really think I've unmanned his only son by leaving him to peel his own apples? He seemed rather keen on me as a potential catch for Ciccio at the Olive Improvement course – embarrassingly so, in fact. Has he perhaps found out that I have fewer olive trees to my dowry than he imagined? Surely not. My sister calculated, shortly before she left, that our olive earnings had at last overtaken the princely sum you would get on the dole in England. And since she's abandoned the olive groves of Italy for the white stilettos of Bulgaria, leaving her share to me for now, I'm an even more substantial olive-holder than I was before. Twice the woman, you might say. Next harvest, I shall be on more-than-double-DHSS rates. But then, has Salvatore heard, maybe, that his son and I have shared a bed without any mention of holy matrimony? Or has it reached his ears that when he refused to countenance the Drastic Pruning heresy on the family land, I let Ciccio try it out on several terraces of my own trees? Oh, God. Almost anything is possible. With such a catalogue of sins to my name, I should be glad he's speaking to me at all. How do I manage to hold my head high?

The chickens he's brought are too old to be worth eating, says Salvatore now he's got over whatever-it-was. They're a pair of his old layers, well past their prime – but they'll make a fine stock simmered up for a few hours. He thought he might as well start slaughtering the ones that aren't laying so well. No job for these old hens any more, eh? That's you finished, he says, giving them an encouraging prod. He just won't bother replacing them any more, that's all, now that he's going to have to give up keeping chickens altogether.

Ciccio stops in his tracks. What does Salvatore mean, give up keeping chickens? His son has just paid a fortune in fines for that chicken run of his, and now he's giving up keeping chickens?

Salvatore switches in his usual alarming way from good cheer to black rage, and roars his reply in hundred-decibel Calabrian. I am not too hot even in the local Ligurian dialect, and have no chance at all with this exotic Southern one. Luckily, I get half a conversation to guess from, because although Ciccio and his sisters understand Calabrian perfectly well, having grown up listening to their parents talking it, they always answer back in Italian.

Salvatore roars a long roar, incomprehensible to me, at his son.

That was the whole point of paying the fine! answers Ciccio. So you didn't have to knock it down!

Another, even longer, contribution from his father, whose

oaken features are now turning an interesting shade of violet.

Well, why didn't you ask me first? Before you started knocking it down?! shouts Ciccio.

Off goes Salvatore again, accompanying himself with that what-on-earth-are-you-on-about fig-weighing gesture, just the way his son does it.

Of course I explained it to you! answers Ciccio. Do you think I'd spend four million lire on it, and then not explain it to you?

More roaring from Salvatore.

Four million lire! Ciccio roars back at equal volume, looking ready to tear his hair out. Or his father's hair, perhaps. I paid up so you could keep that *maledetto* accursed chicken run, so you didn't have to knock it down! he repeats.

Fortunately for my eardrums, Franchino now sticks his head through the hatch, gesturing agitatedly for to us to keep the racket down, and calls his partner away. Ciccio is wanted in the garden by a table of regulars who are about to leave, and wish to thank the chef.

Ciccio leaves. Salvatore shouts on anyway.

Nightmare. All alone with a shouting Salvatore and two dead chickens. An even louder volley of shouting from Salvatore: I shrink back in terror. No, it's all right. Not aimed at me. He just spotted his son passing the hatch and fired off a quick insult or two. Now he turns to me, full of good cheer again, and launches into some English practice.

Chicki! he shouts joyously in my own language, picking one up by the neck and waving its beak in my face, its hapless partner dangling upside down by the foot from the other end of the orange rope.

Ah. Maybe there isn't a problem at all? Yes, I agree. Chicken. But I know from experience that Salvatore won't have it that any word might exist, in any language, that doesn't end in a vowel.

Chicki! he repeats, giving it another shake and a ferocious eyeball-to-eyeball glare. Now he mimes wringing its neck. *No speaka Englisha, no jobbi*! he tells it triumphantly. Eh? he adds in international-speak; then prods me in the ribs and roars with laughter.

A snappy critique, I gather, of one-time Australian attitudes towards Italian immigrants. Relieved though I am to find that (apparently) there's nothing personal in Salvatore's disapproval of my connection with his son, I'm too perturbed to follow the knockabout comedy lead.

Funny colour, your chickens, I say feebly, speaking in his own language. One of his languages, rather. It's true enough: their skin is dark brown, like a game bird or something. Not like any chicken I've ever come across, anyway.

Oldi! says Salvatore, unwilling to give up on the English. *Very oldi*! But here his vocabulary fails him. Tough as wood, he adds in Italian: but the broth will be full of flavour. He raises his knuckles to his lips and gives them a big smacking kiss to give me an idea of just how full of flavour.

Inspired, I ask whether Salvatore will be staying here to lunch with us?

Certainly not! Firstly, he has already had lunch. Like all sensible folk, he does not wait till (consults watch) almost two o'clock to eat. He values his digestion too much for that sort of nonsense. (I consult my watch too, surprised by how fast time has flown. Salvatore's going for poetic licence here, though: it's only a quarter past one.) And secondly, his son has no decent wine left in the place, so he wouldn't have been able to eat here anyway, would he?

Naturally, nobody of Salvatore's generation would dream of eating their lunch without a glass of wine: *l'acqua fa ruggine*, they will say if you suggest such a thing – water makes rust. Can Salvatore be such a connoisseur of wine that he'd refuse to eat here because the wine list is not up to his standards? Seems pretty unlikely, Salvatore being a bit of a string-and-knotted-hanky man himself.

Now, though, I remember Ciccio telling me (in some irritation) that if his father ever has to eat away from home, he takes along his own bottle of his own wine, made with his own hands, and won't touch so much as a sip of anything else. Positively embarrassing to his son on major social occasions like weddings and christenings, when the whole clan goes out to a restaurant to celebrate. Salvatore's personal wine supplies stick out like a sore thumb, packaged as they always are in those proper manly litre-and-a-half bottles and hence impossible to slip discreetly on to the table among the restaurant's namby pamby half-size ones. It falls to Ciccio, as the only son, to get a *brutta figura* trying to explain its mammoth presence to the management. 'I hope you don't mind – my father insists on bringing his own wine because he thinks yours is full of chemicals . . .'

Here at his son's establishment, though, Salvatore is usually able to eat and drink with no fear of foreign substances, since he supplies a large part of the house wine himself. Has it run out already? I ask.

Of course it's run out! Trust his son not to keep back a few bottles so his old dad could eat with him occasionally! Sold off to strangers from God-knows-where who probably don't even appreciate it, people who'd probably rather have that rubbish you buy in shops! And worse still, Salvatore tells me confidentially, he knows perfectly well that Pierino the landlord must have a good dozen litres of last year's vintage hidden away in his private *cantina*. He takes seven demijohns a year, as part of his rent. Work it out, says Salvatore, doing that tapping-the-finger-under-the-eyeball gesture to show me how hard it would be for Pierino to slip anything past him, especially anything concerning wine. How could he not have enough left to offer a few litres back to their maker, just in case he might like to eat his dinner up here, in the bosom of his family? Fat chance! There he sits . . . !

I certainly don't dare mention that there's a whole demijohn of the wine in question – fifty-six litres of the stuff – sitting in the larder up at my house, having been transported along my ghastly path in a wheelbarrow by Ciccio and Marco. What a terrible person Ciccio is. I shall have to have words with him about the way he treats his poor old dad. He hardly said thank you for the potatoes and the chickens, either. Still, I say soothingly, not long till you get the new year's wine made now, is it?

Wrong topic. I've set him off again.

Bah! The new wine won't be drinkable for another forty days, will it? If it ever gets made, that is, which it probably won't if his son has anything to do with it . . . And if the grapes are left too late the wine'll be ruined, which means buying in a year's supply of wine for the restaurant, so the restaurant will be ruined too. And they're forecasting rain for next weekend, so the *vendemmia*, the grape harvest, will have to be over before that, or else it'll have to be left to the week after, because if you pick the grapes wet, then they have to be pressed right away, the same day, or the wine will be ruined anyway. And the restaurant too, which will show his son what's what! (The volume rises to a crescendo.) And pressing the grapes on the same day as harvesting is too much for anybody, especially a man of his age, even if two of his sons-in-law do come to help; though who knows if they will because they're as bad as his son and you can't get them to do anything, even though they're happy enough to take their share of the wine, oh yes, no problem there . . .

Don't worry! They're coming! I shout at the top of my voice as soon as there's an audibility gap.

Are they? says Salvatore incredulously.

Yes, I say. I heard Ciccio on the phone to Osvaldo and Giovanni this very morning, and all three of them are coming. Definitely. Not this next Day of Repose, but the one after. And Ciccio's taking the Monday off, too. Some aunt of Franchino's is coming in to cook in his stead.

Salvatore subsides at last.

Where do you do the winemaking, anyway? I ask, looking for a nice neutral subject. Up in your *campagna*, where we mended the pizza oven? (Oh Lord, why did I bring that up?)

Certainly not! Whatever gave me that idea? Why would he be making the wine there when his vineyard is way up near Pornassio, fifteen miles inland? Have I not been there yet? Why don't I come too? There's plenty of work for everybody, no fear!

Help! Is this some kind of test? I'll come, of course, I say, if you think I'll be of any use . . .

Amazingly Salvatore pats me on the shoulder and tells me I'm a good, simple girl. Phew. Can't have done anything too bad, then. Maybe he secretly loves the pizza oven repair?

Ciccio returns, unaware of the major breakthrough in my relationship with his father, with Franchino following close behind him. Franchino seems to be exploding with suppressed mirth. Yes, as soon as they're well out of view of the customers, he collapses on to a stool and laughs his head off.

Salvatore and I look at one another bemused. Ciccio

glowers at his partner. It's not funny, he says. Franchino goes on laughing anyway. Ciccio glowers on. And suddenly cracks up laughing too.

One of the regulars, it turns out, a fat cat from Turin who'd come in to book a table for tonight, was keen to know about the intriguing-looking game birds the old gentleman had just delivered to the kitchens. Something special, was it? Ciccio replied, just for a laugh – he could kick himself, he should have known the man had no sense of humour – that these birds were reserved for himself and his staff. They were a pair of chickens that had escaped their run and lived off the land for a year, he added, improvising wildly. The diet of fresh mountain herbs gave the meat that dark colour. A great rarity; he'd been told that if you ever got to eat one, the flavour was unforgettable. No way was he wasting those chickens on mere clients.

The customer did not spot the joke. On the contrary, he began to insist that as a regular and valued client he and his party should be given at least a taste of this gourmet food. Ciccio stood paralysed, wondering how on earth to explain without giving offence. By now the Torinese's lead was being followed by a table of regular German customers, people with holiday homes nearby and enough Italian to follow the conversation. Somehow Ciccio couldn't find a way out of the situation. So there you are. Eight people are coming tonight specially to eat a pair of old broilers. He's going to have to find some way to make those chickens not just edible but delicious by then, come hell or high water. What else can he do? At least with only two small birds between eight people they won't be expecting more than a taste. Still, it's going to have to be a pretty spectacular taste.

Ciccio's eyes are already roaming his kitchen shelves, checking out the broiler-tenderizing possibilities. I can see he is going to enjoy rising to this challenge. Salvatore, who has seemed till now to be enjoying the story, does another of his lightning mood changes. He's off a-roaring again. His son is a fool! Thinks he can run a restaurant? What's the matter with him? Nobody could make anything out of those old broilers, unless it was a pot of minestrone! . . .

Wait and see, says Ciccio.

Well, Ciccio may be mean to his father, but you couldn't say his father wasn't mean back. I'll reserve judgement here. And make myself scarce for now, while the De Gilio family sorts itself out. No customers left indoors; and only one pair outside, on their coffee already. Good. I'm starving. As soon as they go we can get on with the staff lunch. Nephew Alberto is standing chatting to Pierino down at the far end, waiting till he can clear their table. Pierino beckons me over, waving his wine-glass at me in a companionable manner. Looks a better bet than the raving relatives.

What a temper your grandfather has! I say to Alberto, now I can breathe freely at last. Where does he find the energy for all that shouting? Alberto giggles. I should get Uncle Ciccio to tell me the story of Grandpa Salvatore's court case in Australia, he says, the time he shouted at the judge for twenty minutes solid without drawing breath.

My mind boggles. What was Salvatore doing in a court in Australia?

Somebody shot at him, says Alberto.

My mind boggles some more.

Pity they missed, says Pierino, casually dusting off a glass for me with his napkin. Ignoring this sacrilegious remark, I take a seat and sip in a Sherlock Holmes style at my wine, while Alberto dashes off to see to the customers. I know Salvatore's wine rather well, since I've been drinking it at home almost every night. No. Salvatore has underestimated

Pierino's drinking ability. This is something much rougher altogether. How's life been treating you, then? asks Pierino.

I launch into a dramatic description of bee-attacks over coffee, of crumbling beams, of the scary larvae of scary beetles called *tarli*, which Umberto says are nothing to worry about; of Sicilian roofers and their estimates, and my hopes all pinned on a man called Ulysses . . .

Tarli? Pierino is amazed. Umberto is right; nobody would worry about a few *tarli*. Pierino himself has been sleeping these ten years and more on a bed whose legs are full of *tarli*, and it doesn't bother him a jot.

Doesn't it? I am amazed at Pierino's *sang-froid*. How could anybody settle down in the dark of night over a set of spongy bed-legs that dribble sawdust and produce loud munching sounds?

Pierino's nonchalance vanishes. Munching? Who on earth told me my problem was *tarli*? No, no, *tarli* make tiny holes, holes the size of a pinhead. And no noise. Am I sure I described the size of the holes in question to the Oldest Inhabitant? Or the noises?

Maybe I didn't . . . I can't remember exactly what I said.

Well, Pierino knows the things I mean, and they're definitely not *tarli*. No, those things can really bring your roof down! And I've got them in the floor too? I'd better watch out!

I see now that *tarli* must just be woodworm. No wonder Romeo looked at me as if I was mad when I said they were *tarli*. What are these big things really called, then? I ask desperately. How am I supposed to find out how to get rid of them if I don't even know what they're called?

Ah . . . Long pause while Pierino racks his brains. He himself would just call them Those Big Beetles That Eat Beams – he knows the old folks would have a proper name for them (what, older than Pierino?) but it won't come to him. It wouldn't have been an Italian name anyway, he says, but a dialect one, so it wouldn't be much help. And in any case, the cure for any type of beetle in wood, large or small, *tarli* or not, is simple. Everyone knows it: saturate the lot with diesel.

I thank Pierino gloomily. I've already saturated the bedroom beams, though. Twice. And the munching's still going on. I want the German Poison. I'm definitely going to Diano Marina and the DIY shop. Onward to Imperia, if I get no satisfaction there. Immediately. Now.

19

Some three hours later (no point missing my lunch, was there, and it was siesta time anyway) I am hurtling back down-hill towards the level crossing and the rule of law. Hurtling, because I now have half a sack of potatoes roped on to the carrier on the back of my bike. I've had to take them with me to make sure of my *gnocchi* lesson, and their weight is im-proving my downhill speed quite dramatically. Next stop, Diano Marina's newly reopened hardware shop, all painted up and Under New Management.

When I reach the level crossing, it is closed. On either side of it the usual swarm of Vespas and *motorini* has pushed in ahead of the waiting cars to sit revving impatiently, like two opposing battle lines, among the crowd of pedestrians pressed up against the barrier poles. I scuff my way through cars and crowd to join them. Time to put the helmet on. Except that now I realize there's nothing but a sack of potatoes in the carrier where I usually keep it. Ciccio must have taken it into the house without think-ing. That's what comes of riding the bike right up to the door, you see? Bother Ciccio! The man's making my life a misery! Apart from a couple of venerably ancient gents, who are no doubt exempt from the law on both sides of the level crossing due to length of service, I'm the only person without one. The train thunders by, bodies and bikes pour into the vacuum left by its passing as the barriers rise, and I am sucked across the road among the throng. Nothing for it. I'll have to walk the bike the rest of the way into town if I don't want to risk a fine.

★

By the time I've got into Diano proper, parked the bike and the potatoes, and made my way to the hardware shop, I have bumped into two people I know. Both of them have got on my nerves. First Mario the German, known locally as Helmut because Mario doesn't sound German enough, who was on his way home with his latest haul of kitsch knick-knacks from the second-hand markets of Imperia. Come over here, he said, he just *had* to show me what he'd found. Then Ciccio's sister Annetta, who burst out of the coffee shop to thank me from the bottom of her heart for agreeing to come to Rome with her – *la mamma* told her, she's so glad, she really couldn't face going alone . . .

I have brushed aside the beautiful 1940s Alessi espresso pot, refused to agree that I was going to Rome – I certainly didn't say any such thing! – and explained my mission to each of the timewasters in turn, my quest for a cure for life-threatening giant wood-eating Nameless Horrors, the terrible tunnels in my beams, and the imminent collapse of my bedroom ceiling. Each of them in turn has told me that I am talking about *tarli*, and *tarli* are nothing to worry about. No, I have said twice, these things are not the homely woodworm, but something a hundred times more menacing. They make holes *this* big, I have added, waving my little finger at them to show them just how big.

Pair of disbelieving looks. Why haven't the darned creatures got a name? Helmut and Annetta accompany me to the hardware shop, since they've nothing more exciting to do, but I can tell they're not taking the thing seriously.

Mr New Management, a very sleek-looking gentleman, finally appears from the bowels of his emporium after we've opened and shut his door a dozen times to make his bell ring, and takes his turn to listen politely to my wild exaggerations.

Ah, you mean *tarli*, he says.

No. I do NOT mean *tarli*.

What do you mean, then? he asks.

That's the trouble. I don't know. But they make holes THIS big, I squeak angrily, holding up the little finger again.

He smiles indulgently at the hysterical foreigner, disappears again, and eventually returns with a tin covered in yellow-and-black swirly stripes and bearing the legend '*vernice preservativo legno*': wood-preserving paint. Any other hysterical foreigner might easily fall for it. Not me though. I know that tins bearing this sort of curt legend, and no instructions or other information, are extremely ancient tins – tins, in fact, from before the birth of EEC regulations. Your man is either an ignorant fool, or he's cunningly trying to offload some unsaleable old stock on me. Once upon a time all Italian household chemical products looked like this, with monosyllabic labels – or as close to monosyllabic as you can get in Italian – and attractive designs in primary colours; closed books to anyone who hadn't been brought up to know their uses. In my earliest days here, I took a helpful shopkeeper's advice and boiled up the innards of my blocked espresso pot in something out of a bottle whose label, of a very pleasing lapis lazuli blue decorated with a golden yellow sunray motif, simply said '*acido muriatico*'. Noticing, some days later, that all plant life for yards around the patch of earth where I'd emptied the saucepan had turned pale yellow and collapsed, I dug out the dictionary and looked up *acido muriatico*.

Sulphuric acid, it said dispassionately. Sulphuric acid! (It also claimed that you could say 'muriatic acid' in English, if you wanted. But then it was an Italian publication, whose editors had never found the time to eliminate from their dictionary all sorts of extraordinary archaic words, names for parts of stagecoaches and types of manservant and varieties of whalebone underwear. Maybe we really did once say muriatic acid?) Anyway, it was sulphuric acid, without so much as a warning on the bottle, or a recommended dilution, or anything. And I'd been sloshing it about neat all over the place, certain that it couldn't be dangerous or it would say so on the label! Fortunately, thanks to the benevolent bureaucrats of the EEC, Italian containers these days are as nicely smothered in how-to-use-it information and dire health warnings as they are elsewhere, and such outrages no longer occur.

Oddly, the hardware man hasn't even mentioned diesel. I can't resist bringing it up myself. Does he think it might possibly be the solution to my problem?

What on earth gave me that idea? He stares at me as if I was deranged. So does Annetta. So does Helmut. Very annoying of them all, since it wasn't my idea in the first place. The shopkeeper points out, in a gentle nice-to-madwomen tone of voice, that even if diesel were an effective insecticide – not that he believes it is for a moment – it would be a very smelly and also a very highly inflammable thing to be slopping about the home.

Yes. All right. I know that. I've been saying it myself for weeks. Why is it that things that are perfectly sane up in the hills are utterly mad down here by the sea? And vice versa? You could easily believe that the level crossing between Diano Marina and the rest of the Diano villages was not a mere level crossing after all, but the gateway to a parallel universe.

The shopkeeper stomps off ungraciously on the madwoman's instructions to look for something else with a proper label, and returns with a lovely shiny bright green can, festooned with small print and illustrations of beetles and moulds and rots and all other possible ailments of wood, each in its own little white square. A bold red cross is superimposed on each square, prefiguring total elimination. This is more like it. Here you are, he says. German Poison. (Aha! There are some points of contact between pre- and post-level-crossing folk, then.) Helmut/Mario the German claims never to have seen the brand in his life. But then so far he hasn't shown a lot of *savoir faire* in the matter of wood-beetles and their annihilation. It says it's harmless to humans, it's colourless, and it's odourless too. What more could I want? The makers were inspired by the greatness of German Poison, then, whatever their nationality, says Helmut helpfully. Annetta, who has been poring over the label, points out that it says an awful lot about prevention, but nothing about cure. Will it actually get rid of the things once they're in the wood?

Well, says the shopkeeper, if it's poisonous enough to stop them getting in, it'll be poisonous enough to get them out, too, won't it?

This is maybe not flawless logic, but I am keen to get out of here and on with the job. Okay, I won't bother going all the way to Imperia. I'll take it.

Soon I'm on my way back home with my German Poison strapped on top of the potatoes; chafing at the bit when, once I've reached the level crossing and can actually get on to the bike in this helmetless state, I find myself caught up in a traffic jam composed mainly of various other hill folk, mostly women also travelling homewards on *motorini*, but more sedately and with more traditional items on their carriers. Nice bundles of grass and leaves for their rabbits, for example, or a selection of vegetables from the *orto* for dinner. At their head, a pair of extremely unhurried *Ape*s. Six long, slow bongs from the direction of San Pietro confirm that I have hit the getting-the-supper-on rush hour.

A good time to stop for some refreshment, then, at the fount of all knowledge, Luigi's bar, and wait for the roads to clear. Within minutes everyone is asking me how my *tarli* are doing.

They're not *tarli* after all, I say. That was a misunderstanding. They're something else much worse. They make a loud clicking, munching noise, and holes this big, I add, waving the little finger and managing, just, to keep the squeak under control.

A clicking, munching noise! Why didn't I say so before?

Destroy a beam in no time at all, once they've got in there, says Pompeo, leaping straight into the debate now that I have no rival dominant males with me. A hundred times worse than *tarli!* Your roof'll just suddenly crumple and fall in after those things have been at it for a year or two! Nothing you can do about it! Nothing at all. My heart sinks.

Utterly destroyed, *ah, si, si*, Pompeo goes on. No hope for it. The roof will be falling in on your head soon. In the winter, probably, he adds comfortingly, when some big storm arrives – one that goes on for hours and hours, so the weight of the clay tiles doubles and quadruples with all the water they absorb.

Pompeo does one of his famous impressions for us, awful creaking and cracking sound effects, beams collapsing in all around him, weaving and ducking to escape cascading tiles. Hilarious. Pompeo cackles away to himself at the thought of it; the rest of the bar joins in. Can nobody ever mention the peril my roof is in without bringing a completely over-the-top storm into the equation? I could cheerfully murder Pompeo. Eventually he spots the homicidal glint in my eye, and backtracks a bit. It may not be that bad really, he says. He'll come up and have a look at it, if I like. If my young man won't mind, that is.

Oh, for goodness' sake!

What about my trying some German Poison, then? I ask,

pointing through the window at the tin on the back of my *motorino*.

Euh! The company is horrified. Where did I get that from? That's not the proper German Poison tin! I should take no notice of that hardware shop man – he isn't a local, or even a countryman, but a city person from Milan or some such place. A lazy Longobardo from up on the high plains, where no one ever lifts a finger. Nobody in here would dream of taking his advice. No, of course they don't actually know him! But what would you expect from some townsman who decided to retire to the seaside to run a restful small shop, and just happened to hit upon a hardware one? He knows nothing of the products he is selling, and cares less. What could his products be but rubbish? Stick to the diesel!

The topic of the deficiencies of Lombards and other *mangia-polenta*, polenta-eating, folk unleashes a storm of debate. Once upon a time Luigi would have taken a strong stand against these outbreaks of regional chauvinism in his bar. But since the vilely xenophobic Northern League presented itself some years ago as the political voice of the polenta-eaters, demanding separation for the rich and superior North from other, less deserving parts of Italy, I notice that he's given up the unequal struggle and just lets it flow. Also noticeable is that the term Longobardi, the rather ridiculous-sounding archaic form of the word Lombard, has become very fashionable in this bar.

I take my Cynar (an *aperitivo*, the approved drink for this pre-supper time of day: this is a strangely bittersweet medicine-flavoured one made from artichokes, which you can also use as a digestive aid after your meal) on to the nice quiet empty terrace outside, away from the racket, and sit gazing hopelessly at the church opposite. I've lost my nerve. What if it really is the wrong German Poison? What if the diesel treatment has started to work at last, and this stuff stops it penetrating? What if it reacts with diesel? It might asphyxiate us in the night. Or explode. Especially when I light my bedside candle. I wish I was in England. I would go to a lovely big DIY store and read the backs of all likely products, and I could ring up the manufacturers and ask for help . . . And there would be actual official pest control companies . . .

The *campanile* interrupts my train of thought, emitting the wheezing, clacking noise that lets you know it is gathering up its strength to announce the time of day across the valley. So much for peace and quiet. I brace myself for the long-drawn-out bongs that vibrate your very bones when you're this close: six of them again, and then, after a bit more wheezing and clacking, a cracked-sounding bing. Now, where was I? Pest control . . . But wait! I've seen labels stuck on the sides of the *comune* wheely-bins – haven't I? – with the legend 'Pestakil Italiana' printed on them. International Pest Control experts! I remember a Pestakil team coming to our home when I was a child, wearing very impressively coordinated overalls, and doing something to the dry rot in the floorboards that made my parents extremely happy. I nip over to check the bins. Yes! And a phone number, too! I don't suppose I could actually afford to get Pestakil to come and sort my Nameless Beasts out, but I might get some proper advice from them. Off I dash to the public phone in the piazza – might just catch someone before they leave, businesses here don't shut till seven – only to get through to a man who seems amazed that anyone should ring him up; and even more amazed that they should think he might know something about pest control.

We just put rat-poison down behind public bins, says he, and give them the odd swill out with disinfectant. That's all.

Clearly, I say to myself, I am speaking to some particularly ill-informed receptionist. Or a night watchman who's come on early.

Well, I say politely, might there be anyone else in the company who could perhaps give me some advice? I need some information about eliminating pests in wood, I add. Long silence. No, there mightn't.

What do they do, exactly, at Pestakil Italiana, then?

Just the *derattizzazione*, says he: the de-rat-ization.

I wander sadly back to the *motorino* and check the back of my tin, just for the hell of it. A postal address in Hamburg. Natch.

Now what? Would there be a DIY pest control book of some kind? If so, where would I find one? In a library, you might think. But you would be wrong. Perhaps Diano Marina hasn't got a library, you'll be guessing? Wrong again. Some years ago, I discovered that the beautiful twiddly-stuccoed *palazzo* that stands in its own lovely shady little palm-tree laden park in downtown Diano Marina, once some aristocrat's wintering-on-the-Riviera pad by the look of it, was secretly a public library. I say secretly, because you'd never find this out unless you made a habit of going right up the steps of unknown and apparently unfrequented buildings in order to read the extremely small brass name-plaques by their bell-pushes. Yes: once I'd got close enough, it really did say '*biblioteca pubblica*'. And a local library, I said to myself in my innocence, was bound to have the thing I needed: proper ordnance survey maps of the area, maps of the old mule-tracks and pathways round my house. I hadn't found one anywhere in the province so far, not even for ready money. Pushing open the door I found myself in a large empty hallway. Not so much as a sign saying 'entrance' or 'this way to the library', never mind the profusion of posters and community notices associated with libraries in my own land. Was it really a library?

Tentatively I opened a second door. A vast musty brown hall the size of a ballroom. A deathly, echoing silence. No sign of any books. Just two small tables standing forlorn in the middle of the room, a motley assortment of chairs scattered around them. A quiet rustle – or a sigh of despair? – attracted my eye to a distant cubicle away in the shadows to my right. Behind a desk sat what I supposed must be a librarian. Over I went to greet her. But alas, she seemed positively affronted by my request. No, no ordnance survey map; certainly not. No map of the old salt trails up in the hills; no. Not so much as a tourist plan of the town; no, no maps of any kind, none at all. Thank you, goodbye.

Thoroughly chastened, I crept back off through the gloom towards the exit and the sunshine. At the doorway, though, I just had to look back to check. Where on earth did they keep the books? Or did they not really have any? Then I spotted them. What I had taken for musty brown walls were in reality musty brown books. Thousands upon thousands of them, going all around the room and right up the twenty feet to the ceiling. Every single one of them wrapped in an identical camouflage jacket of flyblown brown paper.

I soon gave up trying to get hold of an ordnance survey map, anyway. Down here at Luigi's, shortly after my assault on the librarian, I witnessed a large amount of after-dinner guffawing about a bunch of poor little soldier-boys, young lads doing their compulsory military training, who'd been sent on some sort of practice manoeuvre up in the hills, and ended up trapped for hours in a deep gully full of some sort of horrendously spiky and tangly plant, name only available in dialect. They'd had to radio for reinforcements with machetes to come and get them out. All this pain and humiliation down to the fact that ordnance survey maps here are hopelessly out of date.

No, the map I needed, everyone told me, was the one belonging to the Electricity Board, the ENEL, which is based on up-to-date aerial photographs. Has to be accurate, of course, so the ENEL can track down their pylons scattered about the hillsides when they fall over in storms and earthquakes and what-have-you. Or crumple under ferocious beetle attack, I daresay. Sounds good, but just you try getting a map off an ENEL employee. First, find your ENEL employee . . . I've still never managed to get hold of a decent map of the area to this very day. I rely on guesswork and my famous sense of direction. Why do you think it's so important to know about the Madonnas-at-the-crossroads?

20

Absurdly Anglo-Saxon of me to expect to find anything out from printed matter, in any case. I've been privy to plenty of horrified talk in my time, here in San Pietro, about the weird habits of foreigners who come all this way just to sit about on beaches and in bars *reading books*. (Even more so in the bars of Diano Marina, where holidaymakers are much more in evidence. Ciccio's BarLady, for one.) Do these tourists have no inner resources, no healthier interests, no other way of entertaining themselves? Have they nothing to say to one another at all? If not, why do they go away on holiday together? What a tragedy!

Ciccio himself has complained, on occasion, of finding my constant reading unnerving. I suppose he can't help this, coming as he does from a nation that (a) is compulsively sociable and (b) buys fewer books than any other nation in Europe, according to some recent statistic or other. Reading is a social activity as far as Ciccio and company are concerned, a thing you do in bars, with newspapers. In the bar, though, people stop reading every few minutes and wave their paper about, read the good bits out loud to their fellow customers, argue about whether they're right or wrong. No silent sitting. I'm restricting silent reading done in Ciccio's presence to ten minutes a day at the moment. When he stops finding this painful, I shall slowly increase the dosage. One day, if my plan succeeds, I'll be able to read a whole thriller in his presence. Without being taken for a social inadequate. Which reminds me that I've got a book of my own to finish: time to go home and turn that computer on.

Back at the house, I go first to the bedroom to check. Munching, but maybe a smidgeon less of it. The gas-station aroma down there is so powerful now that I fear it may well explode or asphyxiate us even without my adding any extra German chemicals. I move the bedding to the spare room. Now I give everything another squirt of diesel and cross my fingers. It's great how I don't even care about the roof any more. Some day the Saviour Ulysses will turn up and all will be resolved. Off to work, then.

But within the half hour I have left the laptop and am standing on a chair at my bookshelves, researching. Can't help my Anglo-Saxon roots, can I? Among the stuff I relegated, some time ago, to the unreachable top shelf are several of those publications that tell you how to survive in a wilderness / desert / river full of piranhas, books left here over the years by friends and relations who have trouble distinguishing between an olive farm in the foothills of the Maritime Alps and a bivouac in the Mato Grosso. Surely there will be some information on Beetle Life in one of them? Tossing aside *Where There Is No Doctor*, a survival manual for Latin America, and the *SAS Guide to* – yes – *Survival*, I go through the index of a Zimbabwean publication that tells you how to feed a family of six on half an acre. Insecticides! Here we are. Collect up forty cigarette stubs and boil them up in a litre of water. Spray the resulting liquid on to your vegetables, but don't eat them for at least a month. I should think not. Puts things in perspective, though. Absurd to get worked up about a few beetles in the beams when you could be trying to maintain a family of six on a postage stamp. What about *Wildlife in House and Home*, then; an ironic gift from a brother who had a rather wildlife-packed visit here. (I seem to recall a small scorpion in his shoe.) I've never done more than flick through this book till now. What a fool I've been! It's a supremely gripping read, all about cockroaches and dust mites and creatures that chew through your electricity cables – count your blessings, at least that wouldn't matter up here with only a safe twelve volts in the system – and, yes! a section on every variety of creature known to eat wood.

Depressing news. Wood-eating beasts only make their holes to the outside world, I learn, once they've already eaten as much of your beam as they fancied and are ready to pupate into beetles. So if you can see a hole, the creature's probably already left. There's no guarantee you'll hit anything at all by squirting stuff down it. Poison on the outside won't get them, either, till they take that last mouthful. Which may not be for years. You will be calling in experts to get rid of the things, it seems, so there are no DIY hints. Experts who will seal up the house and raise the temperature to eighty degrees for forty-eight hours. At least, that's the only one of the things they might do that's actually described. Could we manage to do that if we lit the old paraffin heater as well as the stove and the fire, I wonder? Not till after the diesel fumes have worn off, of course . . .

Some hours later, when I've already gone to bed, Ciccio returns home, full of the joys of a job well done. He bangs about, humming happily to himself and waking me up; silence falls as he discovers the empty bedroom. He tracks me down and, humming again, clambers into bed. You managed to create a gourmet recipe for ancient laying fowl, then? I ask sleepily.

He did. They loved their broilers. They really were good – he marinated the creatures for hours and then cooked them incredibly slowly *in civetta*, a kind of sweet-and-sour game recipe with chopped pickled vegetables in it. Would have brought a bit home for me to taste, but they ate every last scrap. Still, they had cost him a fortune in gas and labour by the time they got on to the table. And if he was to include the fine on the chicken-run, now, they'd be easily the most costly fowls he's ever cooked . . .

Anyway, he asks, what are we doing in this room? Pierino told him that the things in the beams aren't *tarli* after all . . . did I put some more diesel on them?

Yes, I did. But check this out, I say, showing him by candlelight the fascinating *Wildlife in House and Home*, which I have naturally brought to bed. It seems there's hardly any chance of poisons working, I add. And it doesn't even mention diesel.

Ciccio yawns, grabs the book from me, and looks sceptically at its front and back covers. What makes you think the people who wrote this know what they're talking about, though? he says.

Well, I say, they must know more than we do, or they wouldn't have written a book about it.

Ciccio leans authoritatively back into the pillows. It's probably all a load of old rubbish, he says. You've never met them, have you?

What, met the authors of *Wildlife in House and Home*? No, of course I haven't.

Well then! says he, weighing the offending publication in the palm of his hand. It stands to reason. You don't know them; they don't know you, either. Why would you believe what they say?

Positively Kafkaesque. Is this what lies behind the behaviour of the non-reading nations of Europe? A conviction that all books are nothing but a tissue of lies? Or is there perhaps some confusion going on here between the novel and the work of non-fiction?

You don't have to meet the writer of a book to believe it, I say. Unless it's fiction, in which case you aren't supposed to believe it anyway.

See what I mean? says Ciccio infuriatingly.

I take a deep breath. Why on earth, I ask, trying another tack, do you think someone who knew nothing about the subject would go to the trouble of making up a lot of lies about wood-beetles?

Why not? says the madman. You wouldn't know if it was rubbish till it was too late, would you? They've made their money anyway. So have the publishers. Why should they care?

We are in deep waters here. Can I, a woman who always has her nose in some book or other, who is even writing one herself, seriously be planning to have a long-term relationship with a man who views all printed matter as nothing but a repository of lies and deceit?

I flick on through the pages, seeking something to change Ciccio's mind about this great reference work. Look at this bit, I say, there's a whole photo section here, so you can identify your culprit by the kind of tunnels and debris it creates. (It looks even scarier by candlelight, too.) We can check it out in the morning.

Ciccio doesn't know why I care what the creature's called. You don't need to know your enemy's name to kill them. Look at wars! It's better if you don't. And how is he supposed to take a book seriously when it claims to deal with insect elimination and doesn't even mention diesel? There wasn't one single person in Luigi's bar that didn't say 'diesel' straight away, was there?

The bar, you see! That's why nobody bothers with books

in this country. They have bars instead. Well, in my opinion, I say crossly, there are certainly a lot more lunatics and liars in bars than there are on bookshelves.

Stick with the diesel, says Ciccio, stroking my hair in a soothing manner. We'll do it again tomorrow morning.

No prizes for guessing which side of the level crossing you were born on, I reply. Ciccio, ignoring this peculiarly meaningless remark, wraps himself around me and changes the subject completely.

Next morning, tracking a delicious breakfast aroma that has percolated down to my bed, I arrive upstairs to a startling sight. Ciccio is not only reading *Wildlife in House and Home*; he is so engrossed in its pages that he hardly notices me come in. Marvellous! What an easy victory! Next stop, Shakespeare. No, Dante, of course, keep him in touch with his roots. I may have to train him up to a slightly more orthodox reading position, though; at the moment he is standing on the kitchen table to pursue his studies. I would normally recommend an armchair, I say, if you're going to be taking up reading seriously. Or the sofa, perhaps.

Wharfborers! he says excitedly, ignoring me. That's what they are! Oh, no. Look, it can't be – wharfborers leave empty tunnels, our ones are full of sawdust. (Small cascade of ditto confirms these words.) Is it the sawfly larva? No, their tunnels are too narrow . . . Ciccio is utterly gripped, head amongst the beams, comparing and contrasting our tunnels with the illustrations. Eventually, by a lengthy process of elimination, we have it. Our visitor is the House Longhorn Beetle: *Hylotrupes bajulus* in Latin. Using the rules Latin has usually followed as it evolved into Italian, you ought to be able to update *Hylotrupes* to *Ilotrupe*; but Ciccio has never heard of such a creature. Here is its portrait, though: an innocuous-looking thin grey beetle, only half an inch long. You wouldn't look at it twice. But its larva is another matter altogether; a bulging white blob with a ferocious pair of jaws to it, and no other features to speak of. The parent beetle can lay up to a hundred eggs, we read, and each blob-with-jaws can spend up to seven years slowly digesting your beams before it pupates. Awesome. We stare up at the roof. Seven years! How many of the things might be in there?

I was wrong, it seems, to claim that we had no such thing in my own country. Further reading indicates that the House Longhorn Beetle has, thanks to the international wood trade, begun to infest some parts of rural Surrey, where its activities are causing consternation among homeowners and building-insurance persons. Luckily for Surrey, the things only fly about looking for love and infesting beams with their vile munching offspring if the temperature is above twenty-three degrees Centigrade, a thing that doesn't happen all that often in England. Sadly, from the beetle-eliminating point of view if no other, it is an all-too-common occurrence here in Liguria.

21

Our union has been blessed by the gods. It's official. Not by the Christian God, as yet. We have begun at the pagan beginning, with the original reigning deity of this valley: the woodland god Bormano. A most generous god, who, when we took his name – in vain, as we expected – for the first time, kindly performed a miracle for us within the hour. A miracle that quadrupled our electricity supply at a stroke.

Until now, not a lot had been heard from Bormano for a millennium or two. When the Roman Legions first arrived here, rather a long time Before Christ, they noted that the wild tribes of the Liguri had consecrated this valley to Bormano – even wrote '*Lucus Bormanii*' on their maps out of respect for local tradition. But later, when their Empire had bloated up to encompass almost the whole of the known world, and their egos to match, they reneged on the deal. Bormano, they now said, was in all essentials the same being as their own hunting Goddess, Diana. They would call the place after her instead, in the interests of Imperial Unity.

Bormano clung on to existence by the skin of his teeth. With all the might of Rome against them, the best his supporters could do for him was to slip in a surreptitious vowel-change: from goddess Diana to god Diano. At least that got him his manhood back. Then Christianity came. For centuries that vestigial 'o' on the name of his valley was all that remained of Bormano's once-proud dominion; while his woodland shrine languished untended down by the river in Diano Marina. Eventually, some time in the nineteen-eighties, a team of archaeologists arrived, documented the site carefully, and reburied it for good. Sounds bad, I know, but put yourself in the shoes of a poor Italian *comune*. Dig a hole anywhere in this country, for any reason, and as like as not you'll come across some important bit of World Heritage. The World will now expect you to maintain it, and will complain bitterly if someone's left rubbish lying about, or scribbled graffiti on it, or there aren't enough public conveniences. More trouble than it's worth. So now the *comune* of Diano has solved the problem for good. Dumped a few lorryloads of fine gravel over the spot; rolled it all nice and flat. Now for a good strong fence around it, fifteen feet high. And here it is, a potent new temple to a nice, modern source of National Unity. Introducing – the *Lucus Bormanii* football pitch.

And here I am, the night before the afternoon of the miracle, a novice worshipper at this multi-layered shrine. Floodlights have been installed high above it: the team sponsored by Ciccio's restaurant is playing tonight. I have been dragged down here by force. Of course people will notice if I don't come to cheer the boys on! I am Ciccio's official companion! No, it doesn't matter how little I know or care about football. They will feel disrespected, and Ciccio will get a *brutta figura*. Worse still, if they lose, they might think it was my absence that brought the *sfiga*, the bad luck, upon them . . .

Oh, all right then, I say graciously, as usual.

Is there no end to the responsibilities loaded upon a woman who foolishly takes up with an Italian? Evidently not. Still, the shed at the back of the ground turns out not to be a shed at all, but a small and well-stocked bar; so at least I have a large glass of deliciously cold and fizzy Berlucchi to see me through the event. Chatting to some other spectators in here before the game began, I also discover one slightly interesting thing about Italian football. The reason why there are double teams in Italy's great Northern cities – in Milan, Inter as well as A C Milan; in Turin, Juventus as well as Torino – is that, when the first waves of Southern Italians began to migrate up here in appreciable numbers, they were not made welcome in local teams, and had to create their own. Well I never. A sort of Italian version of Celtic and Rangers. And that is why persons of Southern extraction, a generation or so later, are still so obsessed with Juve.

If you've never been initiated into the deeper mysteries of the game of football, though, no amount of fascinating background information can help. I sit gazing mindlessly at the hypnotic movement of the ball, to and fro, back and forth, now lost in a wild tangle of multiple shadows and muscular calves, now hurtling across unnaturally purple-orange skies. And as I gaze, I find myself wondering whether, in fact, the cult of Bormano may never have died at all. Could it have been going on under cover for all these millennia? Could someone in the *comune* of Diano be a secret initiate? Soon the Berlucchi and I are slipping back, back through the mists of time . . . the wild Liguri of Bormano's valley have assembled here to propitiate their forest god . . . the tribal elders have chosen their youngest and strongest men, fleet of foot and swift of eye . . . twice eleven of their bravest youth playing out the ritual hunt scene before us, straining every sinew to do homage to their deity, all the skills of the chase brought to bear upon their symbolic quarry, a hare-sized, bloated-looking fetish object, some sort of inflated animal offal, is it? The creature is captured now, entangled in a great blurry mesh of rope . . . A great deep-throated roar rises from the worshippers all around me . . . Goooolaaaa!

Next day, Ciccio and I are sitting celebrating last night's football victory by drinking our very last bottle of Salvatore's wine, the end of last year's vintage, with our lunch. From now until this year's brew is ready, we'll be drinking, O horror, stuff bought in shops.

It has been boiling hot but completely overcast for the last two days, and we are fretting about electricity as we eat. None left in the solar batteries, which are winking their red empty-light at us. No sun to charge them up; so no music, and no chance of watching the video we've been looking forward to seeing this evening. It's ridiculous, Ciccio is saying, that we only have lots of electricity on a good sunny day, which is exactly when you don't need it. How lovely it would be, he adds seductively, if, once winter evenings come, we could snuggle up together in front of the fire, certain sure of our light, our music and our moving pictures. Shall we get a generator?

Strange what love can do to you. When it was just me and my sister here, TV and videos were an entertaining luxury, a surprise bonus. So was the music machine. On evenings in, we would sit companionably by mini-bulb and candlelight with our noses in our books or the radio on. Or both. Happy as Larry. Now, though, I want more electricity too. Desperately. Yes, it's love that's caused this change of heart. First there is the expression of transcendental suffering that comes over Ciccio's face when I sit down with a book. Then there is the way he starts clutching at his head after five minutes whenever I try to listen to the World Service of the BBC, to which I am heavily addicted, and asking plaintively when I'm going to turn off the *trapano*. A *trapano* is a drill: or a person who goes on and on about utterly tedious matters to an unwilling audience. A bore. (I've just realized, as I write this, that we use the exact same metaphor in English too. To bore a hole: to drill a hole! Duh!) Ciccio hates the chattering World

Service: and he loves his music, of which he gets constant new supplies from his DJ friend Luca, and which he would have on day and night, power permitting. I am enjoying this outbreak of melody. My head is too full of words, I think, and the music is doing me good.

Just an afternoon of sunshine would do us for now, says Ciccio. Let's say a prayer to Bormano. He did us proud with the match.

True, say I, and if he was going to be rooting for anyone, it'd be us two, away up here where cultivation ends and the wild oak woods begin; the last human beings to enjoy living in his beautiful wilderness. I take my very last glass of the very last bottle of wine ceremonially over to the oldest oak tree, the ancient gnarled one just above the house that I've always thought looked like a forest-god altar, and raise it to Bormano, making a prayer for an evening's electricity. My whole heart is in that votive swig: I desperately want the solar panel to prove its worth. I can't stand the idea of a nasty noisy generator that will run out of petrol or break down at vital moments all the time, just like the dreaded water pump.

Ciccio goes one better than me. He takes a sip of his wine, then pours the rest slowly and ceremoniously out into the deep hollow at the bottom of the trunk.

Extraordinary! Seconds later the sun comes out. We thank Bormano from the bottom of our hearts, and promise to light him a candle in his hollow tonight. Little do we know that this is only the beginning. Bormano is back on top form from the limbo of forgetfulness, and so thoroughly energized by his regular weekly libation of footballers' sweat and blood that he is raring to go, and ready to do a lot more for us than just a few rays of sunshine.

We wander off for a walk; and, as you do in all the best

tales of the supernatural, we soon come across a tiny over-grown path we've never noticed before, ever, in all these years. We follow it, of course, and after half a mile or so find a strange little ruin at the end of it – a ruin that somebody seems once to have started to fix up. It must have been years ago, though, because you can only just detect the traces of their work; a bit of new cement around a bone-dry well, already wildly overgrown; a patch of new tiles on the roof, just visible behind a thatch of creepers and brambles. And then, the bush. A big round bush: a biblically burning bush. Except that the flames at its heart are not flames after all, but the sun's rays reflecting on some wide, flat, shiny surface. Something is caught up right inside it, amongst the tangle of twiggy branches at its core. We draw closer. It can't be! Can it? We plunge our arms into the foliage, elbow deep, and start to rip away at the knotted tendrils – bush, bramble, creeper, old man's beard – that bind the object of our desire tight to the bush's breast. A thousand scratches later, and we have it. Yes! A four-foot solar panel! And it looks intact! Holding the thing aloft in triumph, we dash for home. Ciccio gets out a light bulb, finds a couple of bits of electric flex. A few quick twists, and halleluiah, the bulb blazes out across the hillsides.

Do we dare go up on to the roof to fix our new panel next to the old one, though? I fear that our combined weight on the beams might produce a similar effect to the much-predicted wild winter storm. But Bormano's not going to let the roof cave in after he's gone to all this trouble, is he? Dawn breaks next morning to find a nightlight still burning in the hollow of Bormano's altar place: and our joint power source jutting proudly on high, giving us music in our home – even on a cloudy day.

★

Some days later I get home to find Ciccio, Marco and Paletta playing poker at the kitchen table, surrounded by an awful lot of bits of electrical flex and pairs of wirecutters. Go and look downstairs! they say excitedly. I do. And there, next to my bed in the spare room, is the electric bedside lamp of my dreams. Ciccio has followed me down to watch me switching it on. And off. And on again. A real lamp! I am overwhelmed. Maybe I don't have to finish writing the book after all, now I have such a competent man at my side. And a little help from the gods, of course.

You can unplug the lamp, too, Ciccio says, and plug it in in the other bedroom. And we've put another socket upstairs next to the sofa, too.

Brilliant! We could saturate both bedrooms in diesel, now, if we felt like it, and still be able to read in bed with no fear of raging infernos. Still, I have high hopes of the anti-beetle terror campaign I've mounted in our proper bedroom, to back up the regime of diesel injections. I simply whisper menacingly into the darkness each night before I go to sleep: *Hylotrupes bajulus! I know you now! There is no escape!* By now the creatures must be quaking in their boots. I knew it was vital to find out their name.

Ciccio pulls out the lamp plug: it is a strange, cigar-shaped object, unlike any plug I've ever seen before. He found the lamp in the car accessories shop at a motorway service station, says Ciccio: it seemed ideal, twelve volts and no adapting needed. It plugs into a car cigarette lighter.

But what are we using for a socket, then?

Yes indeed. Attached to the wall next to my bedside table is a large plastic cube. Set into its heart is my own genuine in-house car cigarette-lighter socket. There's another one just the same in the other bedroom, and one on the living-room wall too. Not only do we have a movable electric lamp, but we need never fear running out of matches ever again.

22

Tiny jellyfish. That's what they are. We've floated in Ciccio's little motorboat into a swarm, a shoal, a galaxy of the things, dotting the deep blue surface of the sea everywhere we look, right to the horizon. Some are no bigger than a fingernail, some a couple of inches across. Does this mean they're all different ages, a gigantic family of jellyfish? Each one has a tiny, transparent helix of a sail to catch the wind and transport it, along with its myriad brethren, to who knows where. At the core of each transparent gelatine ring, a compact heart of intense, vibrant violet blue, set against the equally intense blue-green of the water. Stunning. The two colours together make your eyeballs positively vibrate. How could there possibly be so many of them? Where could they be going? They certainly can have no say in the matter; just a million playthings of the wind. Awe-inspiring. But, on the other hand, not as good as dolphins. Everyone who's been out on the boat this week has met the dolphins. But today, my first attempt at meeting them, they've stayed tantalizingly on the horizon, playing with one another, and refused to come and play with us. We start the motor up and creep closer. They like that game, and dash off, daring us to follow farther. And farther, till we're nearly out of sight of land. They've won: we're nearly out of fuel, and we'll have to turn back. Never mind. Time to get home to meet Marco and Laura. And our doom. They have captured Ulysses at last, and are bringing him up to inspect the roof this very afternoon.

I may as well give you a hand, since I'm up here, says

Laura, nipping off and getting the mop and bucket out of the cupboard. My heart sinks. Laura often does this. I get a choice between watching her do all my housework by herself, or participating in the job, thereby doing more cleaning than I usually do in a month. The Third Way, where neither of us does anything but lounge about chatting, is not available. Even though it's boiling hot again. She's already off in a flurry of dustpans and floorcloths. Should she take the curtains down? Do I think they could do with a wash? Groan. Still, at least it'll stop me brooding. I put on some music, just to prove I can if I want; then I grit my teeth and fill the bucket.

I brood anyway. Ulysses has been: and Ulysses has gone. He turned out to be a large, blue-eyed, gangling man, oddly uncoordinated-looking for someone who spends his life balancing about on roofs, and most unlike any idea of a Ulysses I had previously formed. But he certainly knew his onions – and, as advertised, did not suffer from Romeo's conviction that my roof had to be replaced with a concrete one. His conclusion, after the proddings, cascades of sawdust and horrified *porca miseria*s to which I have become accustomed, was that the Horrible Hylotrupes has eaten the whole end of the last joist, and most of the next one along. They could shear away at any moment, and the roof collapse in on top of us. Probably, he added, during some winter storm . . .

Ulysses is not available to do the job, though, being fully booked up for the next decade or so. This at least means he has no ulterior motive for condemning the thing. Marco has taken him away now, leaving Laura here to help me get over the shock. Supposedly.

Why, I say crossly to Laura as I mop, does everybody feel the need to add this raging storm to the roof scenario? It's bad enough imagining the thing falling around my ears; no need to beef the business up with thunder and lightning and cold and wet. My friend Rose is meant to be coming over from England for a visit soon, too. It now seems she'll be risking her life. Should I ring her and cancel? Laura doesn't think so. There shouldn't be any really bad storms for a good month or two yet.

A mere couple of months till the storms arrive. Ulisse can't do the job. Romeo has vanished off back to the South, having been offered a better one. With, I daresay, no squiggly path to get your materials along. He left Anna to bring up a depressingly large estimate, and the information that he might be able to fit the job in next summer. Next summer! Ulisse couldn't think of anyone else, either. Had I thought of Franco?

Franco? Was he sure about that? Franco the Knife?

Ulisse was. The only thing with Franco, he said, was that you just had to keep your eye on him. Well, said Marco, who couldn't think of anyone else either, he wouldn't recommend it. You're always hearing of some trick Franco's played on some poor innocent bunch of holiday-home-buying Longobardi or foreigners. Making them pay over the odds for property or labour; deceiving them about how soon the electricity is likely to be connected, or how easy it will be to get water piped up to some farmhouse way up in the hills; and, of course, finishing jobs months beyond schedule.

Exactly, was Ulisse's unruffled response to this litany of misdemeanours. You just have to keep an eye on him. Franco isn't dishonest. It's just that he always looks on the bright side. Franco is an optimist.

He certainly is. Last year I was shown, by a very cross Milanese neighbour, the bathroom extension Franco had built for him: and plans for the said bathroom, to which Franco's creation did not, it is true, correspond very closely. I don't believe he can read a plan at all! said the neighbour angrily, waving them at me. And although I didn't mention this, having rather a soft spot for Franco myself, I am sure the Milanese was right. Because Franco can't read, full stop. No doubt, optimist that he is, he will have been sure he'd get round to learning before he started the job.

Laura, who is now helping me eliminate diesel residues in the bedroom – I managed to find us a job that needed doing, even in my own opinion – definitely does not agree that Franco could be our man. I admit privately to her that, much to the annoyance of all right-thinking people, I can't help being fond of Franco. Moreover, I say, in spite of Franco's constant eye to the main chance, I know he is fond of us too. This spring, just before my sister left, for example, he appeared at crack of dawn with a pair of spare horses in tow to take us for a ride over the almost-forgotten mule-track to Pairola, down in the Faraldi valley, where he was meeting a business associate for breakfast. Business that was transacted in almost impenetrable dialect, and involved moving Beasts across the French border over various other almost-forgotten mule-tracks. Nudge, nudge. Finger under eyeball.

Breakfast in Pairola! says Laura. On horseback! No wonder he's keen on you two. Who else would he get to join him in such acts of folly?

Ulisse is right, though, I say: most of Franco's bad behaviour really is down to his being an incorrigible optimist. Except for the money stuff, which is down to culture. Franco expects people to haggle, so he proposes a ridiculously high starting price. The clients are meant to propose a ridiculously low one: and the haggling process would end up somewhere in the middle, at the correct price for the job. But if the client just accepts the starting price, as they sometimes do – especially if they're not from round here and have no idea of the right price anyway – even the most principled person wouldn't be likely to say, Oh! Sorry! I suggested a ridiculously high price because I thought you were going to haggle. Would they?

Laura gives me a long, suspicious look. She's right: I can hear it myself. I'm talking myself into hiring Franco.

Laura can see my heart's not in the cleaning today, she says. Why don't we give up for now, and she'll take me back to her place? Arentino *festa* tonight!

Yes! I have the cleaning paraphernalia away, and my loins girded, in a trice.

We leave early for the *festa* to make sure we get a good table for our dinner, one right near the dance floor, to keep little Michele entertained. Collecting Maria Chiara, we head downhill to the piazza where the *festa* is held. The monastery, sorry, seminary, explains at least one of the puzzling features of this Arentino *festa* – why it is not held in the piazza in front of its church, where all the other villages hold theirs. Obvious. The priests would miss out on their beauty sleep. The other puzzling feature, though, is the food. Arentino's is a Ravioli Festa. All the other villages in this valley cook something seasonal and local for their *festa* dinner – they have a wild mushroom *festa* or a frogs-and-eels *festa* or a wild boar and rabbit *festa*. Or whatever. Surely spinach-and-ricotta ravioli is an odd choice for a festive delicacy? It's a local dish all right, but you can get it all year round, in supermarkets even. Did Arentino perhaps just not have a food element to its *festa* until quite recently? Had all the more fascinating possibilities been snapped up already?

Here, under the usual tree, sits the usual pair of young girls selling tickets for the food from the usual rickety desk. The menu board is nailed to the tree trunk above them: and, yes, there, heading the list as always, are the ravioli. We collect our starters from the trestle booth where a good fifteen excited Arentino folk, shining red faces under chef's hats, are cooking away at an array of giant gas burners. Off we go with piles of crispy borage leaf fritters, *frisceui*, and the local salad of peppers, tomatoes, olives and red onion, *cundiun*, back to our table under the fairy lights strung across the piazza from tree to tree. The band has struck up, and the strains of accordion and saxophone fill the air. Marco goes off to get us some wine. Michele tucks in, gazing mesmerized at the musicians in the frilly shirts on the brightly-lit stage under the chestnut trees. Good moment, I decide, to ask about the ravioli. But Laura doesn't know. It's always been a spinach-and-ricotta ravioli party since she was tiny. Marco, returning, has no idea either. Of course he hasn't. He grew up in Diano Borganzo. Laura's mother can't believe we're all so thick.

Do I see all those iron rings set in the wall over there? she asks. I do. Well, in the old days this *festa* was for the beasts of the field, too, and there would be animals tethered there, one from each family. Surely Laura must remember that from when she was little, doesn't she? The point of the *festa* was to celebrate the return of the milking herds from their summer pastures away in the hills. The priest would bless the animals first: then it was time to party the night away.

I see, I say hopefully. I mull this over for a bit, but find that I'm not getting the connection between milking herds and ravioli. Some element is missing, either from the information or from my brain. And I've only had the one glass of wine. Now Laura's father Carlo has joined us; and, yes! he claps Marco rather hesitantly on the back as he takes his seat and deposits another two bottles on the table. Laura is making a huge fuss over him. Papa! I'm so glad you came! Marco is trying hard not to look as if he just sucked a lemon. I'm going to be distracted at any moment from my ravioli investigations, either by the wine or by the fascinating spectacle of the long-awaited reconciliation. I give up mulling and just ask.

Simple. The connection is not the ravioli themselves – *che idea!* What an idea! – but the ricotta. Before the days of fridges and supermarkets, says Laura's ma patiently, how would you get any fresh soft cheeses while the animals were away? Ricotta is made out of the whey that's left over when you drain the curds for the big rounds of hard cheese. That's why it's called ri-cotta: you re-cook the whey to get the last of the goodness from it. People couldn't afford to eat their own hard cheese; they made that to sell, a cash crop, and ate the ricotta instead. But ricotta doesn't keep, does it? So while the cheese-makers were away in the hills they just ate it themselves. Making the end of the summer, and the return of the herds, the signal for a ricotta feeding-frenzy. All the women of the village have always got together and made cartloads of ravioli the day before the party; and this year, her mother tells me proudly, giving her daughter a pat, Laura joined in too, for the first time ever.

But her mother needn't get all excited, Laura announces fiercely. The Good Old Ways are fine, and it's great to be up here among her family again, but no way is she going to become a dependent wife without a few bob of her own in her pocket. Which seems to be the ambition everyone has for her, she adds, giving her husband a glare from under her lashes. Laura's mother smiles indulgently at her daughter, does a bit of fond head-shaking, and strokes her arm soothingly.

Now I've understood, at last, the deep cultural significance of the ravioli, I naturally feel bound to honour them, and the history they embody, by falling greedily upon a large plateful and devouring a lot more than is good for me. I do such thorough homage to them that, to my consternation, I can't finish my *secondo piatto*. Tragic: it's one of those lengths of lovely spicy sausage curled up into a snail, speared through with a rosemary twig, and grilled *alla piastra*. With a bowl of peperonata on the side and polenta chips. (Yes, sometimes the dreaded polenta makes its way down here to the foothills: but Diano folks know how to tame it. Slice it up into slivers and fry it in plenty of good olive oil.) The reconciliation has so far been disappointingly unspectacular. Carlo shook Marco's hand when he sat down – and mine too, when we were introduced – and since then has hardly spoken to him. I suppose he doesn't have to. The simple fact that they're sitting together, in public, at the same table, is enough to transform Marco's status from undesirable to desirable son-in-law.

The polkas and the mazurkas start up, several more bottles of wine go down, and although Ciccio still hasn't arrived, a large contingent of his family has come along – his sisters Giusi and Grazia, their husbands Osvaldo and Giovanni, the two small boys and two tall teenage girls who are the offspring of both couples: and, leading the pack, Salvatore and Francesca. Instead of joining us as I'm expecting them to, though, Salvatore leads his clan to a table right over the other side of the dance floor. All I can do is wave hello across the heads of the eaters and the mazurka-ing crowd. But Francesca must be keeping a very close eye on me indeed, because the second I admit defeat and put down my knife and fork, she dashes over, excuses herself to Maria Chiara and the rest of my table, and claims me for her own. I must come and sit with The Family to take my coffee, she says.

Public recognition, or what? Eat your heart out, Marco! As we squeeze through the packed diners at the trestle tables filling the piazza, threading our way to the De Gilio table, Francesca clutches my arm and pulls me down so she can whisper in my ear. She had to come over and get me herself, she hisses, even though it should really have been Salvatore who came. (Should it? I'm beginning to think I need a book on Ligurian family protocol. Oh, no, of course, there won't be one.) They would have joined us, but then Salvatore saw Carlo at our table. What's he doing here? He never comes to the *festa*! Has he given up his vendetta against his son-in-law? Carlo is a terrible man. There has been bad blood between Salvatore and Carlo, she goes on, ever since the bad times forty years ago when they lived in Diano Castello. Salvatore still refuses to have any truck with him. I'll tell you later! she adds as we arrive at the table.

Before I've even finished sitting down, Salvatore is raising a familiarly huge-looking bottle – he must have had some secret supplies stashed away – and insisting that I have a glass of proper wine before my coffee. Something to wash away the rubbish I'll have been drinking over there with That Lot, he says, curling his lip in scorn. For goodness' sake! says Francesca. Leave the girl alone! His whole family starts telling him off in chorus, but Salvatore, unperturbed, fills my glass, his own, and anybody else's who doesn't physically stop him, and proposes a toast to Carlo's downfall. Really, papa! comes the chorus. Stop it! Carlo has obviously mended his ways at last; look at him over there, sitting down with Marco!

About time too, says Salvatore. He knocks his wine back in one go, rises from his seat, grabs his wife, who is doing her best not to laugh but can't help herself, and whirls her off on to the dance-floor, where they do not just the very energetic polka currently playing, but the waltz that comes next as well. Giovanni and Grazia and the two girls take to the dance-floor as Salvatore and Francesca return, giggling like a pair of teen-agers, to their seats; I go for a mazurka with Giusi. When I return, Ciccio has arrived. He only got here this early, he tells us, by inviting the last four customers to come up here with him. God knows what they'll make of it. Now he spots Marco and Carlo sitting at the same table for the first time ever, and goes to shake their hands, overjoyed. I see now that there's a small queue waiting to do just that, as if this was an official, ceremonial occasion. Blimey. There I was saying it wasn't very spectacular. And now it looks like a scene from *The Godfather*.

The band is great, rough-and-ready Ligurian country style, none of that smooth *Come Dancing* mallarkey. I take a turn around the dance-floor with Giovanni, while Ciccio sits down for a rest and a couple of quiet glasses of wine. But my blood is up now. When the next mazurka starts up, I just have to drag him from his seat for a swirl round the packed dance-floor. I can't help it. I love this sensation, being part of a great herd of humans, all moving in time together. Can't think of anything better. Maybe I should have been born a jellyfish.

23

What with the relentless pace of life round here, Ciccio still hasn't got round to giving me my potato *gnocchi* lesson. This afternoon, though, the *gnocchi*-master should be back nice and early, and I shall have a pan of potatoes ready boiled, as instructed, when he arrives. Strange to find myself peeling spuds; an occupation so unusual in this land of daily pasta that it makes me feel quite nostalgic.

Ciccio appears unexpectedly early, with Marco. Have they finished the wall already? Some hope, says Marco. They never even got started.

So much for escaping the lunacy of restaurant customers, says Ciccio. Wall customers are infinitely worse. This one, for example, hadn't bothered to mention that the rest of the village was implacably opposed to her wall. So they arrived on site at seven-thirty to find a couple of dozen angry neighbours standing where the wall was meant to go, and the *signora* in her doorway, arms akimbo, hurling abuse. Just shift those *cretini* out of the way, she told Marco and Ciccio as they climbed out of the *Ape*, and you can get started. A couple of *poliziotti* were on their way, she added, to stand guard while the job was done.

What? Shift them out of the way! No way was Marco going to stand there being heckled, or worse, by angry neighbours while he built some highly controversial wall whose use he knew nothing of, and cared less about – and under the indignity of police protection, into the bargain!

They went to talk it over with the opposing team instead,

who told them they'd even been to court to try to stop the woman and her wall. She won, because the land was legally hers. But the judge was a fool, and the village was not having it. Thirty people would have to drive an extra three kilometres each way to their olive terraces and back if she put that wall up. Work it out: nine hundred pointless kilometres between them a week. She didn't need the wall for anything, it was just part of a stupid feud with her brother-in-law. So from now on, whenever any builders turned up, they would just be standing peaceably right here on this spot. That was all. And they looked long and meaningfully at Marco and Ciccio.

Damage limitation: which would you rather have, one *signora* out for your blood, or a whole village? Time to go. As they were clambering back into the *Ape*, the two *poliziotti* arrived. Now the *signora*, beside herself with rage, grabbed Marco by his T-shirt and wouldn't let go. She would have him arrested, she said, unless he got on with building her wall *pronto*! Ciccio had to drag her off, and Marco, who is not known for his even temper, started thumping his fist on the *Ape* – better than thumping it on the *signora*, at any rate – and shouting his head off about trickery and deceit, to much applause from the anti-wall contingent, whose numbers were swelling by the minute – while the policemen explained to the *signora*, with nervous glances at the small army gathering across the road, that their job description did not include interfering with the free market in labour.

But the judge said they had to! screamed their putative employer, beside herself.

No, madam, said the *poliziotti*, nobody actually had to build a wall for her if they didn't want to. As Marco and Ciccio made their getaway, the *signora* was baying for their blood, saying she'd see them in court for breach of contract and calling upon the embarrassed *poliziotti* to be her witnesses.

186

Still, Ciccio is not despondent. First, it's a good thing Marco isn't going to get the chance to wear himself out heaving stones about. He should stick to cardboard boxes for a while yet. Marco sighs. He's already got a wife and a mother, thank you, and he doesn't need Ciccio going on at him too.

And second, says Ciccio, thanks to Marco he now knows what huge sums of money people will pay for dry stone walling these days. Loads of money! For a job with nothing but a few piles of nice quiet stones to handle! Compare that to dashing about at the beck and call of all those deranged *rompicoglioni* ball-breakers of diners, who have too many opinions about cats, and probably won't go away in time for him to come and join us down by the sea for a drink tonight. As usual. Or to being stuck miles up in a nasty spiky palm tree with a hysterical hotel owner complaining that you're dropping your prunings on to her lawn. Or to working up in the *campagna*, for that matter, with that other deranged *rompicoglioni*, his father, who's too proud to admit he actually needs a lot more help up on the land now he's nearing seventy, and just gets more and more bad-tempered. There's masses of drystone walling work around, too, because hardly anyone knows how to do it any more, and there are all these new laws about not ruining the landscape with concrete. Think of that! He remembers, when they were kids, him and Marco sulking horribly at their fathers for making them learn to rebuild the stupid old terrace walls in the *campagna*.

Marco laughs. We were convinced that the whole lot needed re-doing in nice, modern reinforced concrete that would never fall down again, he says. Kept giving them lectures about it. Till a terrible flash flood came, and demonstrated that when a concrete terrace wall goes, it collapses in one huge chunk and destroys everything in its path – like your *rustico*, or half your olive trees. He never heard the end of the crowing and I-told-you-so-ing from his father after that. So whatever you do, he tells Ciccio, don't go mentioning the price of a drystone wall these days to Salvatore.

Do I detect the hatching of another plan for leaving the restaurant? I certainly do. A whole portfolio of part-time jobs, Ciccio says, so he'll have more spare time to help his father in the *campagna*. Walls, gardens, removals with Paletta . . .

But he has already spotted the potatoes draining in their colander, gone and got a bowl and tipped them into it, and started to prod meditatively at them with a fork. The man is positively addicted to cooking. How could he ever abandon his restaurant?

I got those ready for the *gnocchi*, I say quickly, in case he's forgotten.

What, make *gnocchi* with these? Of course we can't make *gnocchi* with them! Peeled, they can easily absorb too much water, and your *gnocchi* will come out heavy as lead. We'll have to use these for something else.

Great. Thanks for telling me.

Anyway, Ciccio's starving; he and Marco went up to Arentino and got his olive nets ready for laying, seeing the wall job was off, and they just grabbed a sandwich at the bar for lunch. They may as well have a few potatoes now. With some anchovies, maybe.

Sorry, I say. I don't think I've got any anchovies up here.

Of course you have, he says; *la mamma*'s anchovies. They're in the larder.

He may well be right. The longer Ciccio and I stay together, the vaster grows my collection of nameless jars: a collection founded with Anna's engagement present of *passata* pots, and since then enlarged with many others full of mysterious things created by Francesca. Ciccio brings another couple down every time he's been working up on the *campagna*, and he alone is able to identify and use them. I hardly dare open one. Even when I can spot, say, mushrooms, I can't tell if they're those pickled kind of mushrooms you use for starters, or the fried-with-garlic kind for a pasta sauce. And you'd only want to open a jar if you were going to use all of it. Because once they're opened, they dribble oil, and collect dust, and mess up the lovely new shelves in my lovely new larder, built on to the cool, north side of the house with my own, and my sister's, hands just before she left for her wanderings among the Slavs. Or else they turn out to be something you have to keep in the fridge once it's been opened, and then there's no room for the milk.

Why can't you just work full-time with Salvatore, though, I ask, if the whole point is to get more time to help him? There's enough land and olives to support the pair of you, isn't there? And a vineyard as well. You'd escape the *rompicoglioni* customers, and have a happy father into the bargain.

Ciccio shudders. Work full-time with his father? Have I never seen *Padre, Padrone*? Father and boss at the same time! And he certainly wouldn't be happy at all unless it was on those terms.

What, they couldn't be partners?

No. Salvatore's too set in the old ways, says Ciccio, cutting my potatoes up into bite-sized chunks as he goes.

You'd understand, says Marco, if you saw either one of our fathers doling out our share of the olive earnings. They wouldn't so much as dream of telling you how much you'd made for your year's work together, even. That's their business, not yours. They just hand you some arbitrary amount as if it was pocket money. That's how their generation was brought up; with the son under his father's thumb, however

189

old he was, until the father kicked the bucket. Why do I think he was so glad to get hold of Laura's derelict groves to work by himself? Why do I think he does his paper-recycling round? Not because his father's short of land. Do I know that some time in the last century, when your land was still your whole livelihood, there were so many fathers treating their adult offspring like slaves all their lives and then, at the last moment, punishing them for some imagined slight by leaving all their land to the church or whatever – and leaving them with no means of support – that the government had to make a law forbidding disinheritance?

All right! I say. Calm down!

He's right, though, says Ciccio. It has half-killed Salvatore to see that his son can make a perfectly good living without his precious *campagna*.

But have you tried talking to these fathers? I say. If they were only made to think about it, they might enjoy being loving, sharing, partner-type fathers more than boss-*padroni*.

Some hope. I should have seen Salvatore's reaction when Ciccio suggested putting up a couple of greenhouses on the flat ridge-top by the *rustico* and doing some commercial growing of his own – asparagus or basil or a snail farm, maybe.

Marco rolls his eyes. Snail-farming is not a sensible plan. Asparagus is too temperamental. Go for the basil.

Good idea, I say. You'd have to clear all that junk away to fit your greenhouses in, and that would improve the place no end. And the outlook with the neighbours over the eyesore question, too.

Irrelevant, says Ciccio. It's not going to happen anyway. Salvatore just decided that his son thought he was on his last legs, and was making some sort of murderous takeover bid.

Still, he says casually, the two of us could maybe try the basil plan out up here. We could fit a couple of greenhouses in down by the well, where the terraces are nice and wide; and rig up a rainwater-saving system so water wouldn't be a problem.

Basil? Greenhouses? Together? Aren't we going a bit fast here? Still, maybe it's only in England that you shouldn't mix business and pleasure.

24

Ciccio nips out and makes another of his ferocious attacks on my parsley patch, slashing off a gigantic handful. I'm going to have to plant a whole terrace of the stuff myself, I can see, if he's going to be staying around. Which it sounds as if he's planning to do. He rinses it under the tap and niftily chops it between the knife and the ball of his thumb, sprinkling it over the warm spuds as he goes. Will one of us pass him out *la mamma*'s anchovies?

La mamma! That reminds him; have I got organized with Annetta for the trip to Rome?

No, I say. I'm not going.

What? says the dutiful son. But you can't let *la mamma* down now, at the last moment, with only a day to go . . . !

What does he mean, let Francesca down? I never said I was going at all! In fact, I definitely told Annetta I wasn't going.

Well, *la mamma*'s sure you are, says Ciccio.

Yes, says Marco, they bumped into her at the Bar Marabotto taking her after-lunch coffee with *la Zia Mela*, Auntie Apple, and Francesca was showing off like mad about how Ciccio's *affidanzata* was going to Rome too, to keep an eye on Annetta for her.

I am speechless. Annetta is leaving tomorrow. I'll drive down now and tell Francesca she must have misunderstood, I say. But is Ciccio just making this up, I ask suspiciously, to get his own back for my lack of enthusiasm for basil greenhouses?

No, he isn't. Oh God, he knew this would happen if I got

involved with his family! She's paying me a big compliment, conscripting me on to this trip. If I'd been brought up in this country, I'd know that's how it was meant. Come on, it won't be that bad! And he'll get a terrible *brutta figura* if I turn up now, saying I'm not going.

He certainly will, says Marco, playing the Greek chorus. And Francesca will worry herself sick if Annetta goes on her own.

This is ridiculous. First Ciccio's family decides, without consulting me, to send me on a mission to Rome. And then I have to worry about giving him a *brutta figura* if I don't do as I'm told! What'll it be next, the scold's bridle?

Light is beginning to dawn, anyway. To go round to visit a mother, bearing the fatal bunch of flowers, or as it were bag of snails, is to put in an official request to be accepted into the family. That's why it's so surrounded by ceremony. And if you're accepted into an Italian family, you get pushed around, not to put too fine a point on it, by *la mamma*. Even if *la mamma* is a kindly, unassuming person like Francesca. The role is bigger than the individual. *Ergo*, this piece of outrageous behaviour is meant as a sign of acceptance. Well, I suppose I'm pleased. I don't really mind going to Rome. I'm just shocked to discover that I have symbolically handed over control of my life to his mother by the act of eating her salt.

Oh, all right then, I say ungraciously from inside the larder, where I am hunting for anchovies. There were already an oppressively large number of jars even before we went round to his mother's; I'd forgotten she gave me another couple of dozen from her provisions out in the wine shed. Another sign of acceptance, I suppose. What sort of pot would they be in?

I pass Ciccio out the enormous Kilner jar he's after, and soon he is digging something from under a crusty tomb of rock salt deep within it. Yes, an anchovy. At least twice the size of those long thin slivers you buy in shops, though.

Ah! says he. Nobody makes anchovies like *la mamma*! I try one: he's right.

You should be glad you're going to Rome, anyway, he says, shredding anchovies over his warm potatoes with what seems to me a hint of snugness. He's sure I'd rather be sitting on a nice quiet train with Annetta than wrapping another thousand jars of *sugo* in newspaper. And if I stayed here, I'd be dragooned into his family's tomato harvest-and-*passata*-making event. In fact, he has strong suspicions about his little sister's motive for taking these exams in the first place.

He is getting the tiny ice-cube tray, a thing I never use, out of my tiny fridge now. He empties a couple of bright green cubes out of it. What are those?

The remnants of the rocket pesto, of course. Fresh pesto will keep for months if you freeze it. He sets a couple of pesto-cubes to melt in a cup on the side of the woodstove.

I dig out another anchovy. How do you make these, then? I ask. I'll get myself a cookery lesson tonight, by hook or by crook.

Some hope: I get one of Ciccio's usual unfollowable recipes. It begins like this: 'Wait till you hear that the shoals of anchovies have come in; then go to Imperia harbour and buy a crate.' And how would you hear such a thing? By endlessly popping in and out of bars to catch up on the gossip, that's how. In Marco and Ciccio's account of today's events at least two droppings-into-bars have casually cropped up; and there will have been several more. I've begun to grasp that Ciccio isn't quite as overworked as I first thought. If he has even the smallest task to do, he will be away by seven a.m. to do it, not because it has to be done that early, but because he can't bear to miss the essential men's pre-work espresso-and-gossip session at the bar. As often as not he's back by nine, bearing fresh rolls and hot news. This is how the men of this valley keep their fingers on the pulse – not only of the movements of anchovy shoals, but also of such matters as whether to do the *vendemmia* now or wait another week or two, what jobs are going where, how the year's olive crop is looking and likely prices for it at the mill; also whose husband has been seen in the car of somebody who wasn't his wife, and vice versa; the life histories of drug-dealing goat-herds; and, even, in extreme cases, wood-beetle elimination techniques. Agricultural information network, stock exchange, labour exchange, and Neighbourhood Morality Watch all rolled into one.

The anchovy recipe continues thus. After the harbour, you go to a *tabacchaio*, a tobacco shop, and get a load of sea salt, the chunkiest kind. Now you pile the anchovies one by one into your jar, covering each one with a good handful of salt crystals. Press down hard, shut the jar. Then wait till they're ready.

What, don't you have to gut the fish first? I ask.

Of course you do! Fillet them too, if you like, though *la mamma* doesn't bother. Then you just wait a few weeks while the salt cures them.

Will I ask how long you wait? I bet I can guess anyway. Everything always takes forty days round here. Wine, cheese, olives, fresh salami, anything at all that has to mature takes forty days.

Forty days? I ask.

Well done! says the chef. How did you know?

I'm surprised, though, to hear that you really do buy salt in tobacco shops. They always have that dark blue enamelled sign hanging outside them with a big white 'T' on it, it's true, and a small inscription below saying 'Salts and Tobaccos', but

I've always imagined that these were of archaeological interest only, a hangover from some former time when salt was expensive and hard to come by. I just haven't noticed, Ciccio tells me, because the San Pietro grocery shop doubles as a salt-and-tobacco shop anyway. Salt is still a State Monopoly as far as he knows. Like tobacco.

Would they have State Monopoly bits of coastline, then, for the sea salt? I ask. With minefields around them and the odd Cruise missile and suchlike? Going on my own experience of the rigours of the tobacco monopoly, this seems only too likely. A while ago I found myself in the tobacco-growing heartlands of Italy, admiring the high curing barns with their walls pierced to the wind, the great thick ropes of golden-brown leaves hanging within. Idly I decided to get hold of a few tobacco seeds while I was here. I would plant them back home in Liguria and see what organic home-grown tobacco might be like. I nipped into the first *Consorzio Agrario* I saw. Could I buy some tobacco seeds, please? Woman looks at me as if I'm mad. Or do you sell seedlings, perhaps? I add, guessing that it's the wrong season or something. Woman and a local tobacco farmer, who turns out to have been lurking in a dark corner among the sickles, soon put me right. *Magari!* they say: some hope! When they say State Monopoly, they mean State Monopoly. Even a tobacco farmer can't get hold of tobacco seeds. The State grows the seedlings itself, in some sort of top secret Tobacco Silos, and delivers them, counted out, to the farmers each spring. Then they count them back in again at the end of the growing season. They've done something to the plants, too, says Tobacco Farmer with a bitter laugh, so that even if you collect up seed from your tobacco, which of course he and his neighbours have tried doing, most of it is infertile. No way to circumvent the Salts and Tobaccos Inspectorate.

★

Now Ciccio has got out the *Olio dell'Amore* – oh, all right, the Love Oil – and sliced a lemon in half. He trickles the one on to his warm-potato-parsley-and-anchovy salad, squeezes the other. Marco adds a pinch of salt, a turn of black pepper. Dollop of pesto on the side. They sit down and start to eat. I'm feeling quite hungry again myself. Ciccio passes me a fork so I can share, and pours us each a glass of wine. Not proper Father's Wine, of course, but some concoction of grapes and chemicals bought in a shop. Marco is most concerned. Why didn't we tell him? He would have brought some of his own Father's Wine up for us. Or even some of Carlo's, which he and Laura have been given a whole demijohn of, fifty-odd litres, to celebrate his new status as *persona grata*.

Bring some up, yes, says Ciccio. We're on this bought stuff till Saint Martin's day now. *Il giorno di San Martino, il mosto diventa vino*, he recites. 'At Saint Martin's time, the must turns into wine.'

When is this Saint Martin's day, then? asks the foreign ignoramus.

When do I think? Forty days after the grape harvest, of course. Which we'll be doing next week, as soon as I get back from Rome. Right after the tomato harvest this year, worse luck. No peace when Salvatore's running your life.

Thinking of your father's temper, I say a few mouthfuls later, Alberto told me there was some story about him shouting at a judge in Australia . . . ?

The first, condensed version of this story, told by a man desperate to get on with his potatoes, goes something like this:

Scene: A courthouse near Melbourne. Salvatore is led into the witness box. Ciccio, aged nine or thereabouts, waits on the sidelines. His English is a lot better than his father's, and he is to translate if Salvatore gets into difficulties. The Judge sits on his throne, the Jury on its benches. The Accused stands in the dock, on trial for firing three shots at Salvatore while he was on his way to the beach with his son, unarmed and unsuspecting.

Spotting the Accused, Salvatore utters a loud roar of rage. The judge asks if he recognizes the man in the dock. Salvatore does his best to answer in English, adding an extra vowel or two wherever he feels it will improve the flow. The judge begins to look perplexed. Salvatore gives up the unequal struggle and storms off in his own more adequate language, with plenty of ferocious stabbing of the index finger in the direction of the accused. Some ten minutes later he begins to run out of steam. The judge turns to Ciccio.

Judge: What did your father say?

Little Ciccio (thinking hard: what was the actual content of his father's remarks?): Um . . . He said . . . He said . . . He's angry.

Courtroom collapses in helpless mirth.

Satisfactory enough, as stories go, but where is the background? Is it a tale that can never be told, some Australian Mafia saga, to be veiled forever in *omerta*? I wait until the potato plate is almost empty, the second glass of wine going down, and inspiration perhaps flowing more easily, before asking the burning question.

Why, I say, bracing myself for the *omerta*, was this man shooting at your father in the first place?

But *omerta* doesn't come into it. The story is too weird for that.

Salvatore had taken his son to collect mussels on a shore somewhere near Melbourne. They used to do this regularly, take the bus to a nearby beach and get a nice big sackful, enough for a fine family dinner. Australians, apparently, looked askance not only at snail-and wild-artichoke-gathering, but also at mussel-eating: it was something only foreigners did. (They also looked askance at people with big dripping wet sacks full of the things sitting next to them on buses, and Ciccio was always mortified by the mussel outings – but that's another story.) To get to the mussel beds, you had to go along a sand-dune footpath that passed close to the home of an Australian who, unbeknownst to Salvatore and son, particularly disliked foreigners. Especially mussel-collecting ones. Today, after a drink or two, he'd decided that if any came by this afternoon, he'd give them a good blast with his shotgun to teach them a lesson.

Hearing the first shot ring out, Salvatore, as you'd expect from a man who had survived the Nazi occupation of his country, hurled his son to the ground and threw himself over him for protection. The defender of Australian mussels fired another couple of rounds, but had to stop before he'd done any permanent damage. This was because another Australian had appeared, coming up the path from the sea. And this other Australian disagreed so violently with the shooting of unarmed Italian mussel-gatherers that he went straight off and got the police.

And so, to court.

25

I board the train at Diano Marina with my charge, Annetta, a gentle pussycat of a girl with big brown eyes and a huge infectious smile. We are bowed down under the weight of the provisions Francesca has supplied to keep us going for the next forty-eight hours. We'll be staying two nights in Rome, because otherwise we'd have to get a very slow night train back tomorrow. We've been given double, or possibly triple, rations to make up for the absence of my own mother, who would naturally, Francesca explained, have provided me with several tons of snacks for the trip herself, if only she were here. *Magari*. Luckily we've found an eight-person compartment all to ourselves. Let's hope nobody else tries to get in with us; not till after lunch, anyway.

Annetta has brought some cribbing equipment with her, she says, so she can do some last-minute revision on the train. As the train clanks slowly out of the station and cleaves its way through the crowds at the level crossing, she mounts a major hunt for it among the piles of garlic-and-rosemary-perfumed roast chicken and slices of *frittata*, the foil-wrapped packets of stuffed onion halves and *focaccia*, the carrier of tomatoes from the *orto*, the dribbling pots of grilled aubergine and stuffed red peppers *sott'olio*, the brown paper bags of cheeses and whole salami.

Until now I've believed that only foreign travel would produce this obsessive fear, in the breast of an Italian mother, that her offspring might be looking starvation in the face. The Naples–Calais train I once used to catch from here at the end of summer was, I recall, a positive travelling cornucopia, packed with every type of delicacy a few thousand fearful *mammas* could pack into their migrant-worker offspring's luggage. Delicacies that, handily for a foreigner provided with nothing more exciting than a couple of limp ham rolls, the travellers would always insist on sharing round the compartment.

It now appears, however, that even in Rome, Francesca's own capital city, we can expect to encounter famine conditions. If, that is, we survive the muggers and thieves who will be dogging our every step. Francesca has warned us to remove every scrap of jewellery – and don't forget your watches! – before setting foot outside our hotel.

How did *la mamma* get you to change your mind about coming? asks Annetta, still hunting as the big blue Mediterranean comes into view: this line runs alongside the sea all the way to Genoa.

I'm not quite sure, I say darkly.

Annetta gives me one of the huge sunny smiles. That's why my brother kept putting off taking you round there, she says. You'll be dragooned into everything now. And you'll both be round for supper at least once a week, or it'll be the worse for you. Poor Ciccio! *La mamma*'s dead keen on you, though, isn't she?

Pity about your father, though, I say. I don't think I've made much of a hit with him.

Mah! says Annetta, just the way her dad says it. Salvatore makes it a policy never to approve of anything. Do I know he's never once said aloud that he loves his children? Heaven forbid he should show such a sign of weakness! Good job we have to stay two nights in Rome, too, or he'd have had us both up in the *campagna* slaving away over his tomatoes.

Annetta has found her revision equipment at last: a pile of pads, like blocks of long thin raffle tickets, one for each of her subjects. I flick through the Italian literature one; it is packed with information in minute print on both sides of the book-mark-shaped page. Nine essays on each of the major literary figures of the last three centuries: their social and historical background, their major works and significance, their place in literary innovation. Amazing, I say, you don't get nice pat essay-type summaries like this in English cribs. I suppose they'd think it was a bit too much like cheating.

Really? says Annetta. But that's exactly what these things are for. Cheating. You tear them off, sheet by sheet, and fold them up concertina-style so they fit perfectly into the palm of your hand. She demonstrates. I am amazed. What, publishing houses actually print these things? And sell them openly?

Of course they do: Annetta bought these in a university bookshop last time she was in Rome.

But what, I say once I've digested this startling information, about the exam supervisors? Or the other students? Wouldn't they notice you fiddling around getting the things out?

No problem. Everybody cheats; there are hardly any super-visors; and anyway there are hundreds, sometimes thousands, of students all sitting the same exam at once, spread about ancient halls and corridors and anterooms full of columns and niches.

So there's no danger of your exam being invalidated, then, if you get caught?

No, of course not! says Annetta, horrified. If they do catch you, they just tell you off. They don't even confiscate your cheat-sheet unless you're unlucky and get a grumpy one.

Oh well, that's all right then. I'd been thinking for a horrible moment that my chaperone-and-guardian job description might mean I was supposed to persuade her out of the cheating plan.

They're very good cheat-sheets, too. By the time we get to Genoa, I am much better informed about the Romantic movement in Italian literature – or rather, the lack of one, thanks to Napoleon Bonaparte, whose perfidy towards Italy nipped it in the bud.

At Genoa things get even odder. We have a half hour wait here, so we leave our stuff in the compartment – the other travellers will all have their own gargantuan supplies of food, won't they, so why would anyone pinch ours? – and go off to the station bar. I lick the cappuccino-froth off my teaspoon, as you do. And I let out a howl of agony. Examining the implement, I find that somebody has drilled a rough DIY hole through it. No wonder it ripped my tongue to shreds. Are they mad? Why have they done that? Annetta shows me her own spoon, also perforated. To stop people stealing all the teaspoons to boil their heroin up in, she says.

Licking my wounds, in so far as this is physically possible, I set off to find the station loo. On the train they only had those vile so-called Turkish lavatories; things where you have to balance on a pair of abominable-snowman-sized raised ceramic footprints, crouching over a murky hole, and then leap nimbly backwards as you pull the flush to save your footwear from the tidal wave of sewage that would otherwise overwhelm it. Never a great experience: and even worse with dark, clattering sleepers rushing past below, clearly visible through the hole, and the streaming wind of the train's passage upon your delicate nether parts. Crossing my fingers, I enter the station Ladies' Room. Yes! A row of shiny spanking-new cubicles. But a huge and very slow-moving queue. Eventually I grasp that a mere two out of the fifteen or so loos are in working order. How can this be? I ask the lady in front of me.

Lemons, she replies grimly. Choked up with lemons.

I'm not sure if I've heard this aright. Lemons? I repeat.

Yes, lemons, say all the other women in the queue in equally outraged tones.

Drogati! they add. Junkies! I teeter about indecisively at the end of this queue of Surrealists, trying to imagine what interest junkies could possibly have in filling public toilets with lemons. Revenge, perhaps, for the teaspoons? I give up. I'll miss the train if I wait much longer. Back to Annetta. Turkish loos it is, then.

Could I have misunderstood, though? *Limoni* . . . No, there is no getting away from it. They definitely were saying 'lemons'.

Back on the train, Annetta fills me in. Junkies in this country, I learn, as hard-up as their cousins elsewhere, prefer to grab a free lemon off a tree than to pay for citric acid to boil up their drug with. If they can find a functioning teaspoon to do this in, that is. And being, like the rest of their kind, thoughtless of the conveniences of others, once they've squeezed the juice out, they just drop the rest of the lemon down the loo. Obvious.

Our compartment starts to fill up. First a friendly couple in late middle age, then a younger man in a suit; a doctor, we discover, on his way home to Naples from a medical conference. Now a woman in her mid-fifties, just off the connecting train from Turin, dressed in a vaguely overalled way that I can't decode. Countrywoman? Feminist? Both? Neither? Strange how that rapid automatic pigeonholing you do in your own culture always eludes you in another, no matter how good you get at the actual language. You go on having to take people at face value. Probably a good thing, but sometimes too much like hard work.

This unknown type of woman has a small basket on her lap,

and soon we are all admiring the monstrous *porcino* mushroom lying inside it on a bed of fern leaves. She found it this morning, she says, growing in the field beside her house; and she's taking it as a gift to the gentleman friend she is off to meet. This is her first romantic appointment since her husband left her for his secretary after twenty years of marriage, she confides, and she is worried that she may faint.

Faint? we all ask.

Yes. She has a history of fainting in these situations. She fainted on her wedding night when she was about to get into bed with her husband. Then, fifteen years later, after she'd caught him in bed with the aforementioned secretary, she went and picked up a man to prove that she could if she wanted to; and she fainted that time too, before she could actually commit the act. Though she didn't tell her husband that – she just left him to hear the rumours and stew in his own juice, as was only fair. (We all agree fervently.) Although, strangely enough, she adds, on the actual day when she came home unexpectedly to find him in her own bed with the secretary, she didn't make a fuss. She just went quietly back out of the room, pulling the door to behind her, and got the week's shopping in as if nothing had happened. She never did mention it at all, not for five years, until the last of their children was fully grown. Then she told him it was time he left.

The doctor is now advising the mushroom lady to have a stiff alcoholic drink before facing the bedroom situation; Annetta is disagreeing; you're more likely to faint if you suddenly raise your blood pressure with alcohol. Everyone's giving advice at the top of their voices, all at once, as so often happens in this country. But is this really a perfectly ordinary Italian train conversation? Everyone else is acting as if it is. This will be why they don't need Oprah Winfrey here.

Once our lady has left the train, I ask Annetta what sort of person she was. Just a typical Piedmontese woman of a certain age, she replies. I make a mental note to get more familiar with the Piedmont.

26

Things in our carriage now go from bizarre to very bizarre. Annetta asks if I'll help her fold up her cheat-sheets. She wants to have them ready folded when we get to our hotel, so she can put them under the mattress right away. Then they'll be nice and flat by tomorrow.

But everyone in the compartment will see what we're doing, I say. Leave it till later. I really don't want to be shocking these nice respectable people.

Waste of breath. Who would be a chaperone? Annetta gets her pile of pads out anyway and starts studying the best way to fold the sheets so she can still see the numbers at the top of each one. There is, of course, a little foldable index for speedy selection.

As I suspected they might, our fellow travellers soon begin to show great interest in what she's doing. That, however, is the only thing I suspected right. Everybody spots straight away that the things are cheat-sheets; and nobody is remotely shocked. The doctor wants to show us his own folding technique from the good old days when he was still doing exams; the couple reminisce happily about the various hiding places they used at school. Mr Couple says that those military pants with a pocket on the outside leg are the absolute best; Mrs Couple says that things are always easier for men, she and the other girls in her class used to have to sew an inside pocket, kangaroo-pouch style, down the front of their skirts. Amazing, says Annetta, that's exactly what she's done! Soon she has her bag down off the rack, her Exam Skirt out, and we're all admiring the hand-stitched secret pocket, the cunning way she's chosen a sarong style so the bulge won't show.

Soon all five of us are folding away, a pad each; and I have foolhardily tried to explain the attitude to cheating in my own strange land. Everyone sympathizes deeply with me. It must be terrible to grow up in a place where human fellow-feeling and camaraderie hardly exist at all, in a nation of cold-hearted moralists happy to betray their friends and colleagues, or (in the case of exam supervisors) their own students, at the drop of a hat. Everyone agrees that it might make some sense – though it would still be appalling – if the betrayer expected some personal gain from such treachery. Am I sure they don't? Do supervisors get paid more, or students gain better marks, by unmasking cheats?

No, of course not, I say desperately, and start all over again. Imagine, if you will, a world where it is actually more normal *not* to cheat than to cheat . . .

Luckily it is almost seven o'clock by now, and debate turns, as it will at this hour in Italy, to food. Collective folding is suspended for a competitive tasting session where everyone tries a bit of everyone else's stuff. And in my opinion, Francesca wins by several heads.

Once we're off the train and on our way to our lodgings, I have another go at explaining my nation's view of cheating to Annetta. I would like at least one person to grasp that I am not a mere apologist for a nation of creeps, stoolies and grasses, but am seriously trying to suggest that a culture where cheating at exams is not the norm might be a good thing. I tell Annetta that the word 'cheating' in the English language has no positive connotations, unlike the Italian version, which suggests something more like 'being naughty'. Annetta has just been telling me, hasn't she, that the Neapolitan doctor was a nice bloke, but he worked as a night locum; and only useless doctors end up with that job? Am I right in thinking, I ask Annetta, that there are cheat-sheets like yours for medical school exams? Probably, she says; there are bound to be. (Until this eye-opening trip I have assumed that Italians' deep mistrust of their doctors was part and parcel of their general mistrust of everything, like Information Found in Books or Food Cooked Outside a Thirty-Mile Radius of Home – now we see there is a real basis for their paranoia.) Well then, I say triumphantly, does Annetta not think that eliminating cheating would produce a new breed of doctor who could be relied upon to genuinely know their subject? Annetta supposes it might; but the likelihood is so remote that she hardly finds the idea worth thinking about.

We arrive at the Porta Maggiore to find that Annetta has booked us into a student place full of American backpackers. And as soon as we've got our luggage stowed in our room and sat down for some refreshment in the atrium, what does Annetta do but pull out her cheat-sheets and make a great heap of them on the communal coffee table? I can already see several shining scrubbed honest American student faces turning interestedly towards us. I give it minutes, if not seconds, before somebody asks what they are.

Put those things away, I hiss at her urgently. I've explained to you about cheating in the Anglo-Saxon world!

She can't, she says, she needs to get them under her mattress straight away. And she goes on ordering them neatly by number, running her nails along the folds to make them lie even flatter.

What are those all about? asks an interested Texan accent.

For exam, says Annetta. Thank goodness her English is pretty basic.

They're just revision sheets, I say nonchalantly, in English.

She's studying Italian literature. Don't explain what they're for, I say to her in Italian, doing my best to look as if I was just making gay chitchat. They won't understand that you could be a nice person and still cheat at exams.

So much for my advice. My idiot protégée interrupts me midstream, still speaking English.

I hide! she announces with a big innocent smile. Examination! she adds. Look! And she demonstrates how she will slip the things down under her waistband. No see! she points out triumphantly. Our fellow-guests gaze at her, horrified. Wait for it. I knew it. Is she *cheating*? Three of them say this together, in appalled chorus.

Cheating, yes! she says triumphantly, recognizing the word I just taught her on the train. I put now under bed! she adds conspiratorially. Make very small!

The young citizens of the United States of America turn to one another with disgust writ large across their faces. Why, oh why did I tell her that word? Within a few minutes everyone in the place – except me and the young manager, an Iranian refugee – is pointedly ignoring the self-confessed Cheat.

Annetta, who is used to being found *simpatica* by new acquaintances, is hurt and mystified. What has she done to deserve this savage boycotting? Still, she enjoys chatting to the nice Iranian, Majid, who tells us, in English not unlike Annetta's own, that although he's been working here in Rome for a year, he hasn't learnt a word of Italian because he never gets out of the building, and the clients in here are all English-speakers. Still, his English has got a lot better, and that's what matters, because his plan is to get over to his sister's in Canada as soon as he gets his papers sorted out.

Our fellow guests are fascinated by my English accent. They all seem to be fans of *Absolutely Fabulous*. Go on, say something else, Edina! they keep saying to me. Cruel of them. Edina? Could they not have chosen Patsy? This is a shattering blow to a woman who spent her childhood dreaming of growing up to become Joanna Lumley. And they go on determinedly cold-shouldering my friend the criminal. Evidently Americans have even firmer anti-cheating principles than us English. Nobody will so much as look Annetta in the eye. My feelings do a sudden loop-the-loop. Poor Annetta! How do they know she doesn't have some good reason for cheating, like having to maintain an aged granny with Alzheimer's or put a brother through college? I can't work out where to put myself at all. They are explaining to me at this moment that Rome doesn't just belong to Italy: it is part of World Heritage, and they are appalled by the way Italians leave rubbish and dirt and graffiti all over it. I certainly can't tell this bunch of strict young moralists that, going by my experiences today, the whole of Italy thinks it's entirely normal to cheat, can I?

What are they saying? asks Annetta, spotting my dyspeptic expression.

They want you to get off your butt and go clean up Rome, I tell her.

Next day, while Annetta is cheating away at her exams just like everybody else, I go off to check out a few Roman ruins and get my fill of the Ancients. *Magari!* In the park opposite the Colosseum a young Senegalese man is trying desperately to entice a wounded baby seagull out from under a parked car. It will surely die, he says, nabbing me as I pass by, if it's just left here. Together we catch the poor seagull chick, and since my new friend hardly speaks any Italian, it is down to me to harass passers-by for help. Why, oh why have I got myself embroiled in this? In Diano San Pietro, if you stood about the streets asking passers-by for information about organizations devoted to saving the lives of infant seagulls, you would be laughed out of town. Knock it on the head with a rock and put it out of its misery! Try roasting it! they would tell you. Luckily, things are different here in Rome. A park-keeper, summoned by somebody's mobile phone, arrives and takes over at last.

Emotionally drained by this experience, I give up on tourism and stop in a bar for a rest and a cappuccino. Marvellous! Romans are so used to the mad behaviour of foreigners that they don't bat an eyelid when you order a cappuccino in the middle of the afternoon. No puzzled look on the waiter's face when you place your order: no remarks about whether you've just got out of bed: no quizzical glances from the other customers when they see what you've been served.

I pick up the Roman daily paper lying on my table and read that there are fifty-six thousand and two students taking the exam today. And that the Ministry of Education has announced that examinees must not use their mobile phone text facilities during the exams. But, the journalist points out, this is only an announcement. It has not been propounded as an official rule that would disqualify examinees who broke it. So, he concludes, it's probably not too serious if you send and receive the odd message.

Annetta returns from her exams triumphant. She had a very nice supervisor, she tells me, who didn't mind helping out at all when asked for a few clues about one of the answers.

It's nearly suppertime by now, and we decide to eat in some local *trattoria*, see a bit of Rome away from the tourist areas. We end up, just round the corner from the hotel, in a place remarkably like a Toulouse-Lautrec painting. From one of his seriously low-life periods. Bawdy revelry, plunging cleavages, semi-conscious drunk in corner, jugs of wine overflowing on to tables, electric blue eye shadow and blurry vermilion lipstick, the lot. I catch myself thinking that you notice the smells of poverty and drink a lot more in three dimensions than you do in the picture.

As soon as you sit down and say you're eating here, the waitress (haphazardly pinned-up candy-floss hair, bright green mascara and plenty of black stretch lace) plonks a bowl of minestrone and a basket of bread rolls down before you, and a litre jug of wine; then you order your *secondo* from the day's menu. We eat the soup, heavily loaded with pasta, wait rather a long time, and drink most of the wine; now the waitress returns to tell us that whatever-it-was we ordered has run out. So we order something else; another lengthy wait; more wine; same thing. By the time we're finally told that the only *secondi* left are tripe or sweetbreads, we're too drunk to leave. We'd fall over. And anyway, we're enjoying ourselves much too much to go now, even though, what with the thick Roman accent, the shortage of teeth among the clientele, and the surfeit of drink, we can hardly understand a thing anybody says. So we choose the sweetbreads, *animelle*, because neither of us can remember quite which unappealing part of the anatomy a sweetbread actually is, whereas we're only too sure about the tripe. Whatever the *animelle* may once have been, they come to our table sliced thin and fried in breadcrumbs, and are perfectly edible, something like very tender chicken. No, don't tell me, thanks.

As we leave, song is turning to scuffle, and cuddle to grab. Still, though we completely forgot to take off our watches before we left, not one person has tried to steal them.

Back at the hotel, we sit and chat drunkenly to Majid the manager, who turns out to be virtually a prisoner here. The owner promised him an Italian work permit if he stayed for six months, but nothing has happened. And Majid can't even check if he's really applied for one, can he, without betraying himself? He doesn't know what to do. And he is stuck in Italy unless he gets some sort of legal document. As we go off to bed, we discover that he doesn't even have a room of his own: he sleeps on a mattress that he puts out on the kitchen floor each night.

Luckily for him, Annetta is so outraged on his behalf that she vows to devote her highly developed cheating skills to his cause. Within the month he has miraculously procured some nice false documents and, after a heart-in-the-mouth transit through Heathrow, he succeeds in escaping the clutches of the hostel-owner and making it to Canada, where his engineering degree may perhaps be of some use.

27

What a relief to get back to the normality of my nice quiet valley. Ciccio collects me at Diano Marina station. Hurry up, he says. He has a surprise for me at home. Surprise number one meets my eye as soon as we open the door. There has been another huge outbreak of nameless jars. The kitchen table has vanished under a sea of the things. *Passata*: of course, he's been off bottling tomatoes with his dad. Surprise number two: Ciccio has come up with a brilliant interim plan for dealing with the offspring of the hylotrupes while we wait for our dream roofer. Look up there! he says proudly. I do: and see that the noisiest bit of beam, over in the corner by the window, has been completely stuck full of three-inch nails. It looks like some sort of aerial pincushion. Or a larger-than-life voodoo doll. A beetle trap, is it?

No, it isn't. Ciccio was sitting here listening to the munching, he tells me, when it came to him that the thing to do was to take careful bearings on the exact position of the sound, and then simply hammer a nail into the spot: kill the vile blob-with-jaws stone dead. A great success! He is certain that at least one of the creatures has fallen silent for good. He could ask his sister Grazia the nurse to get hold of a stethoscope for us. We might be able to pinpoint them all, one by one . . .

I am speechless. There must be about fifty nails up there, and all for one muncher. Ciccio may be a genius in the kitchen, in horticulture, possibly also fishing and drystone walling, but I'm beginning to suspect strongly that DIY is not his forte.

Neither of these surprises, anyway, was the one he had in mind. Downstairs, he says, leading me by the hand to the bedroom. He has put our bedding back in here, even though the place is still powerfully perfumed with attar of garage. I do my best to look pleased, not wanting to hurt his feelings. Maybe proper men don't touch sheets and duvets, and this is something like peeling apples, another great blow for sexual equality?

Just shut up and listen! says Ciccio. I do. Deathly silence. I hear nothing. Ciccio waggles his eyebrows questioningly at me. Still nothing. Then I get it. Nothing! My God! Has the diesel worked at last?

It certainly has. Proving conclusively, Ciccio claims, that you don't need a book, or indeed a name, to exterminate a beetle.

I'm not so sure about that myself. They lost the will to live, probably, once they knew how thoroughly we were on their case. I wouldn't be at all surprised if that last menacing hiss of mine before I left hadn't made all the difference. Marvellous, anyway. The floor is not going to fall in. And who needs oxygen when they have blessed silence?

Moreover, says the genius, he has got everything ready for my long-awaited *gnocchi* lesson. See how much he's missed me? The potatoes are ready and waiting, should be cool enough for peeling by now.

I am touched. Let's have a coffee, though, first, I say. I've brought some seriously classy whole beans back from Rome, so we can try out the lovely little wooden mill at last . . .

A coffee at this time of day? says the restaurateur. Am I sure? Won't it make me nervous?

Agh! Not that again! I've just been on a train with no coffee at all for five hours. I've spent two whole days in his sister Annetta's company, being pestered by mad Italian theories about coffee. I stamp my foot like a petulant Alice. I am NEVER nervous, I say, no matter how much coffee I drink, and I'm not having any more silly conversations about it. Moreover, coffee is packed full of antioxidants, I read it in the *Guardian*, so there.

You sound nervous already to me, says Ciccio idly, taking an egg from the fridge and setting it carefully on the marble top near the potatoes. I wouldn't have one if I were you.

I take a deep breath, manage to remain calm, and get out my bag of lovely aromatic beans. I dust off the pretty coffee-mill, open the slot in the top and pour in a great shiny handful. I remember wistfully, as I grind, the day my sister and I moved up here. We drank three whole pots of coffee that morning, one after the other, to celebrate our newfound freedom from anxious Italian eyes, from local coffee rules and regulations. Now look what I've done. A representative of Italian coffee-neurosis practically living in my home, sitting there telling me I mustn't have a cup of coffee because it'll make me *nervosa*!

No hope. My man holds inexorably forth, as I grind, on the agitating effects of coffee. I may feel all right for now, while I'm still young and strong: but the effects of my habitual coffee overdose will slowly mount up until, later in life, I suffer some sort of unspecified total collapse. I do my best not to listen, winding and grinding, busily opening my little drawer every few turns, partly to see if I've ground enough yet, but mainly for the sheer joy of it. Wrong type of sleep indeed! As far as I know, I say, Italy's the only country in the world that's turned coffee into a medication. Four ferociously strong teaspoonfuls to be taken with every meal, or you'll suffer systems breakdown, and a poisonous taboo the rest of the day.

At last the drawer is full. I empty it carefully into the espresso pot's coffee-ground-holder. There is nothing wrong, I add firmly, as I put the pot on the stove and stick the kettle on next to it, with drinking coffee as a refreshment, the way I do.

Silence falls. Ciccio knows that when I say this, I mean that I add a load of hot water to my coffee – one of those concentrated thimble-sized ones he drinks will make a whole mugful for me, and it's still pretty strong as far as any non-Italian's concerned. He always averts his eyes in horror while I carry out this act of sacrilege. It is behaviour so revolting that the added water, the weakness, can't possibly count as a mitigating circumstance.

The pot starts to hiss as the water whooshes its pressurized way up into the top half of the pot. A series of loud gurgles announces that it's ready. Lovely aroma! I take it off the heat, pour some out, add my large dash of water, and turn, cup in hand, to make my last stand. I am sick of talking about coffee, I say fiercely, and I refuse to keep having this conversation over and over again. I've learnt to be tolerant of your culture, I add, and if we're going to live together, you'll just have to learn to be tolerant of mine!

I raise the coffee defiantly to my lips and take a large swig. Effect utterly ruined as I swallow, pause for a horrified second, and almost explode, gasping for breath. It's horrible. Not just horrible: painful. Agonizing. Burning hot: not stove-hot, but Madras-curry hot. I dash for a bit of bread, stick it in my mouth and chew desperately, trying to suck out the pain.

Ciccio is staring astonished at my extraordinary antics. What on earth's the matter with you? he asks.

I still can't speak: I'm standing panting, mopping and fanning at my face with a dishcloth. Did the man in the coffee shop put something hot in with the coffee beans? A joke? But why would he do that? I don't even know him.

Ouch! Ouch! I say, jumping from foot to foot. Could

Ciccio have spiked it? Some Macchiavellian plan to put me off coffee for life? No, he can't have, I've only just taken it out of my bag. Eventually I manage to choke a few words out.

It's hot, I say, *piccante*! As if it was full of chilli! I go on chewing manically on my bread. Still no relief.

The explanation has dawned on Ciccio now. Big grin. It really is chilli! That's why the coffee mill was on the top of the pile. Salvatore used it to grind his lethal dried chillis, to make chilli powder for his pasta.

The evil Ciccio, who loves chilli almost as much as his father does, thinks this is hilarious. Has he no finer feelings, no sympathy for the sufferings of others?

A punishment from God, he says smugly. The final proof that He is with us Italians on the coffee question.

Off we go, then, into the world of *gnocchi*. Move number one: get the potatoes mashed up nice and fine. Ciccio hands me a fork and I start work; and hard work it is, too, with just a fork. I wonder whether to get out my English potato masher. You'd think it would be ideal for the job. On the other hand, ten to one there'll be some compelling reason why Italians have no desire or need for such a thing. I screw my courage to the sticking point and open the drawer anyway.

What if I use this? I say diffidently.

Ciccio looks suspiciously at the implement. What is it?

It's what we use in England for mashing potatoes, I say, and demonstrate the potato-mashing tradition of my homeland. Brilliant! he says, snatching the bowl away from me. Let me have a go!

He mashes: he marvels: he mashes some more. Still, mashing potatoes is probably the only element of *gnocchi*-making I definitely don't need a lesson in.

Mashing done, I'm amazed, not to say outraged, when Ciccio takes a bag of flour and simply empties the whole thing straight out on to my nice clean marble draining board. Now he unceremoniously dumps the panful of mashed potatoes on top. Honestly! Why does he never think about how much mess he's making? Fine in a restaurant, I daresay, but hard to handle in the home.

Oy, I say, or words to that effect. There's no need to make a horrible mess all over the place. I've got plenty of bowls, you know.

But this is not a mess, I now learn. It's part of the lesson. You always make *gnocchi*, or any sort of pasta, straight on to the work surface, and never in a bowl, where you wouldn't have enough mixing and kneading space, not to mention rolling and cutting space. Once he's got me straightened out on this one, Ciccio makes a big well in the middle of his pile of flour and potatoes; and in goes the egg, salt, a dollop of water. No measuring of any kind, naturally. I stand by him, observing closely, as he mixes with his hand from the centre, leaving a rim of flour to the very last to hold the runny middle in check, the way builders mix water into a pile of sand-and-cement.

The *impasto* gets rolled with a light hand into long thin sausages, which you cut with deft slashes of the knife into *gnocchi*-sized chunks. Ciccio's ones come out all the same size. Mine don't. First sign of coffee-poisoning, I dare say.

Now you roll-and-flick each one on your floury marble surface with a nifty one-handed fork move that turns each lumpy dollop into a pretty oval with a four-pronged dent-and-fold at its heart. Looks incredibly easy: let me have a go!

I begin by creating half a dozen flattened squashed blobs, horribly reminiscent of the offspring of the *Hylotrupes bajulus*. Eventually I start to get something like the right effect, but my heavy handling is making the *gnocchi* all sticky on the outside. And it's absurdly slow work. Can't we just cut out this fiddly decorative bit, I ask, wouldn't they be just as good in the chunk shape?

No, they would not. The fold-and-dent is no mere decoration. It lets the heat into the centre of the *gnocchi* to cook them. I don't want them to have raw gluey middles, do I?

I suppose I don't. I hand my fork back to the expert and stomp off to get on with a task I know I'm up to: chopping up a bush-sized pile of basil plants and half a head of garlic for the pesto.

Scorbutica, says Ciccio, laughing at my expression.

You what? This new word turns out to mean grumpy, or bad-tempered. The more I mull it over, the more it seems closely connected with the word 'scurvy' in English. Deficiency in a-scorbic acid, otherwise known as Vitamin C. I check this out: is there an illness called *scorbo*? No, but there's one called *scorbuto*, something sailors used to get. So! He's just called me a scurvy knave! I've always imagined that scurviness was to do with the look of you, scabby or scruffy maybe. Not a character trait. Is grumpiness one of the symptoms of scurvy?

Ciccio doesn't know; he doesn't think I ought to worry about it. Perhaps I have some book I could go and look it up in?

Bah. While I'm trying not to worry, and enviously watching the deft flipping of *gnocchi* on the marble draining-board out of the corner of my eye, I have an inspiration. Not about seafaring sicknesses of the past, as it happens, nor even about *gnocchi*, but about the draining-board itself.

This modern convenience, with its accompanying sink, was added to the house round about 1944 by Pompeo's father; but it is two or three hundred years old at least, maybe older than the house itself. Pompeo's father stole it, or rather liberated it, from some local church building whose priest had run off and left his flock in the lurch when the Nazis invaded. This priest didn't deserve to find his kitchen intact when he returned, because if he wasn't going to stay put and suffer alongside his parishioners, he should have gone up into the hills to give help and succour to the partisans, as Pompeo will explain to you in some detail, given half a chance.

The round sink part is hollowed out of a cube of marble that can't be more than two feet across, and I've often thought that the draining-board part, carved from a separate, thinner block almost five feet long and curving out to a good six inches wider than the sink, was oddly out of proportion to it. And it has no runnels to carry water back into the sink, either; so, annoyingly for a draining board, it doesn't drain properly. The sort of little glitsch, you say to yourself, that soon got ironed out a bit later in the history of kitchen design. Still, it's such an object of beauty that you'd never want to replace it. And it does have a raised inch of border sculpted into it, so the water doesn't go all over the floor. But now, as the *gnocchi* go to sit on their floured tray and settle for an hour or two before we cook them, I find myself idly pondering how I'll go about cleaning this new and horribly sticky *gnocchi*-mess up. Blinding flash! Suddenly it comes to me that the thing has no defects at all. It is not a dodgy prototype draining-board at all, but a perfectly designed pasta-preparing surface. If you have to make large quantities of seriously sticky *impasto* for your daily pasta, not in a bowl but on a flat marble slab, what could be more sensible than to have a wash-it-off-straight-down-the-sink work surface? Thank you, Ciccio. And a big hand, too, for the pasta-preparing priests of yore.

28

Dawn is just breaking as our convoy grinds and roars, three carloads of us, over the steep mountain pass into the Imperia valley. Our own valley is closed off to the north by high ridges that no road could be driven over. You have to go to Diano Arentino and over this westward ridge to continue inland towards the Piedmont and the Alps, or to the land of the Longobardi. We're not going anything like that far, though. Ten miles or so on, near Pieve di Teco, a lovely old town with a low-vaulted main street paved with great slabs of slate and unchanged since the Middle Ages, we turn off into the valley of the Arroscia river, where terraces of vineyards are already starting to win out over terraces of olives. Around and above us, velvety with distance, thickly forested mountains rear up, a landscape too steep and rocky ever to have been worth terracing and cultivating. We're only a few miles away from the vineyards where the noble Ormeasco wine comes from. Most of them actually lie around the town of Pornassio, says Ciccio, a few miles downhill from Ormea: and, yes, the name 'Pornassio' does have the same dubious ring in Italian as it does in English. That'll be why the wine gets called after Ormea instead.

Till now, my only experience of wine-making round here has been with the late and much lamented Domenico, our first mentor, whose vineyard was nothing like big enough to produce all the grapes he needed for his year's worth of wine. You would never waste good olive-growing land on grapevines, which are happy to grow in places where the olive can't survive; so common practice is to grow a small vineyard of your preferred grape, enough to give your wine the flavour you're after; and make up the bulk by buying in a cartload from the vast selection of grape-laden transport that congregates, at this time of year, from all over the grape-growing areas of the country, down at the Diano crossroads. Unless, like Salvatore, you have a bit of land further up in the hills, where the olive won't grow anyway, to devote to grapes. I'm looking forward immensely to having a go at a proper *vendemmia*: although I'm having to keep the enthusiasm under wraps, because any sign of it produces an outbreak of cackling party-pooping predictions from my fellow-travellers about the backache and exhaustion that I will (they say) be complaining about later.

Salvatore, in the lead car, is driving Francesca, Annetta, Marisa who is married to the shameful shirker Beppe, and her son Alberto. Grazia and Giusi are in the next car with the rest of the children: Grazia's two teenage daughters and Giusi's sons aged ten and twelve. Ciccio and I are travelling with Osvaldo and Giovanni, the other sons-in-law. Unfortunate, because I can't be more than five minutes in Osvaldo's company without getting into a blazing row. It was bad enough when he was a supporter of the Northern League, which at the time was going around fomenting racist feeling against Southern Italians and calling for secession. How weird is that, in a man who's married into a large Southern Italian family with whom he gets on extremely well? The worst of it is that I can't help liking Osvaldo. He is good company, as long as he keeps off politics, and he has an enjoyably lively mind, if pottily confused. One moment he will be loudly supporting his noxious League; the next he will be raging against his own Northern parents for refusing, after they'd come to the Confirmation of his eldest son, their first grandchild, to come to the traditional Confirmation dinner. They could not sink so low, they said, as to go and eat in a public restaurant where somebody might see them, with a bunch of Southern Italians. Osvaldo was outraged.

Then, last time I met him, down in Diano Marina, we had the usual row, during which I announced, rudely as I thought, that his precious Northern League were a bunch of proto-fascists. Imagine my surprise to hear that there was nothing wrong with fascism, or at any rate its modern Italian version: which organization Osvaldo had recently joined, abandoning the League. That put me in my place. So here I am, stuck in a car with an avowed fascist. Please let him keep his mouth shut. I don't want to talk to anybody, as it happens, because it's much too early in the day for talking. But I really, really don't want to talk to a fascist.

Hopeless: he's already off, holding forth on the absurd thesis that homosexuality does not exist among genetically pure Northern Italians. It was imported into this country, he says, from North Africa and the Arabs. (There is a kind of deranged logic to this if you know that the Northern League often hints that all Italians from Rome southwards are 'contaminated' by Arab blood.)

What, I say, about the ancient Romans? They certainly weren't famous for their rampant heterosexuality.

Exactly! says Osvaldo triumphantly. (Bother. I'd forgotten he hated Rome too.) They'd been contaminated by their Empire in North Africa, hadn't they? But up here, where the blood line is pure – and he doesn't means the cesspits of big miscegenating cities like Milan and Turin – there are no homosexuals. He challenges me to name one homosexual in our valley.

Anyone who's gay round here, I say, has to run off to some big city to get away from the likes of you.

Osvaldo rests his case. She's admitted there are no homo-sexuals, hasn't she?

Ciccio gives his brother-in-law a long, pitying look in the rear-view mirror, and says quietly: '*Eppur' si muovono.*'

A bit of concentration tells me that this is Ciccio's version of the rebellious words muttered by Galileo Galilei some centuries ago as he left the Inquisition court where he'd been forced, under threat of death, to renounce his evil heretical theory that the earth turned on its axis. '*Eppur' si muove*': 'Still, it moves.'

Osvaldo, dumbfounded, falls silent at last. And Ciccio uses the airspace to fret aloud about his restaurant. It's the Day of Repose today; but he's had to take tomorrow off too, to get the grapes crushed and into the fermenting vats. Franchino's aunt Nandina's a grand cook, but if she gets a bunch of those demanding foodies from Milan or Turin, she might well lose her nerve. They've decided that if any of their serious *buongustaio* customers ring to book, Franchino will say that there are no tables left. But what if he doesn't recognize their voices till too late?

Ten more minutes of twisting narrow roads, and slivers of sunshine start breaking through the hills to the east, picking out the laden vines above and below us, floating ghostly in the mists rising from the Arroscia, the landscape of sloping vineyards only broken by the occasional ramshackle hamlet. Our convoy comes to a halt at last, and we stumble, half asleep, out of the cars. So near home, but several degrees colder already. A jumble of houses and tiled roofs, walls and yards, all looking half abandoned; down a grassy alleyway we go, and stop at a big wooden door, grey with age. No sound but the invisible, rushing river somewhere at the end of the vineyard. Francesca takes a huge iron key from her apron pocket, and leads us in. Here it is: the family *taverna*. We enter an enormous vaulted room where there's not a perpendicular line to be seen, its limewashed walls curving gently up from the floor to a central boss in the ceiling. A *taverna* is not, as you'd think, a tavern, but a glorified *rustico* – not just a store, but a workplace where you create your stores as well: and much more domesticated than a *rustico*. Another one of those big tables that are a De Gilio speciality, a large number of ill-assorted chairs, a woodstove; a series of marble worktops all along one wall, and an enormous white ceramic sink. Smaller archways lead to more shadowy rooms beyond; there's a wooden-slat staircase in one corner. From a cupboard Francesca extracts a strange object that looks like a fifties sun-ray lamp; a heater that runs, it turns out, off a big gas bottle. It's not worth lighting the woodstove – it'll be hot soon anyway, once the sun gets over the hills. Once it is hissing some welcome warmth into the room, Francesca turns her attentions to finding a coffeepot. Salvatore and Ciccio, Giovanni and Osvaldo have vanished into one of the back rooms. I follow them. An overpowering aroma of wine-lees: a row of four great wooden barrels, head-high, each one wider than the span of my arms, sits on a dais at the back of the room: the *botte* where the juice and skins of the grapes will ferment together for a week once the grapes are gathered and crushed. And a huge stack of crates for the grape-picking.

Back in the main room Grazia and Giusi are unloading vast quantities of supplies on to the marble sideboard; Marisa and Rosi are digging cups out of a lovely old dresser (yes, I want that too) while Annetta rinses them out – they haven't been used since spring, when the last demijohns were bottled. Alberto stands in front of the heater warming his hands and complaining bitterly, as seventeen-year-olds will, at the injustice of it all. He's already been made to work at uncle Ciccio's place all summer; now he's back at school having to study for exams – and he still gets dragged out of bed at dawn to come up here and freeze to death, all to make a load of stupid wine he doesn't want any of anyway. He hates wine. Wine is for boring old farts. He only likes beer.

That's enough, Alberto! says his mother Marisa. Of course he has to do his exams – how else will he get on in life? Uncle Ciccio interrupts, on the topic of Ungratefulness in the Young and how many of his mates would have liked that job in the restaurant . . . Salvatore chips in, roaring over the top of both of them. Rather have beer than wine!? Has Alberto lost his wits? Beer is a terrible thing for your health! He has seen plenty of beer-drinking folk in his time, and they're not a pretty sight, Alberto should take his word for it! A bevy of aunts now strikes up, on various topics along the lines of family duty and all the things the relatives have done for him and the moral obligation to look after grandparents who need his help now they're getting on in years . . . The entire De Gilio family is now shouting at once, over the top of one another, as usual. All, that is, except Alberto's four younger cousins, who have snuck off among the vines, from whence muffled giggling can now be heard.

Francesca is alternating between laughing helplessly, shouting, '*Calma, calma!*' in the special high, squeaky voice she uses to make herself heard on these mass-shouting occasions, and wiping the tears from her eyes with her apron. She comes round and takes my arm, still shaking with laughter. I'm not sure whether it's me or her family she finds funniest; she keeps peeking up at me for a quick expression-check; then taking another look at them; the result, each time, is that she has to grab her apron-tails and press them to her mouth to keep the laughter in.

Salvatore eventually wins the audibility battle for his closing remarks on the topic of beer. Alberto should take his grandfather's advice, leave the beer alone and stick to good healthy civilized wine! Alberto should have seen Australia, people reducing themselves with beer into drooling morons! That would have put him off the stuff soon enough!

Alberto responds with one of those insolent blank looks that seventeen-year-olds are so good at: and lounges boredly off to help the brothers-in-law and the younger children carrying armful upon armful of bright plastic crates off into the distant reaches of the vineyard, where they disappear among wreaths of mist and mellow fruitfulness.

Not wanting to look like a shirker, I knock back my coffee, grab a pile of crates and follow. They're dropping off a couple at either end of each run of vines. The vineyard stretches right down to the rushing waters of the Arroscia, shallow pools on this side, a deep ferny rock face opposite. Along the river, now the mist is clearing, you can just see an improbable-looking hump-backed arch of a bridge, no wider than a footpath and so narrow in section that you can't believe it wouldn't blow down in the first storm to hit it. Giovanni, handing out the secateurs, disabuses me. It's the mystical powers of slate, at its strongest under compression, that allow the arch to be so narrow and delicate-looking. But it's been there since the Romans; and while other, more recent bridges have been swept away in storm and flood, this one is solid as a rock.

Now we're off: we start at the river end so that when we're all tired at the end of the job, we'll be nearly at the *taverna* anyway and won't have too far to carry the crates. The sun has come over the hilltop behind and begun to warm us as we start snipping away, piling the fat dewy bunches into our crates.

Salvatore's family having fallen silent for once, moving slowly along the rows of vines absorbed in their picking, he decides to continue today's apt theme, lecturing us through the vine leaves on the evils of beer. Thanks to this noxious beverage, he tells us, Australians do not have a social life, and have lost all self-respect. All they do, once their working day is over, is pour beer down their necks as fast as they possibly can until they fall over or the bar closes, whichever comes first. You will see grown men stumbling home, mumbling and gurgling to themselves like infants, at closing time. Does Ciccio remember going to the bar with him once, when he was a kid? Ciccio does. Salvatore bought him a lemonade, and the place smelled horrible, like rotting bread.

Exactly! says Salvatore excitedly. Because that's what beer is, rotten bread! Or rotten grain, anyway, which is virtually the same thing.

Ciccio also remembers finding a drunk Australian in a ditch, sinking ever so slowly into six inches of muddy water . . .

Alberto, are you listening? shouts Salvatore across the fifteen yards that now separate him from his grandson. (Alberto seems to be going rather a lot slower than everybody else.) Do you hear what happens to beer-drinkers?

Yes, grandad, says Alberto wearily.

The drunk in the ditch! Salvatore lets out a cheery guffaw. We went over and tried to help him, didn't we? . . . Couldn't just leave him there to drown. But he took a look at us, all squiffy-eyed, and said, clear as a bell, 'Eff off, bloody Eyetalians!'

Yes, says Ciccio, and we gave him another heave anyway, just to get him clear of the water, but he said it again.

He did, too, says Salvatore, chortling some more. And if somebody would rather drown in mud than be saved by an Italian, that's all right by me. So I just pushed him back in. See! he says, raising his voice again to make sure Alberto doesn't miss the moral of the tale. All down to beer! he shouts triumphantly.

This wasn't the end of the story, either: after they'd walked on, they saw a pair of neighbours of theirs, Yugoslavs or something, draw level with the man and stop too. Salvatore shouted to them not to bother, but they didn't understand. The drunk did exactly the same thing to the Yugoslavs; and ended up back in his ditch again. Maybe he died.

Within the hour, I have learned that the muscles you use to snip bunches of grapes from vines just above your head are ones you never use in ordinary everyday life. My arms are screaming to be let down. It is also getting quite remarkably hot. What a wimp I am! I force myself to go on working, keeping the upper lip as stiff as possible. But it turns out that Salvatore has planned his vineyard with this very problem in mind. One half of his vines is trained tall and pergola-style, so the grapes dangle above you from on high; the other half is neatly espalier-tied, shoulder height. Come over here, says Francesca, spotting the stiff lip, and join me on the low ones. Brilliant. I am renewed. The only problem now is that, while under the pergola you got a bit of shade, out here the sun beats down mercilessly on your head. Salvatore has put the classic knotted hanky over his head for protection: the younger men are too conscious of their *figura* for such behaviour. I wish I had one: I would definitely put it on. Also, although most of the bunches grow at shoulder-to-waist height, you have to remember to bend right over and poke about for the odd one hidden among the lower leaves. If you don't, you will soon find Francesca following along behind you with an extra crate, chuckling away at your incompetence as she harvests the *grappole* you've missed.

Ten out of ten to Salvatore for vineyard design, though: by the time your head is boiling and your back aching on these lower rows, your arms have recovered enough to have another go at the shady pergola department. And vice versa. I compliment Salvatore next time we pass, plucking on opposite sides of a row.

Yes! says he. He has a bit of imagination, that's why! Not like that lot next door, he adds, gesturing at the neighbouring vineyard, where all the vines are trained to shoulder height. Pathetic *cipollini*!

Cipollini are spring onions. This seems a bit of an excessive put-down for what look, to my ignorant eye at any rate, like relatively strong, healthy vines. But who am I to argue? Fortunately, I don't. 'Cipollini', I will discover some time later, is the surname of the unimaginative neighbours in question. Mr and Mrs Spring Onion. The name's imaginative enough, at any rate.

Francesca tells me apologetically, when I ask for the loo, that there's only an old earth closet in an outhouse. I'm not bothered by earth closets at all, having lived for years with one at my own place. Fine, I say. Where is it?

See? says Francesca loudly, addressing all and sundry. She's not bothered by the earth closet! Look at her! she adds, opening her arms wide as if to present me to her family in all my glory. Not bothered at all! So *brava*! So *semplice*!

Every time I see Francesca, I seem to get simpler. It ought to be a good thing: it's the opposite of '*sofisticato*'; which in Italian is a bad word, suggesting something like 'over-elaborate' or even 'adulterated'. But let's face it, there's a close connection, is there not, between 'simple' and 'daft'? In this case, for example, judging by the dark looks I get from Annetta and Marisa, I've undermined some longstanding campaign to get a proper loo up here. Only Francesca is at all pleased with my relaxed attitude to earth closets.

29

By lunchtime we've picked half-a-houseful of grapes. Time to go indoors into the nice cool *taverna* with Francesca and Grazia to get the food ready. There's a big ball of dough rising under a floury cloth on the sideboard, ready to flatten into *focaccia* – lovely job, bash out the big flat rounds, then jab your fingertips hard into them, making deep dimples to hold the olive oil and salt crystals you sprinkle on. And another of those beehive-shaped ovens out in the yard, which the efficient Francesca got lit a good hour ago, so it's already up to heat. No cooking apart from this, just a great pile of salamis, hams and whole cheeses to be eaten with the *focaccia*, a great basket of tomatoes, another of red and white salad onions, plenty of olive oil, and a couple of bottles of wine from Salvatore's secret store. And fifteen *focaccie* to be cooked. We drag the table outdoors and lay the lunch out on it, start putting the *focaccie* one by one into the oven, taking them back out again crisp and golden on the big wooden paddle. Suddenly the air is full of that delicious hot-bread aroma. I'm starving. We'll eat as soon as the rest of the grape crates, now surrounded by a tempest of bees and wasps, have been got out of the sun and the wildlife and into the safety of the cool *cantina*, where they'll be crushed tomorrow. Ciccio and Marisa have started a crazy dash up the vineyard with the last few crates, shouting and laughing as they race Giovanni and Osvaldo, Rosi and Grazia, the teenagers Federica and Manuela, and even little Lorenzo and Daniele, valiantly stumbling through the grass with a crate almost as big as them. Everyone collapses breathless at the table.

Francesca doles out plates and knives and *focaccia*; and once we're all munching away, she decides to entertain us with a bit of old-tyme Calabrian village rivalry. Salvatore's home *paese*, she announces, may be grandly titled Santa Cristina d'Aspromonte, but it's a no-account mountain village peopled by ignorant illiterate shepherds.

Salvatore raises a growl, but he's too busy eating to fight back yet.

In Mellicucca, his wife goes on, the proper decent market town that she comes from, they tell a story about Santa Cristina which goes like this:

Why is Jesus always represented barefoot on the cross? Because he left his sandals behind in Santa Cristina, that's why! He was going around on his Father's instructions distributing gifts to each village; but he soon realized, after a day spent with the inhabitants of this place, that they were so utterly benighted that no gift in his power could possibly help them. (This tale of Jesus distributing gifts seems to be firmly established in Italian popular culture; in our own valley, sniggering inhabitants of rival Diano villages will tell you of the Sack of Ignorance that Jesus forgot in Diano San Pietro. The pagan version must have been so well-loved – and so useful for insulting your neighbours – that it just got grafted on to Christianity.) In his rush to get away from that desperate place, Jesus forgot to put his sandals back on. So relieved was he to be away that he didn't even notice the discomfort till he got right down to the stony bottom of the valley. He certainly wasn't going back up to that godforsaken spot to fetch his footwear, though! Rather than return to Santa Cristina, he decided, he would just finish the job barefoot.

So there you have it! says Francesca, winking naughtily at us. That's the sort of place *he* comes from! And moreover, she adds, whatever smidgeon of civilization his village had to offer,

Salvatore missed out on anyway; he only got two years of schooling. By the time he was seven years old, his family had hired him out as a goat-herd. Had to, to make ends meet. So he didn't even have a mother and father to teach him any more. He hardly saw the village, never mind the school, except on feast-days when his employers brought him down from the mountains along with the goats. He finished learning to read, she says, with her help, when he was eighteen and they'd just got engaged.

Salvatore is poised to get his revenge by telling us what they say in Santa Cristina about the inhabitants of Mellicucca, and trying as usual to refill my wine-glass to the very brim in spite of my protests, when his last mouthful of cheese from the gargantuan spread before him reminds him of an even more entertaining story from his goat-herding days: the story of his Week on Cheese. Francesca laughs expectantly: this is a great tale, she says.

Amongst his goat-herding community up in the hills, Salvatore tells us, baking was done twice a week, down at the *taverna* at the foot of the valley – the place where they made the cheese, and where you would take the goats for milking, too, once they'd had their kids – in the usual outdoor bread-oven, like this one here, only twice as big. And moreover, he adds parenthetically, giving his son a baleful look, nobody had covered the thing with cowshit.

Of course they hadn't, says Ciccio, they were too poverty-stricken to own any cows! And you wouldn't get far using those little pebbly goat turds . . .

Anyway, Salvatore goes on sternly, the bread was made twice a week, and he would walk his herd down to collect the two big flat loaves that would last him till the next baking. He must have been eleven or twelve at the time, and pretty cocksure, as you are at that age. You had to leave your goats on the hillside nearby, go down to tell the bread-makers you were there, then go back to your beasts and wait to be called when the next batch of loaves came out. Somehow, that day, Salvatore didn't hear them call him. Maybe he fell asleep in the sun? Or maybe they didn't really call him at all? He's never been able to make his mind up about this matter. Anyway, he waited and waited; and when he finally went down to see what was going on, there was no bread left for him. He hadn't come for it, they said, so they'd given it to someone else, and now he'd have to wait for the next batch. Desperate situation! Now he would be well behind in his travels with his goats; he wouldn't get back up to the shack he slept in till after dark.

He was sitting brooding in the shade round the back of the *taverna*, when what should he spy through its open window but a mouthwatering stack of freshly made whole rounds of cheese – a dozen of them at least! He was wearing one of those old military jackets, the ones with a great big pocket that went right the way round the back – we know the kind he means (I don't, but never mind)–and suddenly, irresistibly, he knew he had to grab a cheese, stuff it into that pocket, and run off hell for leather back to his goats. He'd be in for a thrashing whenever he finally came back down, but who cared? A whole cheese all to himself!

A week later, he'd not only eaten the whole thing, but had gone hungry for two days into the bargain, for fear of the punishment. Finally he went back down and took his medicine. What a beating that was! Still, no beating could overwhelm the joyful memory. Salvatore's eyes light up at the thought of it. A whole Week on Cheese! He can still taste it to this day, he says with a Cheshire cat grin. And he slices himself another large hunk of pecorino.

★

At the beginning of this rather puzzling story, I had my face composed in an expression of sympathy for one who had suffered the hardship of eating nothing but cheese for a week. Got the whole thing back to front, as usual. Cheese was a luxury item, as I ought to have remembered from Laura's ma, and not to be eaten by the likes of its makers. Even up here in the relatively prosperous North. How would a lowly child herder in the poor South ever get his hands on the stuff?

What did you normally get to eat, then? I ask.

The bread, of course: the two flat round loaves, spiced up with as much chilli as he could get, and if he was lucky a dash of olive oil and a slice of raw onion.

I knew this already, too, if only I'd concentrated a bit. And a bit of ricotta, maybe? I ask, memory working properly at last. From the whey left over from the cheese-making?

I must be joking! The ricotta was the perk of the herd-owners and the cheese-makers. No way would the herd-boys be getting any of that!

I'm having a very strange reaction to this story. It's making me want to cry. Here are Salvatore and Francesca sitting in this modern G8 world before a table groaning with food – no shortage of cheese on it, thank goodness – carrying around in their heads another life where hardship and hunger and child labour are just part of everyday life. The little pile of fresh chillies at Salvatore's right hand, which he still adds to almost every mouthful of his food, bears witness to it. Meanwhile I, like most of my generation of Europeans, only conceive of such things as immensely distant in place or time. Little goat-herd boys far away in India or South America, yes: or a century or two ago in my own land. I know from the *Penguin History of Food in Britain* I once bought in a junk shop, ignorantly expecting to find all sorts of intriguing old-time recipes in it, that country labourers ate virtually nothing but bread for a good couple of centuries. No traditional cottage vegetable soups, no ploughmen's lunches. All just a modern fantasy. Plain bread for breakfast, lunch and supper. Depressing. But, as I say, a long time ago.

For Salvatore, though, sitting right in front of me now, a childhood on bread in a lonely shack; no schooling, and employers whose right to beat him went without question; followed by war, enemy occupation, a collapsing economy and a whole series of migrations. No wonder he and Francesca bully the family to come and work on the land, drive them mad with their conviction that keeping the *campagna* up and running is more important than their Real Jobs. That way they're certain the family will never go hungry again. How could a paid job, a thing that can vanish like the driven snow for reasons utterly beyond your control, be more real than that? As if to point up the contrast, Rosi, the success story of the family – she runs her own agency in San Remo, providing tourist guides for cruise ships to all the cities of the Mediterranean – appears with a tiny state-of-the-art video camera and starts filming us all as we finish our lunch.

Now that everyone's finished eating, the De Gilio family erupts into its usual Tower of Babel re-enaction. So I start carrying the dishes indoors ready to wash up. I'm not sure if the members of this family really do all talk at once and never listen to one another, or whether it is just that, when you're a foreigner, it's harder to set up the mental filters that enable you to distinguish one thread of conversation from another. Still, as I set dutifully off for the kitchen with my armful of plates I seem to distinguish, among the hubbub, Francesca's voice pointing out to anybody who may be listening (nobody, probably) what a very simple girl I am.

While Grazia and Francesca make the coffee, Annetta and Marisa take me to see the upstairs, where the men will be staying tonight: a large airy loft with a big old bedstead and half a dozen Italian Army camp beds set out in it. I've no idea which war these camp beds are left over from, but they are virtually indestructible: you meet them dotted about all over the hillsides, indoors and outdoors, used as beds, sofas, tables, workbenches. Hard to imagine what military genius could have invented them, and why. Bizarrely, they are hardly any smaller when folded up, and so heavy that one person alone can only just lift them and certainly couldn't carry them any distance at all. This is because they are made entirely of solid cast iron, except for the bit you sleep on, which is metal netting. Can Italian soldiers really have been made to drag cast-iron beds about with them when they went to war? Marisa and Annetta don't know. Must remember to ask Salvatore. If they did, I'm not surprised the Italian army got itself such a reputation for cowardice. Once you'd set up a camp furnished with these awesome beds, you'd not be fit to advance for a month.

Next to the big, proper bed is a tiny clay oil lamp; one of those Aladdin-type things with a big wick sticking out of the spout, all blackened and greasy with age. So do these things really work? I ask the sisters. I've got one at home, a repro-duction of a Roman-British one my mother sent me, and all it does is make a lot of smoke and then go out after ten minutes. Very disappointing. Marisa grins. She bets I've been using my good, extra virgin oil in it, haven't I? I certainly have. That's what it's supposed to run on, isn't it? Olive oil.

Yes, says Marisa, but not extra virgin. I need a cheap, acid oil to make light; just go and buy anything that doesn't say extra virgin on it.

Really? Yes. Why do I think there's so much non-extra virgin olive oil grown in the world, stuff that nobody would want to eat, not for preference, anyway? It was never intended for eating. All planted for lighting oil. A major industry for centuries all over Southern Europe and North Africa. What do I think people used before petroleum arrived on the scene? Revelation. And now I come to think of it, we even call those old paraffin lamps with a wick and a glass 'oil lamps' in English, don't we?

Back downstairs, I check out the other side room. Full of great glass demijohns, piles of Salvatore's favourite litre-and-a-half bottles, and several very stylish bottle-drying devices, things like wooden Christmas trees with dowel branches tilted upwards, so you can have several dozen cleaned bottles drying at once. I feel strongly that I need one of these too, though I'm not quite sure what for. Now, on my way back out, I stumble into something ferocious that crushes my foot painfully and skins my ankle. I give a loud yelp and collapse on to the nearest chair. I've walked into an immensely complicated Calabrian mousetrap; a mousetrap made by Salvatore himself from a small collection of rocks and sticks. And see how brilliantly it works! says Salvatore, vastly entertained.

Congratulations, I say coldly, examining my wounds.

While Francesca and Annetta rush off to make cold compresses at the sink, the perpetrator brings all the elements of his trap over and piles them on to the table. He will distract me from the agony by teaching me how to make this useful money-saving device for myself. See? A large flat stone, a couple of smaller stones, a short twig in which you cut a slot with your pocket-knife; and a long thin piece of cane, one end of which you notch so it resembles a giant fish-hook. Balance your flat killer stone neatly on all the other elements, impale a bit of bread on the point of the cane, which is now resting on the slotted twig, and you have a hair trigger. (Waste good cheese on catching a mouse? You English must be mad!)

Salvatore demonstrates how the merest touch on the bread will cause the whole structure to come crashing down, flattening any vermin, or indeed part of the human anatomy, beneath it. The crash takes Francesca by surprise, making her spill coffee all over the sideboard. For Heaven's sake! Do we really have to have a lot of old stones all over the table? Can her husband never just sit quietly?

As the afternoon wears on, I find myself working opposite Ciccio on either side of one of the pergola sections; Grazia and Annetta are on the next row along. Together we drag our full crates to the end of our row for collection.

Your father still doesn't seem too pleased with the oven repair, does he? I say.

Ah, he always carries on like that, says Ciccio.

Yes, says Annetta, he's pleased as Punch really. He loves it when Ciccio goes and does some work off his own bat up at the *campagna*, without needing to be harassed into it.

It's funny, though, I say, that he should have such a great mistrust of Pieve di Teco oven-repair methods. We're only a few miles from Pieve di Teco here, aren't we? And he's had this place for decades?

Yes. But Ciccio thinks there's been a misunderstanding. The cow-manure repair technique was certainly told to him by an old man up in Pieve; but the old man from Pieve had got it from a visiting relative. A nephew from a long-lost branch of the family that emigrated a generation ago, who had come back here for the summer to find his roots. A nephew, not to put too fine a point on it, from Argentina.

What? Argentina! I say. So we were trying out an Argentinian repair, only known by hearsay, on your dad's oven?

Ciccio is not having this. No, he says, on his mother's oven.

Well, whoever's oven, say I impatiently, refusing to be

distracted. I'm not surprised at all if your father didn't want you to experiment on his oven with an unknown technique from the other side of the world! Poor man!

Mah! says Ciccio. It worked, didn't it?

It must have been great, though, I say wistfully, a few crates later, to grow up with a father who would tell all those good stories and teach you to make wine and build do-it-yourself mousetraps and all.

Magari! says Ciccio. He was amazed to see his father showing me the mousetrap, all kind and helpful like that. It was like catching sight of another father altogether.

Certainly was, says Grazia. His idea of raising a son was like raising a fruit tree or something. Prune it back hard, and you'll get a sturdier specimen. And a better harvest.

The skies would have fallen in on his head, adds Giusi, before he'd praise Ciccio to his face.

Poor Ciccio. And poor Salvatore, come to that. What a waste!

It's all right, Ciccio says with a grin. I've not turned out too stunted, have I?

I should think not, says Grazia. The rest of us spoiled you rotten!

Look at *papa*'s own childhood, though, says Rosi. What could you expect? He didn't really have one. And there were a lot worse fathers than him.

There certainly were. Ciccio remembers a San Pietro boy he went to school with whose father would punish him by tethering him to a tree on his bit of land by the side of the road as if he were an animal. Sometimes even leave him there till after dark. Ciccio and his friends would avert their eyes as they passed by, pretend they hadn't seen him at all, to save his shame. It was all they could do for him . . .

30

Time to mount another of my inadvertent assaults on Nino's lands and property.

Rose has arrived, and I have taken her to one of the bars under the wide arched portico that runs along the port at Imperia. Interestingly, the owner, a mate of Ciccio's and a lover of all things Spanish, has made an Italian version of *sangria* for tonight's speciality, and since Patrizia is giving us a lift home we have sat outside drinking a huge jug of it while we watched a great grey Russian ship, away out in the bonded area of the port, unload unimaginable quantities of wheat straight into the bowels of the Agnesi pasta factory. It simply pumped the stuff straight out from its holds; a flowing river of grain that streamed up through a great funnel of a tube, curved gracefully through the air, glistening momentarily in the lights from the port, and then vanished into the grey maw of oblivion in the entrails of the building. No, not oblivion, of course. Pasta is a noble end to come to. And this factory produces a third of all the pasta consumed in Italy, Patrizia tells us.

Surprising, to us foreigners, that the grain should come from Russia. But of course there couldn't possibly be enough flat bits in this mountainous land to grow all the corn Italy would need, not when every man, woman and child expects a plate of pasta at least once a day, often twice. The wide plains of Russia have been supplying the pasta-eaters of Italy for centuries, says Patrizia, except for a few small hiccups – revolutions, wars and suchlike. Have I never looked closely at the Agnesi packet? I confess that I haven't. One is brought out from the kitchens for us to see, with much fussing and shouting, as if there was some sort of emergency going on. And here is the proof: the Agnesi logo, an Armada-style grain ship in full sail, dashing through the waves on the last leg of its voyage from the Black Sea, to reach safe harbour here in Imperia.

An image is coming back to me now through the mists of forgetfulness; I recall having been made to learn, once upon a time, how the Russian Revolution came about. The story began some time in the eighteen-hundreds, when the Russian aristocracy found they could make unexpectedly large amounts of money from their land by exporting wheat to the rest of Europe, and slowly came round to the idea of turning their miserable serfs loose, to be disciplined in a nice modern, impersonal way by the forces of the market. Add a bit of industrialization, a few intellectuals fretting about Democratic Rights, and there you have it: Revolution. It never did occur to me to wonder exactly who was buying up such huge amounts of grain that Russian feudalism was doomed to die. Was it the Italians? Was the Russian Revolution caused, indirectly, by pasta? Nobody is sure. Have another *sangria*, says Patrizia.

Patrizia, owner of a head of the thickest black curls you've ever seen and mother of two young daughters, now reveals that she has just started work in Imperia library. Nepotism and corruption being the done thing in this country, I begin holding forth immediately on the great importance of a local history archive, and in particular a collection of detailed maps of the area. Yes! One day, by hook or by crook, I will find that mountain trail to Testico which has so far eluded me.

Patrizia is a single parent, or rather a widow whose husband died horribly young. And she may well beat Ciccio, whom she was at school with, in the myriad-jobs-at-once stakes.

Sometimes you'll find her working in the primary school, sometimes in the Town Hall; sometimes she'll serve you in the designer-wear shop; sometimes she'll be handing you your walnut bread roll in the Bar Tropical; in summer she'll be way up in the hills giving her daughters some good clean air, and you may come across her in the courtyard of her cousin Ivana, matriarch of the sheep-keeping branch of her family, selling you a fresh *toma di peccora*, a cheese that has an amazingly long pedigree. Pliny the Elder, writing in AD 77, goes on at some length about the delights of Ligurian sheep's cheese; so good that the ancients went to the trouble of transporting it all the way down to the markets of Rome. Once you've tasted Ivana's *toma*, also known as *formaggio d'Alpe*, you can see why.

Patrizia also goes off every now and then and does things called Socially Useful jobs, subsidized by the State. A sort of Widows' Workfare, I gather. That's what the library job is. And is there, I ask, anything Socially Useful about the Imperia library? Doesn't seem too likely, going on my experience of the Diano one. But Patrizia tells me that a wind of change is blowing through the libraries of Italy. There are moves afoot to turn them into centres of local resource, instead of just archives, and battle is raging between the old, archival guard and the young, resourceful one. Making the job feel very Socially Useful, yes.

The evening's Communist and Hispanic theme now continues with a boatload of loud and cheery fishermen who appear in a dinghy, asking us in Spanish to get them in a drink. They are Cubans, they say, and they don't have customs clearance to come ashore; they are meant to be confined to their lobster-fishing boat, which is tethered over there, they add, waving seawards. Their mates wave back to us from the ship; half a dozen men in pirate bandannas, busy hanging their washing out to dry on lines stretched across the ship.

Compared to the great grey Russian thing it's moored next to, their boat looks impossibly tiny, chaotic and scruffy. Have they really come all the way from Cuba on that?

Yes, they have; they spend their lives sailing back and forth between here and the Caribbean, lobstering as they go. They never set foot on dry land here in Italy, though: because they'd need visas. But the Customs men lurking down at the bonded end of the portico kindly pretend not to notice if they just row down here to the harbour bars, where they always find someone to pass the time of day with – and get them a drink if they're lucky. We pass them down a pitcher of Italian *sangria*. *Sangria!* they say. In Italy?

How tangled up the world is, we all agree; a big jumble of cultures and nations, goods and chattels flying to and fro, everyone interconnected, all of us just imagining we're so separate, so different . . .

Tangled is the right word, too, for the next episode. There is no moon tonight, and once Patrizia has dropped us off on our homely hairpin bend, dazed and confused, we find that we've forgotten to bring a torch. Or rather, since I couldn't expect my guests, used to street lighting, to be thinking of such a thing, let's admit that it's me that has forgotten. No moon at all; and no helpful neighbours' bonfires this time, either. Don't worry, I say cheerily, I've done this loads of times. I know that Rose will be thinking about the ten-foot drop and the brambles. So am I. Why did we order that third jug of *sangria*?

As we are nearly at the scary midway point, feeling our way along the terrace wall to the right, something that oughtn't to be there trails horribly, wispily across my face, lightly brushes my arm. I stop dead. Manage not to squeak. Keep the guest calm at all costs. A gigantic cobweb, is it? I wave my arms blindly about in front of my face, doing my best to pretend everything's normal. Another half-step and whatever-it-is is still there, horribly resilient: its filaments stretching right across our way, trailing down from the terrace above, floating across the path and on to the terrace below, draping the terrace walls, looping right up into the invisible branches of the trees above us. Where does it start? Where does it end? Much too coarse for spider web, anyway. Olive net. Nino has been up this afternoon and put his nets out. I said the man was a workaholic. Nobody else has got further than piling their nets up by the side of their terraces. But how are we supposed to get round it? What's it doing in mid-air? Has it got blown into the branches? Has there been some wild wind up here that didn't reach us down in Imperia?

I know that whatever else befalls, it is absolutely vital that we do not rip Nino's nets. Even if we have to go back and sleep in my car. Last autumn our overenthusiastic friend Gianni, helping us get our winter firewood ready, sliced a hole with his chainsaw in a brand new net Nino had only just laid. When Nino, usually the quietest and calmest of men, saw the damage next day, he stood and shouted to himself, and the other side of the valley, for a good five minutes. About me. A litany of my sins against him that went back a decade. The time I left a car in the middle of the parking space so he couldn't fit his *Ape* in when he came up to harvest his olives; the time I snapped a branch off his cherry tree as I jumped down a terrace wall; the theft of his flat stones; the tile on his *rustico* roof broken by somebody idly throwing a rock at it; and now, a hole in his brand new net! Would there never be an end to it all?

I had to go right down to him and apologize, not once but twice, and at great length, before he finally calmed down. (And agreed that maybe we hadn't really thrown any rocks at his roof. Bit academic anyway, the building already having no side wall by now, but still, it mattered to me.) Anyway Nino is, except when provoked beyond belief, a sweet, nice man, and I have sworn never to commit another sin against him.

So, how to get past the thing without damaging it? Nino must have had some plan, which would no doubt be obvious by daylight. Are we meant to go under it? Over it? Around it? Impossible to tell. The total darkness is getting more and more oppressive; as if someone was pressing a swathe of blackest velvet into your face. I have one last try at gently treading the net down, walking carefully over it, one hand on the wall to guide me. No good. The further you tread the tauter it becomes; impossible to keep going without tearing a great hole in the thing to keep your footing, or falling to your doom. We can't pass below, not without a detour of half a mile, because of the precipice. Uphill is the only way. I give up pretending everything's all right really, and make Rose turn back, holding her hand for balance and consolation. I want my nice cosy bed so badly. And it's so ridiculously near.

Back at the car we clamber up the wall to the terrace above, grazing wrists and knees as we go. No good, still covered in net. Up another wall – and yes! No nets. Now we only have to feel our way along Nino's nice flat top terrace towards the house, tree by tree, and clamber down a small cliff face, to be home at last.

But behold! Wonder of wonders, as we come up to the rock, there is a light; the small golden light of a candle burning in the window. Ciccio must have spotted the forgotten torch on the side when he got back from work. How did I ever manage without a man? Home. Necks unbroken. Nets unscathed. Bed.

★

In the morning I discover that, as I suspected he would have done, Nino has been at great pains to leave us a clear passageway. Not over his nets, but under them. A beautiful tunnel of white veil, propped up on long stakes to the precipice side, wired to the olive branches to hillward, leads all the way from our rock to the road. By daylight with the sun gleaming on it, the blue skies and silvery leaves above, it looks magical, a romantic gauze alleyway set up for some improbable sylvan wedding. And it will stay here until February comes, and with it the olive harvest. Beautiful. I'll just tie back that last trailing section, though, to make life easier for any other *sangria* drinkers who may try to reach us some dark and moonless night.

31

Hardly has Ciccio got home and collapsed on to the sofa after
a hard day's work – he's been wringing the grapeskins out of
the *mosto* and getting the wine into the demijohns for its
forty days' rest – when there's a knock at the door. A tiny,
bristle-haired figure stands outlined against the glass. Pompeo,
bearing a bottle of *vino d'uva*. He must have spotted Ciccio
on his way up here, I deduce. How else did he know he didn't
need a chaperone?

He's just popped in, he says, to see how the roof's doing.
Oh, has he? Or did he just fancy getting a good look at Ciccio
in situ? He's chosen exactly the wrong moment for it, too.
Ciccio is lying limp among the cushions, looking for all the
world like one of the lazy foreign holidaymakers of my
dubious past. He drags himself to his feet and ceremoniously
shakes hands with the guest. Fearing that Pompeo may be
drawing unflattering parallels, I quickly fill him in on Ciccio's
day so far. Phew. Saved. Making the year's wine is good:
helping fathers do so even better. I see a definite light of
approval in Pompeo's eye. Ciccio collapses on to the sofa
again. I think he's allowed to now, though.

Pompeo can't believe the roof really needs to come off, he
says, having forgotten, apparently, that he was among the first
to predict precisely this outcome. He met Ulisse, who told
him there was no hope for it.

Ciccio, from his bed of pain, claims that it would be a relief
if the roof would fall in on his head right now; but Pompeo,
noticing our latest home improvement, has forgotten all about

the roof. He hasn't been round for a visit since the sister and I built our larder this spring.

What, he asks disapprovingly, has happened to the other window over there at the back of the kitchen? We've turned it into a door! Did we need two back doors, then?

How does Pompeo always manage to make me feel as if this house is still really his? No, no, I say apologetically, we've just built an extra bit on out there, on the cool north side, for storing food.

What? says Pompeo. But you already had a *cantina* downstairs! And you went and turned it into bedrooms! (Pompeo, like many other right-thinking citizens of San Pietro, has never gone along with this sacrilegious alteration of ours. If something has to suffer the heat, it should be you, and not your stores: because you will survive, whereas the food will go off. And then you might starve. Obvious. It is true that in transforming Pompeo's great-grandad's *cantina* into bedrooms, we were taking a huge gamble that modern civilization would not simply vanish overnight. But then, so far, we seem to have been proved right. And anyhow, when the market economy collapses and we have to return to subsistence farming, we can just move our beds upstairs again, can't we?)

No, I say, it's nothing like as big as a *cantina*. We call it a larder in English; a *lardaio*, I suppose you'd say in Italian.

A *lardaio*? A special room just to store *lardo* in? Pompeo is horrified. No wonder you English have such a bad cholesterol problem in your country!

A room full of lard. I suppose, etymologically speaking, that this must once have been the case. These innocent Italians don't know the half of it. '*Lardo*', the word we're using for convenience here, is certainly not a block of tasteless pallid pure grease like its English cousin, but a delicacy pungent with black peppercorns and thyme-sprigs, eaten in wafer-thin slices;

a kind of superfat smoked streaky bacon that melts in the mouth. There would be some point, now, in having a whole room full of *lardo*.

Pompeo is already inside the larder, which as we know contains no lard at all: only my record-winning accumulation of nameless jars, all no doubt healthily olive-oil-based given local conditions, and now swollen to unimaginable proportions by the new *passata* collection. He is most impressed.

Ciccio's mother's stuff, I say, not wishing to take credit where it is not due. (Potted things are always Mothers' Jars, however many people contributed to them: just as wine is always Father's Wine.)

Good, good, says Pompeo, turning a piercing gaze upon Ciccio. His mother's, is it? So, he says after a thoughtful pause, have you named the day yet?

Ciccio lets out a groan of agony.

Now, most surprisingly, Pompeo tells us that Ulisse is right: we should turn to Frank the Knife for our roof repairs. Can he be serious? Usually the mere mention of Franco's name sets Pompeo off in a paroxysm of disapproval. How come the sudden change of heart?

Obvious, says Pompeo. If our path was meant for anything, it was meant for four-footed beasts of burden. Getting all the gear down our path might be a major undertaking for modern builders, but it would be a piece of cake for a man with the right equine equipment to handle it. That was how the house was built in the first place – with mules and horses lugging all the stuff. And in horsy matters, as we know, Franco reigns supreme. Also, Pompeo goes on, ticking off the points on his fingers, we are not defenceless *stranieri*, foreign strangers who don't speak the language. Franco knows we have friends here to protect us against outrages, as he discovered when he tried

252

to re-sell our well. So all we need is someone to give us an honest estimate, so we know the right price to offer Franco for the job, and we're sorted. We've got them already, I say, one from Anna's cousin Romeo and one from Ulisse. Well, there we are then! Let's open the wine to celebrate!

As he leaves, Pompeo shakes Ciccio's hand and tells him what a good son he is – not like so many of the young ones who just disappear and leave their old dads in the lurch! Ah no!

Now, all of a sudden, I feel a wave of annoyance with Salvatore. Look how people who hardly know Ciccio compliment him on being a good son, while his own father does nothing but carp and criticize, and apparently did the same all through his childhood! I'm surprised Ciccio's not a gibbering insecure wreck. No thanks at all to his father if he isn't.

Ciccio laughs. Salvatore may always have snapped and raged: but Ciccio never doubted that he cared about him for a moment. He didn't show it in the way he behaved to him, perhaps; but he certainly did in the way he behaved to other people. Ciccio remembers, for instance, when he was eleven or twelve, pinching a tent from a shop so he and his mates could go camping and watch the dawn from the top of the mountain on May Day. Salvatore, spotting this impossibly expensive item, dragged him back to the shop by the scruff of the neck, made him confess and give it back. Utter humiliation. Now, as they were leaving, the owner turned to Ciccio. You'll not be doing that again, lad, will you? said he. Or else!!!

In a trice, Salvatore had clutched his son protectively to his side and turned a face of thunder on the shopkeeper. What do you mean, Or else? he asked ferociously. Or else what? The only person who is going to discipline my son, he snapped, is me! Got that? And taking Ciccio by the hand, he stormed out of the shop.

Doesn't sound so great to me, but Ciccio insists that this sort of thing was all he needed to feel one hundred per cent secure in his father's love. Fine, I suppose, if it worked for him. Within the half-hour, anyway, he's accusing me of being a worse underminer of his equanimity than Salvatore could ever be. Rose now returns from an afternoon's wandering to find us having our first serious row. About compost. The compost bucket under the sink being full, Ciccio has set off to empty it: but instead of going down the steps to the heap, he's heading straight along on to Nino's land. Is he going to throw it down on to the heap from up here? Can it possibly land in the right spot from a height of fifteen feet? Will it not miss and end up all over the path?

I have had some difficulty, since Ciccio moved in (if that's what he's done) in getting him to accept the concept of compost. Nobody round here ever seems to have heard of compost heaps. Is this because they've always had livestock to feed all their scraps to? Francesca's still go up to the chickens, or to the neighbour's dog, depending on how meaty they are. Or is it just that, if you live so far from your land, there's no point in making compost only to have to transport it for miles? Or both? Anyway, it's doubly convenient up here at Besta de Zago, where rubbish has to be taken all the way down to the wheely bin at the Colla church. A compost heap eliminates all the nasty dribbly stuff you wouldn't want to be carrying about the place, and its product cheers up the vines and the lemons no end. Still, even though he seemed rather impressed when I showed him the final result, and agreed that it was strange that no one did it round here, Ciccio has only accepted the compost heap under duress. Now he admits that instead of going to the heap, he has as often as not been simply burying the stuff, using an old *zappa*, a sort of pointy hoe thing, that he's left leaning against our last olive tree. He can't always be bothered separating out the meaty bits that I won't let him put in the compost, he says; and it can't do any harm, anyway.

This might be true if he'd been burying it under our own trees. But he's been doing it under Nino's!! Has he lost his marbles?

It's a lot easier to dig the hole on Nino's land, he says. He looks after it better. Your soil hasn't been properly dug over for years, has it?

Oh Lord! On Nino's land! Without asking him! Please God make it rot down quickly, and let him never find out!

32

Rose and I are finishing a peaceful breakfast in the morning sunshine. Ciccio is down on the terrace below, tightening the brakes on my *motorino*. Suddenly he starts shouting, banging, and hurling spanners about in what appears, to an innocent British bystander, to be an ungovernable rage. I am interested to see that Rose finds this behaviour very disturbing: and proud to note that I, by contrast, have hardly turned a hair. Until recently, whenever Ciccio shouted and banged – and especially hurled – my every nerve would stand Englishly on end, telling me to get over there and try to calm him down; to reason and soothe and generally be nice. Mistake. According to the author of the racket, it is a private expression of frustration, unconnected with anybody else who may be about. Especially me. I should just ignore it until it wears off, or I might get shouted at myself.

Easy to say, but back in my own land, if somebody carried on like that, they certainly would not be expecting to be ignored. How could anything so loud and noticeable be a private expression of anything? Even when I managed to follow the manufacturer's instructions and let the raging wear out under its own steam, I would find my efforts to ignore the un-ignorable so stressful that by the time the usual cheerful Ciccio had returned, no major surgery required after all, I would often as not be in a foul mood myself, and ready to do some shouting and banging of my own. Except that in my case it would be in the demanding English style.

But look at me today! I say to Rose, to whom I have just

explained all this. I'm just sitting here quietly, not bothered at all!

Rose says she thinks she might be able to achieve the same result by going into deep Zen meditation: but she'll go and do it in her bedroom for now, where it's a bit quieter. Half an hour or so later, things have calmed down somewhat, and the peaceful twitter of bird and winter cicada is only ornamented with the occasional clang or ferociously muttered *porca miseria di una lurida vacca della putana di* . . . when Tonino appears on the path below. Confirming my words, he doesn't so much as bat an eyelid at the sight of the growling maniac battling with my *motorino*. Just says *Salve* as if nothing at all out of the ordinary was going on. Ciccio *Salve*s back sunnily.

See what I mean? I say to Rose, who has reappeared from her room now the shouting has abated.

Blimey, says Rose expressively.

We will be starting to lay our olive nets today, on the lower terraces and the ones down by the car. We can't put them down close to the house till the roof's sorted – they'll just get ripped to shreds, won't they, with builders trampling to and fro on them. Rose, who has done quite a bit of theatre and costume design in her time, has been greatly admiring Nino's wedding walkway creation since she got over her first unfortunate encounter with it, and is very keen to join in the job of clothing a mountainside in acres of white netting. Then we shall be lunching *alla bracia* down with Anna and Tonino, who are going to be doing the same job down on their own terraces. And since we're bringing a vegetarian with us, I'm digging out some extra vegetarian supplies. Luckily the larder is stuffed with a large selection of Tommaso's cheeses: we finally got round to visiting his premises, in spite of Ciccio being (of course) about to sever all connection with his restaurant, and took Rose off trudging up the dirt road and along the mule-tracks to find the place hidden in the elbow of the valley, in a surprisingly flat and fertile corner full of streamlets, wildly burgeoning cane clumps and fat shady apricot trees. Dotted about among these were a whole hamlet of ramshackle stone *rustici* bordering on collapse; amongst which, variously, Tommaso pointed out his home, his goat-sheds, his milking-sheds, his cheese-making *cantina* and his cave-like cheese-maturing rooms dug into the rock. No Peppinos, though; they were away keeping an eye on the goats up above – or so Tommaso hoped and believed, he said, darting me a stern look.

But before they concentrated on the cheese matters in hand, he had to show us his latest, brand-new venture, in which he was sure the restaurateur would be greatly interested. Refusing to say more, he led us down on to a wide terrace below the rest of the buildings, screened from his hovel collection by a small orchard of pear trees and a large pile of rocks he had just moved, he explained, to allow motorized access to his new enterprise from the Moltedo side. Yes: there was indeed a motorized vehicle already adorning the area. A derelict-looking catering van on whose sides were painted the faded and peeling words 'Hamburger, Hot Dog, Panini, Eis Cream'. Bought for a song, said Tommaso, and ideal for his purposes. Look inside!

We looked. So much for Fast Food. On a bed of straw, a huge hairy sow lay snoring, her head shaded by the zinc serving-counter; while a litter of a dozen tiny curly-tailed pink piglets clambered about all over her, squeaking ear-piercingly and nuzzling for milk. Tommaso was planning, he said, to become a purveyor of porky products as well as of cheeses. Look how nice and fat the piglings were already! All destined, said our host with glee, to become ham and salami such as only he knows how to make. We must make sure to come back in the spring.

Great. Just the sort of sight-seeing to please a vegetarian. How foolishly squeamish I am myself, though. I felt terrible standing there discussing, in front of these live and (relatively) attractive creatures, my intention of eating them transformed, as advertised, into hot dogs, or maybe *panini*, at some later date. All these years in Liguria, and still I have learnt nothing. Yes, of course we'll be back for a salami or two, I said, boldly defying my own absurd reactions and determinedly avoiding Rose's eye.

Now, while Ciccio and Tommaso conducted negotiations in muttered undertones ten feet away, Rose and I checked out the cheese-maturing hovel, dug into the side of the hill, where rows and rows of cheeses sat around the walls in little cupboards of fine netting – so air could circulate but not flies, said Tommaso. And he gave us a free sample to take away; two of each of his smaller styles of cheese, the fresh and the matured version, wrapped in the customary antique carrier bags, recycled a thousand times and still good for anything just that little bit too small for an old sack. Then, once we'd all shaken hands to seal whatever deal had been concocted, Tommaso shot off into the dark recesses of yet another half-ruined building and reappeared with something in a sealed Kilner jar to add to our haul. A delicacy, he said, handing over this beige-coloured cream-cheese-looking stuff, to be saved for a special occasion. It was called, as far as I could tell, 'brouss'. It didn't have a name in Italian – why would it? It was local stuff for local people. Ciccio was very pleased. Hardly anyone makes brouss any more these days.

Next time, though, Tommaso shouted after us as we set off with our booty, apparently having repented of his generosity, next time we would have to pay!

★

Rose enjoys the net-laying even more than she expected to. I tie her pouch of three-inch nails round her waist for her, and explain how, once we've rolled the nets downhill and into position, she just has to use the nails as if they were gigantic dressmaking pins, to fix them together round the trunks, making tucks and darts over any rocks and walls that get in the way. I tell her to roll the edges double, like a French seam, before pinning them, so we won't lose our olives down the gaps. Instructions complete, and off we go. By lunchtime, when we set off down to Anna and Tonino's, Rose may have covered slightly less ground than the rest of us, but aesthetically speaking her work is a triumph. Nino's netting walkway couldn't hold a candle to it. She has created some beautifully complex corsetry across three terraces; and something remarkably like a 1950s pointy brassière now adorns the pair of troublesome rocks on the fourth terrace below the house.

Ah, says Anna, shaking Rose's hand, she'd heard we had a friend staying. An acrobat, isn't she? she asks, looking hopefully at Rose. Does she work in a circus?

No, she doesn't, I say, mystified. Naturally I now question Rose closely about any acrobat-type behaviour she may have engaged in recently. At first she denies the thing, but third-degree interrogation reveals what happens at the end of the early morning wanders she takes down the mule-track to enjoy the sands of Diano Marina in peace and quiet. Once she gets to what she ignorantly thinks of as a deserted beach, she has been doing half an hour of T'ai Chi exercises. Little does she know that for every pair of slatted green shutters overlooking the bay, there will have been a pair of fascinated eyes watching her every move.

As he and Tonino get the wood for our lunch fire ready, Ciccio heaves a large piece of log on to his shoulder and suddenly goes into a paroxysm of agony. His neck has got nailed again. Can't think why: everything's been going just fine up at the restaurant recently. Has the air got to him, perhaps? Rose, usually a dab hand at this sort of thing, makes him sit cross-legged on the ground and does some very professional-looking massage on the painful area, but the patient does not respond.

Anna rises to the barefoot doctor challenge. She just needs three glasses, she says, which we'll find in the outdoor sink round the corner of the house. And the bottle of olive oil by the cooker. Oh, and the box of matches. And a bit of dry rag from the pile in the corner. Yes, over there. It has to be cotton, though, nothing synthetic. She burns a corner, sniffs the smoke to check. Fine. Now, three five-hundred-lire coins (we all start emptying our pockets out) and a bit of thread – ah, here's a bit dangling off her apron. Rose, alternative medicine fan, is gripped; what can Anna be going to do with this unlikely collection of objects?

The cure begins: each coin is wrapped in a small square ripped from the cloth, and is tied in with the thread so it looks like a tiny Christmas pudding. Now the sticking-up corners of the cloth are dipped in the olive oil. Ciccio is made to go and lie down indoors, and the little greasy bundles are laid, flat coin side down, on his back, around the pain. Anna lights a match and applies it to the sticking-up ears of oil-soaked cloth. Once they have caught fire, she clamps the wine-glasses over the flames. I am happy to relate that the flame goes out after just a moment or two, starved of oxygen, so the sufferer is not burnt alive, as the more nervous spectator might have feared. But now, slowly and appallingly, like something dreamed up by Steven Spielberg, the flesh inside the glass begins to rise up into a ghastly bulging lump, apparently of its own volition. The lump gets redder and redder, more and more swollen and rigid-looking, as the blood is sucked up into it until it fills half the glass; while the skin all around puckers up into hugely magnified orange peel. Good job the patient can't see Rose's face, or mine for that matter; our expressions of horror certainly would not contribute to any healing effect.

Now he just has to lie still for ten minutes, says Anna, and he'll be right as rain. And she bustles off outside again to get on with the lunch. Rose and I are sure we've seen this treatment illustrated somewhere, along with blood-letting and leeches, billed as an outlandish and senseless medieval practice. Worrying. But ten minutes later Ciccio reappears, claiming to be completely restored. Now I come to think of it, leeches are making a bit of a comeback too, aren't they, these days?

Ciccio, unable as always to let anyone else do any cooking, has taken over the *bracia*, the fire now reduced to embers – woe betide anyone in this country who tries to cook over a bonfire with even the smallest of flames still rising from it – and is serving grilled chunks of fennel and quarters of red onion, using a leafy twig of rosemary off the bush by the door to brush them with olive oil as he goes. On the side of the grill a cartoon chicken lies sizzling away, looking like it's been run over by a steamroller; he's somehow opened the creature right out flat for ease of cooking. It may look ridiculous, but it's already perfuming the air deliciously. No herbs or spices: just plain chicken. The olive wood will add a flavour all its own. Next on to the grill go wafer-thin slices of some dark meat that goes golden and crunchy as it cooks, like a kind of meat crisp; Anna's contribution to the meal, and delicious. No use to Rose, who is even less impressed when we're told they are slices of cow's heart.

Rose's vegetarianism is very disturbing to poor Tonino, who keeps insisting that of course she can eat some of the chicken; chicken doesn't count as meat. The chickens-aren't-meat theory has been expounded on several occasions already to Rose since she arrived in this country, and I can see she's about to have a fit. Ciccio, fearful that she may starve, grills her some *bruschetta*. *Bruschetta*, however much fuss foreign food fetishists may like to make about it, is toast. In the classic recipe, you toast your bit of crusty bread: you cut a garlic clove in half: you rub the cut side hard on to the toast: and that is it. You don't need to add olive oil or butter, because the heat in the bread draws out the volatile oils from the garlic along with the aroma. But you can if you want; and you can rub half a cut tomato lightly over it as well. Very good too, in an otherwise toast-free zone like Italy.

To save Rose from torment I decide to break all local dietary rules and get out the cheese immediately. Why shouldn't she have it now, with her *bruschetta*, if she wants? Lovely, says Rose. The fresh one is delicate and creamy when applied, unorthodoxly, to her toast. The mature one is pungent and flavoursome. Neither of them has that billy-goat aroma that she feared. She'll try the cheese-in-a-jar now. She opens it: and cowers away, covering her nose and passing it to me in horror, her eyes watering. I sniff. Powerfully stinky. I prod its contents with a knife, holding it at arm's length. Once the first explosion of vapour has worn off, though, maybe it's not so bad. Tonino excitedly grabs the jar from me. Brouss! Is it brouss? he asks, as the local contingent gathers round it joy-ously. Almost impossible to come by these days, it seems; he is delighted.

At everyone's insistence, I try a bit on the corner of my own *bruschetta*. (How easily can centuries of tradition be tossed aside!) Tasty, but incredibly hot, as if it was full of chilli. That's because it's so mature, says Anna. You can get a young version, too, that is much lighter. What the mature version is really full of, I am told – after I have finished chewing – is not chilli but microscopic cheese-mite-type things. If you stare closely into the jar, you can actually see the cheese writhing about. Rose gets up and goes for a short walk.

Conversation turns to the source of this wonderful stuff; who made it? Where did I get it? Can I get them some? When Ciccio names Tommaso, Anna and Tonino are amazed. What, is he out of prison already? Generously, I give the jar away to our kind hosts. Am I sure? Doesn't Ciccio want it? No, he certainly does not, I say, giving him a quelling look. There is quite enough wildlife in our house and home already. Please take the whole thing.

33

Time to take Rose for a proper Ligurian Ordeal by Food. Enough cows' hearts and cheese-mites. We are now ensconced in our favourite restaurant of all time, Da Maria up at Cosio d'Arroscia, Patrizia's home town. We have driven up here with the usual Diano company in the usual half a dozen cars, doing the usual stopping every fifteen minutes to check that nobody is missing from the convoy – an odd Italian habit which I have given up complaining about, since it is utterly impossible to convince any Italians that it is odd in the first place. For years I've simply done my best to avoid participating in it – Lucy and I had the thing down to a fine art, you just had to think up an excuse for leaving earlier than everybody else (not later, because they'd just wait for you) so you could go in your own car and only stop once, at the place you actually wanted to go to. All pointless now I have hitched myself up with Ciccio, who is, as I may have mentioned, Italian himself, and suffers from the same inexplicable convoying herd-instinct as the rest of his nation.

I am looking forward immensely to seeing Rose seeing a mountain village dinner for the first time; I'm not at all worried about her vegetarianism up at Cosio, either, because a huge amount of the cuisine of the Ligurian hinterlands is meat-free, based on the products of the *orto*; and you don't even get on to the meat course until you've eaten your way through a good fifteen *antipasti* and two different types of pasta (in fact, the major challenge at these traditional dinners is to have enough space left to fit in so much as a morsel of the meat course). The husband of the eponymous Maria has our table for fifteen ready set with bread, water and wine, and appears within minutes with the first serving dish. This is the wonder of these places high in the hills; no menu, no ordering, you just take pot luck, safe in the knowledge that there will be such overwhelming quantities of food that you can turn down anything you don't fancy and still go away with a full stomach. I make sure to sit a good long way from Osvaldo, who's come in one of the other cars with Giusi, so nothing can spoil the evening.

So, here comes item number one; Mr Maria goes right round the restaurant doling out a portion on to each plate. Whole borage leaves deep-fried in batter: *frisceui di borraggine*. One each, and does anybody want an extra one, there are still a few left on the dish? Proprietor vanishes into kitchens, returns with platter of *zucchini* flowers stuffed with parmesan, egg and breadcrumbs. Next, slices of *porcino* mushroom; now grilled red peppers with anchovies (whoops – will Rose mind the fish? No.) Tiny rolled-up pancakes with melted goats' cheese inside. Squares of crunchy *focaccia* with olives; others with tomato. A little fat fresh salami each. Piece of melon with Parma ham. Triangles of *torta verde* – spinach-egg-and-rice pie. Artichokes braised in white wine. Stuffed onions, oven-roasted. Slices of polenta, with a luscious truffle sauce. Halves of fresh tomato filled with fluffy ricotta cheese and chopped spring onions. Slices of roast aubergine with creamy tomato sauce. Squares of *bruschetta* with olive pâté. Chunks of *toma* (Ivana's?) marinated in olive oil. A garlicky aubergine purée. Spoonful of tiny pickled wild mushrooms. More pieces of tomato, this time with some kind of cheese-and-pesto mixture. Pastry cup filled with creamy chicken. (Short argument. Of course Rose can eat it, says the Italian contingent. It's not meat, it's bird!) Wafer-thin slice of raw beef marinated in lemon and olive oil. No. Slice of *cima alla Genovese* – cold calf's shoulder Genoa style, stuffed with all manner of things; peas, eggs, onion, cheese, breadcrumbs. No again. Crispy fried frogs' legs. Paletta insists that's not meat either, but Mr Maria has learnt his lesson. He bites his tongue and passes on. Last few things not much use to Rose, and she passed on the Parma ham and salami, but still an impressive amount of vegetable. You can imagine how this cuisine must have developed – generations of women in their kitchens thinking up ways to pad out a load of not-very-calorific stuff from the Father's Land, the only thing you were sure to have plenty of, and turn it into something substantial and filling. Look at the *cima*: each slice is ninety per cent stuffing with a tiny ring of meat around the outside. Or *frisceui*: or indeed pesto, the most famous Ligurian speciality. Add a few more calories however you can, oil, flour, breadcrumbs, cheese, pine nuts. It's easy to forget, in these perverse times, that for most of human history, and for most of the world today, more calories is what you're after in order to survive. Even easier to forget when dining here *da Maria*. Doesn't matter how time-consuming the work that goes into it – budget is tight and your labour costs nothing. Look at pasta – hours of work to make it, but you've transformed what is at bottom nothing but flour-and-water paste into something not merely edible, but actually desirable.

And here comes the pasta – the *primo piatto*. An impossible choice between *trenette*, a local flattened version of spaghetti, and *maltagliati*, big flat rough-cut pieces, and of two sauces; a creamy walnut one or bright green pesto just made from the armfuls of fresh basil we saw going into the kitchens as we arrived. I solve the problem, like almost everyone else at the table, by trying a bit of each. Both so good that without even the slightest remnant of an appetite, they're gone in no time. I am pleased to see Rose's eyes boggling as the pasta plates are cleared away and replaced with another set. But she has done her duty, and can give her digestive system a nice rest now. No meat course for her; while I still have the ultimate test to come. The *secondo piatto*. Yes, here it comes: a platter piled high with meat. Fragrant rabbit *alla Ligure*, full of olives and thyme; and wild boar in a rich, thick *umido*.

Rose seems to be suffering at the sight of so much dead animal, so I suggest she goes out to admire the very impressive loo. It isn't actually the loo itself that's impressive, but I don't want to spoil the surprise. You walk into this restaurant at pavement level, so you naturally believe, as you busy yourself with your knife and fork, that you are sitting safe on solid ground. So the effect is jaw-dropping when you pop casually out of the back door to get to the toilet facilities and find yourself on a narrow balcony poised a hundred-odd feet above a roaring torrent of a river at the bottom of a deep ravine.

Since Rose left the table and walked through the bar end of the restaurant, where the usual collection of old folk sits playing cards and nursing glasses of red wine or digestive spirits, some sort of commotion has been going on; lots of chatting and arm-waving and laughter and pass-it-on type nudging. One of them is some distant relation of Patrizia's, she says, giving him a wave. Is it something to do with her? But no. Eventually the prop comes over with a bottle of wine and a big grin on his face. The gentlemen at the bar have sent it over for the acrobat lady, he says; in appreciation of her morning shows down on Diano beach. As Rose returns from the bathroom, looking gratifyingly moved by her Ravine Experience, the eagle-eyed old gent who recognized her stands up and shakes her hand enthusiastically, much to her surprise.

But how could I have imagined for a moment that Rose would get no *secondo*? No doubt it is a point of honour up here in Cosio that nobody should be allowed to escape with even a millimetre of space left in his or her digestive system. A special individual platter arrives for Rose alone. On it baldly sit two enormous plain hunks of cheese – one of them an entire quarter of a sheep *primo sale* – and a whole beef-heart tomato almost as big as a football. Rose can hardly believe that anyone could suspect her of still being hungry; still less, after such a feast of delicate and laboriously prepared delights, present her with a pound or two of crude, unadulterated cheese and a giant raw tomato. Poor Maria must have been grappling with the *secondo* problem ever since we announced that there was a vegetarian in our midst. And finally given up. What could possibly stand in for a great dolloping pile of first-class protein? It would have to be some chunky, substantial item . . .

Once we're on our coffee and *digestivi* (I pass lightly over the dessert course: I couldn't fit mine in anyway), Rose's aged fan comes over to join us, with the excuse of chatting to our Patrizia, and sits gazing admiringly at her. Rose is nearly six feet tall, and there is nothing an aged Ligurian appreciates more than a big tall woman. Especially if she's not all skin and bone. Patrizia introduces us: he is Orlando, and he lives a few doors along from her cousin and grandmother. Unfortunately, though, Osvaldo is holding forth at the moment, over in the corner, about his vile politics. It is not long before Orlando catches a fragment of the conversation; and all hell breaks loose. What does Osvaldo mean, the Good Old Days under Mussolini? Orlando could tell him a thing or two about the Good Old Fascists in Pieve di Teco, where he lived at the time! Would Osvaldo like to know how they would persuade you, if you hadn't quite got round to volunteering, to come and join their Youth Organization? A couple of weedy spotty blackshirted under-fifteens would turn up at your front door, call your parents out, and slap them around in front of their children, their neighbours and anyone else who happened to be passing: a punishment for supposedly having stopped you joining. Your parents would be powerless to retaliate against the striplings, just had to stand there and take the public humiliation, since the Youth would have a pair of fine figures of fully-grown and fully-armed Blackshirts to escort them on their house calls. So of course you'd go and join, to save them any more suffering. Is this the happy world Osvaldo wants to get back to?

All lies, Osvaldo tells me some time later, as we head for our cars. Communist propaganda. All the old folks are Communists round here, have been since the days of the Partisans. That's why they give their children names like Ivana.

34

When Franco turns up to inspect the roof job – yes, of course I've ended up asking him to do it – Rose has gone back to England and Ciccio is away at work. So I have no moral support to hand when Franco announces airily that he's made an appointment to meet the *geometra* up here in half an hour.

What, the official *geometra*? From the *Regione*? But haven't we been told by everyone we've spoken to that our roof project is one best kept from the bureaucracy of this land, rather than shared with them? This *geometra* person is something akin to a Borough Surveyor! Has Franco been infected by the anti-corruption drive sweeping his country, the judges of the heroic *mani puliti*, the Clean Hands movement? Hard to credit. You'd think Franco was the least likely candidate.

No time to probe further. The *geometra* is already upon us, rounding the rock. Franco introduces us; I've seen him about the place, one of the few thirty-somethings with an education who hasn't left his roots behind him and gone off to seek his fortune elsewhere. He wears the trimmed beard and red T-shirt of New Ligurianicity, and he's speaking dialect with Franco, wearing a slightly self-conscious air. Educated people have for decades been expected to abandon their childhood dialect for Italian: this must be a principled stand the *geometra*'s taking. All very fine, seems a nice bloke, good job some people are starting to take their dialects seriously. But that does not mean I want him here.

And it's even worse than I'd expected: before he's so much as looked at the roof, the *geometra* has spied my small and inoffensive larder, leapt upon it and pronounced that in all likelihood it is *abusivo*.

What happens if you have an abusive larder, then? I ask anxiously.

Ah, says the *geometra*, casually scratching his beard, you have to pay a large fine; or else you can knock it down.

Right. Wait till this man's gone and I shall murder Franco.

And the roof, he continues, were we to rebuild it as it is now, would also probably be abusive; because the porch arrangement out front does not exist officially on the *catasta*, the land register, and it adds a good fifteen unauthorized square metres to the house. The fine would be several thousand pounds. If we were allowed to keep it at all.

But, I gibber, it's always been there!

Well, then, it might be all right, he admits. As long as it was added before 1967.

I've no idea when it was added, I say, but we'd have no shade at all on this side of the house if we got rid of it!

Or, continues Gianluca, ignoring me, we could wait for the next *condono*; which, he says, contrary to rumour, does not only come out when a Pope dies, the way it used to, but also whenever the government is particularly short of money. Every four or five years, usually, he adds gloomily.

In spite of having suggested this himself, he seems to disapprove intensely of my interest in when, exactly, the next *condono* might be expected to come out. His country is a mess, he says, fixing me with a baleful and accusing eye. There will never be an end to bribery and corruption; there is no hope for the place at all. What is the point of having building regulations when everyone knows they can build what they like and just wait for the next *condono*?

I have to agree with him. I would like to ask this *geometra* what he thinks about systematic cheating in exams. From the sound of him, he could be one of the few people in his country who might think it was not a good thing. But this is not the moment to be bringing up matters of principle. Because, of course, our porch is only tiny, its roof is of old terracotta tiles the same as the rest of the house, it blends in perfectly well with the surroundings and is utterly invisible (like the rest of the house) to anyone not standing right next to it. And it wasn't us that put it there anyway. While the new roof will look exactly the same as it does now – we're even going to re-use the same tiles . . . And the larder's only a couple of square metres, and there was a shed there anyway so the building looks exactly the same from the outside . . . Moreover, adding insult to injury, just over the ridge into the next valley a ghastly sprawl of hacienda-type mansions is mushrooming up in an area called, rather appropriately, *Le Monade*, apparently untouched by all the rules and regulations being brought to bear on my poor little house . . .

The *geometra*, who has been looking everywhere but at me while I plead and rage, now turns out to have stopped listening entirely, and leaves me in mid-sentence to go off down my (abusive?) steps for a private consultation with Franco. The debate proceeds behind the thick gnarled trunk of our oldest, widest olive tree; I catch the odd glimpse of emphatic flailing arms (Franco) and jabbing index finger (Gianluca) but this does not give me much idea what's going on. The pair of them eventually emerge from their bosky conference, hands are shaken, and Gianluca goes off down the path without so much as a wave goodbye, as if the entire business had nothing to do with me at all.

All sorted, says Franco, leaping nimbly up on to the patio where I stand biting my nails, and sending a couple of stones flying. (Why, oh why can't anybody use the steps and the paths?)

Why did you bring him here? I ask. Have you lost your wits?

Best to do it all above-board if you can, isn't it? says Franco, all po-faced and correct. Alarming, coming from him. But now he breaks into a grin, does that cunning finger-under-the-eyeball gesture. A job like this, he says, horses and all, it's bound to reach a lot of people's ears. Try and do it on the sly and they might easily be annoyed enough to slap an order on you to stop work. You might end up barred from entering your own house till you'd gone to court to sort it all out. Imagine that, with the roof off. Years, maybe, till the case came up. No, no. This is the best way. Draw their fire first. We certainly have drawn their fire, I say. What am I going to do about the fines? How much are they going to be?

Fines? says Franco, taking his customary seat on the step and tipping his hat into relax-position on the back of his head. Don't go preoccupying yourself about fines. Everything's in order. We can get started whenever you're ready.

Can we? How utterly mysterious this country is.

As soon as Franco's gone chuntering off down the hill in his *Ape*, I leap on to my *motorino* and rush squeaking off to the restaurant to get a second opinion on the situation. And on Frank the Knife's mental health status. No problem, is the verdict from Ciccio and Patrizia, who is doing some wait-ressing now Alberto is back at school. Of course it's nothing to do with anti-corruption drives! Am I stupid? Anyway, adds Patrizia, the *Regione* would only bother about such a paltry matter as my roof if someone forced their hand by denouncing me officially for my abusiveness. But that sort of thing only happens if you upset a neighbour, if you've added a window that overlooks their bathroom, or you've blocked off their view, or something like that. Or alternatively if you've done something else, completely unconnected with building, that's annoyed them, and they just want to get back at you. But I haven't got any neighbours, have I? So everything's just fine and dandy.

But I have got neighbours, I say, even if they don't actually live there. Think of all the times I've annoyed Nino! Look how he stored all his grievances up for ages before he finally exploded at me . . . though I don't suppose he would go telling tales unless he was pushed to the limits. Which he may well be, I add, glowering at Ciccio, if he ever discovers that we've been using his groves as an unofficial landfill site. But what if, say, I unwittingly commit an outrage against Ugo . . . we accidentally blocked the path to his land for over a week last year . . . ? And then there's the strangely silent man with the long beard who owns the land just above my parking space. Plenty of scope for annoying him with my cars and *motorini* and visitors' transport; and I don't know what sort of person he is at all. He's never done more than give me a nod hello in all these years. He could be like anything.

(We are momentarily distracted here by having to establish Mr Beard's identity. My mentors soon work it out. Not a comforting story. He was the apple of his family's eye, brilliant brain, great future ahead of him, started university and all; but then his father died and there was no money to spare and he had to give it all up and come back here to support the family. So he stopped talking and grew a beard.)

We return to the topic in hand: my obsession with having things in official order. Silly idea. Just do the job, wait for the *condono*, pay the fine; act normal.

I have no choice, it seems, but to enter the fascinating house-of-cards world of local favours-and-obligations. I suppose it does work in a way – as long as everybody has something to worry about, they don't dare annoy anyone else. Offend nobody, and you're safe as houses.

Further investigation in *Wildlife in House and Home* suggests that we should make sure, when changing our roof timbers, to burn all the old wood before the new stuff comes on site; and use pressure-treated timber to replace it. What is pressure-treated timber, though? Franco has never heard of such a thing; and naturally he doesn't believe we really need it, whatever it may be. This, of course, means that he won't be trying very hard to find it. I'd better do it myself.

Now follows a very stressful period where I try to track some down, only to discover that Franco is not alone; nobody round here has heard of the stuff, or indeed thinks we need it. The Builders' Paradise of San Pietro looks at me blankly; the IPA merchants in Diano Marina treat me as if I was an idiot. The ancient red-nosed brothers who run the woodyard up at Vessalico, near Pieve di Teco, have heard of such a thing – yes! But alas, they've never heard of anyone round here using or supplying it. You need huge ovens to pressure-treat it in, they tell me; nobody round here has the equipment. I should try somewhere like Genoa or Venice, somewhere where there are a lot of valuable old buildings being restored for the tourists.

Worse than the lack of treated timber, though, is the reaction when the name of Franco comes up. Who's doing the job for you, then? people will ask chattily while they wait on the phone for yet another person to give them a blank on funny foreign timber. Franco, I will say. Silence falls. The salesperson in question starts to look extremely shifty, and studiously avoids my eyes for the rest of our colloquy. Is this meant to be a hint? If it is, it's a pretty poor one. Anyone not forewarned wouldn't have the faintest idea what these awful pregnant silences were about. Still, they work horribly well on me. Have I missed some vital item of gossip? Is Franco maybe not really capable of doing a roof? Has he done one that's fallen down or something? Who could I possibly ask in the village that would overcome their prejudices and answer honestly?

I choose lunchtime to pop into Luigi's bar; likeliest time to find the place deserted and only Stefano in charge. His father's anti-gossip code of honour might get in the way of a straight answer, if it was bad news he had to give me. There is only one old man at the bar, knocking back a quick pick-me-up of *vino nero*. I can't possibly ask in front of even one witness, though. I'll mark time with a coffee and hope no other customers come in before this one leaves. I ask Stefano for my usual Very Very Long Coffee In A Big Cup with a drop of cold milk. Years of practice have gone into refining this phrase, the most verbally economical way of getting a coffee that isn't practically all milk like a cappuccino, doesn't come in an eggcup only a third full, and doesn't blow the top of your head off. In Rome, I discovered, they call this an American coffee. Just try saying that here. You'll find yourself having to explain that it means a Very Very Long Coffee In A Big Cup. Not enough Americans around, I guess.

Stefano is used to me by now, and follows his instructions obediently. As soon as my fellow client has drained his wine to the last drop and left, I go for it. I'm sorry to put you on the spot like this, I say, but I desperately need to know if there is any reason to suppose that Franco the Knife is not competent to replace a roof. Just say Yes or No.

No problem: of course he can do a roof, says Stefano comfortingly. I describe the weird behaviour in builders' yards throughout the Province of Imperia whenever I mention Franco's name. Stefano thinks this will be because, me being foreign, people naturally assume that I will have no inkling of the difficulties I will face in keeping Franco's nose to the grindstone. Phew! Is that really all it is? Praise be to the Lord! I drink down my revolting beverage with gusto, thank Stefano from the bottom of my heart, send my regards to his father, and drive off light-hearted at last up my endless hairpin bends to my beetle-infested hovel.

35

At the restaurant, all has been joy and harmony for a good while now. Although there has been some mention of buying a boat and taking people on fishing trips, and a hi-tech greenhouse brochure is sitting prominently on the window ledge, Ciccio's search for an alternative career has died down to a whisper. This is the time of year when the cultured foreign holiday-home-owners visit for their dose of Mediterranean diet; and there has been a pleasing outbreak of Italian Sloffood aficionados, serious foodies doing the rounds of the valleys of our local Taggiasco olive, buying up extra-virgin oils straight from each *frantoio*, olive mill, to take home to Milan or Turin. Both types of client seem to go home to bed at a reasonable time; and Ciccio has persuaded several of them into trying a nutritious horse sirloin, marinated in the classic plain rosemary and olive oil. I've spotted Tommaso lurking down in the shade at Pierino's table a few times, so they'll be getting some good local cheese too – though whether the taxed or the untaxed version, and whether Ciccio has added the dreaded brouss to the menu, I prefer not to enquire.

But there doesn't seem to be much hope of permanent peace and quiet in Ciccio's working milieu, whatever the price of cheese. This afternoon when I arrive to join the staff dinner Ciccio is threatening once more to dump the restaurant for good. This time it is booking that is causing the trouble. Or rather, as I see it, his and Franchino's failure to make the need for booking clear to customers of foreign extraction. The scene will go like this. A group of (let's say) Germans will arrive unbooked, take their seats and wait to order. Their mouths will water as they watch the table of Italians nearby – Italians who have booked, mark you – being plied with endless exciting *antipasti*. Their tastebuds will leap in anticipation. They will order *antipasti* too: and be mystified when they are only given half the selection they have just seen going over to the Italians' table. (They will, of course, pay less: but they won't know this till later, if at all; and saving money is probably not their priority.) Still wondering about the missing *antipasti*, they will move on to the *primo piatto* of pasta. Would they like *penne*? asks the waitress (Patrizia, probably). Or *tagliatelle*? *Al pesto, al pomodoro* or *al ragu*? Or maybe a bit of each? Or some lovely fresh vegetable soup, *minestra di verdura*?

The clients will point at the serving dish piled high with home-made mushroom *panciotti* ('paunchlets', a kind of jumbo-sized ravioli) in a delicious creamy-looking sauce which is just being delivered to the table next door, and, wondering whether they have got the mentally defective waitress, ask whether perhaps they could have some of that pasta there?

No, alas, Patrizia will answer. There is not enough of it. The other table has booked: *hanno prenotato*.

Even if our foreign guests have understood the word '*prenotato*', they will imagine that booking is just a matter of seating space; and there's plenty of that, so what's the problem? It will not occur to them that the *panciotti*, a kind of big fat ravioli, have been made that afternoon specifically for the numbers of clients who have booked, and in the required quantities. And since it takes a good hour to make a batch of fresh stuffed pasta, which must then rest for a couple of hours before it can be cooked without disintegrating, there is no chance of anyone making any more just now, in the middle of the dinner rush.

The restaurant must have run out of this particular dish.

Was that what happened with the *antipasti* too? Feeling a bit hard-done-by, they will order something from the restricted list now recited to them by the waitress. Only to see, as they eat their comparatively boring pasta dishes, another lot of Italians arriving and being served, no problem, with the entire range of the *antipasti* that they weren't offered; followed by a great steaming platter of the ravioli they were told they couldn't have! Why, they will demand, grabbing the waitress as she passes, were they told there was none of that left?

Hanno prenotato! she will repeat desperately, to no effect.

Franchino, who has some English, and has also been learning German from a *Teach Yourself* book he keeps in the loo – so much more stimulating than the local paper he used to read in there, he tells me – has instructed the staff to call him over immediately these warning signs appear. If only the customers will have a little patience he can, with the help of his English or his book, usually defuse the situation. Sadly, though, it is often too late. The clients have sat simmering through the less-*antipasti* and less-choice-of-*primo-piatto* business, and they reach boiling point when they see a whole selection of delicious-looking *secondi*, meat dishes, that have not so much as been mentioned to them, arriving on the Italian tables.

Do you have to be an Italian to get a decent meal here? They will suddenly shout. Why are we getting this second-class treatment? What have you got against Germans, anyway? they may add, if German. The war was over fifty years ago! And so on. Having suffered greatly myself through not understanding this booking business in earlier times – though since I'm English I just took it personally and not politically when our food was crap compared to what the Italians at the other tables were getting – I have no trouble understanding how Ciccio and Franchino's poor clients must feel. This openly rude business of claiming not to have dishes they patently did have, was, Lucy and I were sure, being done on purpose to drive us away. But why? Did village restaurateurs round here feel that a pair of females should not go out to dinner without a responsible male? Had they heard evil rumours about the hillside squalor in which we lived? Had Britain recently committed some terrible act of *lèse-majesté* on the Italian nation without our noticing?

Until now, though – unless you count the huge and ferociously bearded Norwegian, driven wild by receiving less *antipasti* than everyone else, who stormed right into the kitchens demanding satisfaction – the thing has stopped short of actual violence. But today I've just missed a major confrontation, says Franchino. A whole serving dish of guinea-fowl *sotto bosco* was snatched from Patrizia's hands by a table of outraged foreigners. Since it was destined for an innocent Italian family sitting two tables away – a family, moreover, who had booked a good week ago – and diplomacy showed no sign of working, it had to be forcibly removed from the hands of the six *stranieri* who had grabbed it. They'd seen three other tables being served with this stuff, they said angrily, grappling with Franchino and Cousin Paletta for possession of the dish in question. Yet nobody had so much as mentioned it to them! In the midst of all this plenty, they had been offered nothing more exciting than a veal escalope fried in breadcrumbs or sautéed with white wine, a grilled steak, or some lamb chops *in umido*. This was the second time they'd come to this establishment; and the second time this sort of thing had happened!

Paletta, still in a high state of agitation, describes the scene to me all over again, working himself up into a lather of rage. These foreigners are demented! Why can't they just book like everybody else – or put up with what they're offered if they're too lazy to bother!? How dare they go around stealing other people's food from right under their noses?

Having lost the battle for the guinea-fowl, half of which ended up all over the table anyway (to the consternation of its true destinees, who had finished their pasta course some time ago and were keen to get on with the rest of their lunch), the foreigners stormed out. And of course, what with half their guinea-fowl being ruined, and the unpleasant scene they'd been subjected to, there was no way the restaurant could expect the poor Italian family to pay the full whack. Franchino had to offer them their dinner at half price.

I am sick of telling Ciccio and partner that if they would just write a few things down they could eliminate the problem at a stroke. I hate to imagine how many customers they may have lost over the years – may still be losing, indeed. Because most people won't complain, will they? They'll just go angrily off, vowing never to return to the place again. I've been saying it for years. I say it again anyway. First, write out a menu of what you can get if you book. Then another of what's available if you don't: explaining that only simple dishes, quick to prepare, are available without booking. Translate it into German, French, English, and you're sorted.

Alas, the deep-rooted distrust of the written word in this region is more powerful, it seems, than the desire for a quiet life. Impossible, says Ciccio lopsidedly. (Has his neck pain come back? No, he says, he is just making sure it doesn't.) There is nothing you can't get if you ask for it when you book. Is he supposed to write down every single dish in Italy? Stupid idea. This game's not worth the candle anyway. Ciccio will just return to the land, go and enslave himself to Salvatore instead. It would be paradise compared to this *manicomio* . . .

36

Predictions about Franco's extreme optimism were certainly right. He promised he'd start work right after San Martino's day, as soon as he (and the rest of the valley) had got the wine swapped from the fermenting to the maturing demijohns. But that was weeks ago: we did Salvatore's, too, up at the *taverna*, and now the Father's Wine famine is over, and our own demijohn is sitting snugly in the larder beneath the jars, whose numbers are actually starting to shrink, slowly but surely, now winter is upon us and no one's producing any more.

Are we going to have to wait till Franco's finished drinking his, too, though? Each time I've seen him, he's looked slightly the worse for wear – but maybe that's only to be expected at this San Martino time of year, when everyone has to keep checking that their wine is as good as they thought it was – and he has promised that he'll be starting work the day after tomorrow. When I catch Iole at home alone, she looks hunted, and says that her husband always takes on too many things at once. I feel cruel tormenting her, and go away quietly. Now Christmas is nearly upon us, and if Franco hasn't got started in the next couple of weeks, there'll be nothing doing till after the olive harvest. Still, my own optimism is such that I am still refusing to put the rest of the nets out round the house, whatever Ciccio says, because I'm so sure something's going to happen soon. No nets isn't as bad as it sounds. Olive trees here give you a big heavy crop one year, and a much lighter one the next. And the trees in question are on year two. Could be worse.

With only a week to go till Christmas, I get back from a hard day's Christmas shopping with Patrizia and Laura to find that Franco has begun work. At least, I think that's what's happened. Unless it was some sort of very localized typhoon. My parking space has almost vanished under a forest of beams and rafters, piles of sand and gravel, and stacked bags of cement wrapped in gigantic flapping sheets of plastic. Arriving at the house I find that a large chunk of the shoulder-high terrace wall that retains the terrace to the landward side has been demolished, reduced to a pile of rubble. On purpose, it seems. And there I've been, complaining about people accidentally knocking the occasional stone off the top! I shut my eyes and concentrate on some deep breathing. All right: look again. The pile of earth and stones left by the destruction has been flattened out, I now see, to make a path up to the higher level. Horseshoe prints up and down it. A horse-track, then. Not Franco's fault. He's had to do it, because we've thoughtlessly built steps over the original horse-ways up to the front and back doors, which are now much too steep for any four-footed beast.

Now for another surprise. A large blue tarpaulin is roped over the derelict stone igloo two terraces downhill from the house – an ancient roundhouse built of huge blocks of stone, whose centre fell in some time ago. Local experts tell us that we'll have to fill the whole inside of the thing with earth again – apparently that's how people used to drag the top stones into position in the first place – to fix it. I don't think we'll be doing that job for a while yet. Anyway, why has Franco covered it over? How much more stuff could he have needed to store? And why would he have taken whatever-it-is two steep terraces downhill, only to have to bring it back up later?

Simple. This equipment can get back up the hill under its own steam. Under the strange blue light from the tarpaulin a pair of large brown horses stand gazing hopefully out at me, munching gently on a bundle of hay in a rope net that Franco has hung from a wooden peg high in the wall. I've often wondered why they needed so many pegs in the Good Old Days – there must be a good dozen of the things, cut from olive wood and actually built into the walls. Now we see why. From them, alongside the hay, hangs an array of deeply esoteric-looking horse equipment, stuff that can't have seen the light of day for a decade or two; contraptions of leather strapping and brass and carved wood at whose use I can only guess.

Ciccio and I spend rather a lot of the evening going up and down to look at these lovely creatures, taking them apples and water and handfuls of fresh grass and anything else we can think of. Couldn't we get some horses ourselves? Or mules, maybe, which might be sturdier and less likely to suffer at our ignorant hands? Ciccio wonders whether we couldn't maybe make a living taking holidaymakers for mule-train rambles in the hills . . . ?

Next morning Franco turns up with two helpers, a pair of young men who hardly speak any Italian, and starts getting his horses kitted out. Don't worry about the language, he says, they're good strong workers, and they know how to handle a horse. They're Albanians, he adds. I am not surprised. When we first got to know Franco, his workforce consisted (apart from his two nephews) of a man with severe learning diffi-culties whom Franco sent to live way up in the hills, all alone except for the cows and horses, in a larger version of this very stone roundhouse; earth floor, not so much as a tap, and straw for a bed. Franco had lived for years like that in his youth, he said when challenged, and it had never done him any harm.

Moreover this employee was to all intents and purposes a slave, since his services were paid for in advance and by the year, in cheeses and demijohns of wine mostly, not to the man himself, but to his desperately poverty-stricken family, who had, in effect, leased him out for the year. Which meant he couldn't leave the job if he wanted to, however badly he was treated. (Salvatore's childhood goat-herding job will have been on the same basis, I daresay.)

This horrible Old Way was already illegal here, though; and soon Franco could find no one else to fill the bill. Once slaves were no longer obtainable in his own land, Franco somehow managed to recruit a teenage North African: I suppose you could still find a similar feudal mindset in Morocco. A certain Lekbir soon appeared in the valley, a very bright and busy lad, of whom Franco was extremely proud, because he learnt anything he was required to learn in the wink of an eye. (His name was really El Kbir, he told me, but he soon gave up mentioning that, because nobody here will stand for three consonants without so much as a vowel between them.) But these days if you so much as mention Lekbir's name, Franco will rave on about ungratefulness and backstabbing. It didn't take Lekbir long to learn everything Franco had to teach him about cattle-rearing and horse-dealing, to inform himself about modern legislation regulating the relationship between boss and employee, to insist on decent pay and civilized work conditions; and finally to go off and set up on his own. Franco is disgusted. Is there no honour left in the world?

Still, these days, if you can't find a decent slave, there are plenty of Albanians about, many of whom will put up with almost anything rather than be sent home. And Franco has found himself not just one, but two of them.

Soon, with the help of the Albanians, each of the horses is kitted out in a pair of beautiful barrel-like containers, huge deep things with inner sides that curve to fit snugly round their flanks. They are to be used for carrying the sand and gravel into position; and they have hinged flaps on the bottom for ease of emptying. Franco is delighted when I compliment him on their design; brilliant, I say. The only similar thing I've seen was in Spain, where mules carry big cloth panniers slung over their backs for the same task – except that the stuff has to be as laboriously shovelled out of the panniers as it was laboriously shovelled in.

What do you expect? says Franco. The Spanish are known for their crude and backward ways! But the man who made this equipment was once famous all the way from here to the Piedmont for his great expertise in horse-accoutrements. He only died a decade or so ago, tragically disregarded, his skills already surplus to modern requirements.

Sad. A perfect design and a proud execution; all dust and ashes now, no longer needed, only fit for the bin. Centuries of experience, of trial and error have gone into the design of the things; lifetimes of learning to reach the standards of skill you'd need to produce them. And soon, once Franco's gone, to be lost for ever.

I fret about this sort of thing rather a lot, ever since I saw a historian on some documentary about ancient Egypt, who pointed out that no human civilization has ever lasted more than a couple of thousand years. What happens when this one disintegrates, then, and we all have to run for the hills and start from scratch? This horse-equipment is exactly what we'd need to have about us. We certainly wouldn't be using lorries and bulldozers and stuff, would we? Where would we get the petrol anyway? I have personal experience, thanks to my dreadful path, of lugging building materials about using only my own body; and I can tell you that it limits your aspirations pretty drastically. Where you might once have built a palace, you will build a shed. Or a larder that's not quite as capacious as you might have liked. I shall get out my camera and save at least a record of this brilliant intermediate technology for Ciccio's and my descendants – no, for all humanity – to work from.

Franco seems to miss the point slightly, and spends rather a lot of time adjusting his hat and neckerchief and getting into stylish poses, on horse, off horse, and with his Barbarian cohort in suitably subordinate positions. But then, why should he care? Frank the Knife, Renaissance man, would have no trouble at all if civilization collapsed tomorrow. I suppose he'd have to cut down on his basil-growing, once the refrigerated lorry no longer turned up to collect the vast quantities of the stuff he produces. Otherwise, he'd hardly notice it had gone. He doesn't even watch telly. For now, Franco is so happy at getting back to doing things the good old way that he sings and whistles to himself all day long as his minions cart, or rather horse, all the rest of the materials along the path and into place. He'll get started properly on the job, he says, as soon as the festive season is over.

This means, I now realize to my horror, that the new beams are going to be sitting up here, only yards away from the Beast-infested ones, all over Christmas! I rush over to the barometer under the lean-to roof. Relief. Only seventeen degrees. No danger of beetle courtship breaking out for now. Still, I have already come round to Ciccio's way of thinking. We can't stay here while the roof job's going on. Till now I've imagined moving into the two downstairs rooms for the duration; I hadn't grasped that the outside living areas would be transformed into a war zone. No electricity, either, because the solar panels will come off with the roof, won't they? I may as well be cooped up in Ciccio's flat, then, and just pop over every day or two to keep Franco's optimism in check.

★

But on Christmas Eve, Ciccio returns from work fuming. He went into the flat to get it sorted out for us, only to discover that he could hardly get into the place. It's full to the very ceiling with bundled-up old olive nets! And Ciccio had just organized a poker evening up there for next week, too!

It seems that Pierino did ask, a while ago, if he could store a few bits and pieces in the flat, seeing Ciccio had hardly used the place in months, and Ciccio said yes. Now look! Pierino's bought himself a whole new set of olive nets, and rather than throw the old ones away – though what on earth he thinks he's going to use them for, Ciccio can't imagine – he's stuffed the lot into Ciccio's flat. You can just about squeeze through to the bedroom and kitchen, but you can't even get into the living-room. It's only for a couple of weeks, Pierino says, till he clears his spare *rustico* out; but till then the flat's going to be about as pleasant to live in as the building site. No time to come up with an alternative plan, either: Christmas is upon us.

There will be twenty of us for Christmas lunch at Francesca's, and every adult is making one of the dishes. We have been allocated the *lasagna*, so Ciccio spends the morning making *lasagna* for twenty – so unlike a normal working day – while I finish off sewing the velvet scarves I am making, on my ludicrous old handle-wound sewing machine, one for each of the closer female relatives. Economy is essential now that I have a new roof to support, as well as two horses, a pair of Albanians, and Franco. For Francesca I've made her own special pure silk scarf, in a becoming blurry soft peach print, that I had to sew entirely by hand with a needle so fine it was almost invisible, because the stupid machine couldn't handle such fine stuff. (Electric sewing machine! Finish book!) It nearly drove me mad, and I just hope she appreciates it.

Among the gifts I have for Ciccio is a set of three beautiful framed notices for him to hang on the restaurant wall. I have prepared them with Helmut's help, and they explain, in English, German, and something quite like French, the need for booking in local restaurants if you want to get the best from them. We have put the phone number on the bottom, too.

I am already quailing, as we step off down the path with our bundles of presents and our burning hot *lasagna*, at the mere thought of twenty De Gilios all at once. But things start off well. Several sisters and two nieces actually wanted a velvet scarf. And Francesca is most pleased with hers, which singles her out from the crowd. She wears it all afternoon. Honour is satisfied. Among Ciccio's gifts to me is an IOU for a mule, which he has ordered from Franco. My own mule! But Franco is going to have to create it for us, by impregnating one of his horses by a donkey, so it won't be born for several months. Marvellous anyway. Maybe it will have an instinct for detecting mule-tracks, and I can abandon my search for a map?

Present-giving over, we can get on with eating and eating and eating, and shouting and shouting and shouting. Ciccio regales various of his relatives with the outrageous tale of Pierino and his nets; and by the time we've got on to the *secondo* he has come up with a whole flurry of alternative agro-tourism enterprises he will be launching in revenge, among which mules figure largely. Osvaldo is busy doing conjuring tricks out of a kit one of his boys got for a present, so we manage not to have a row. Lunch over at last, the clan starts to plan the after-lunch Christmas Day constitutional by the sea. This, according to some family members, requires all of us to get into a cavalcade of cars to drive the half-mile to the bit of seaside where we're going to walk. Why? I don't know. Several sisters are already pointing out how absurd this is; while I have turned, as I've begun to do on these mass De Gilio occasions, into a passive, childlike being; a rabbit hypnotized by headlights. Francesca finds this vastly entertaining, and pops round the table every now and then to give me a quick pat on the cheek, or an extra titbit just in case I haven't eaten enough yet. Rosi has brought her video camera, and films us off and on through the lunch, and the washing up, and the walk (we go in the cars anyway) and the game of lotto when we return; and then the next meal too, which we sit down to only a few hours later because all that food can't go to waste. All this time, everybody has been talking, more or less constantly, over everybody else. But at last, even the De Gilio batteries start to run low. Conversation is becoming desultory: some of us have actually stopped talking altogether. Salvatore has snuck off to have a nap. Time to show the video. Rosi plugs it into the telly. Marvellous. We can all go on lying in a quiet, sated heap, making the occasional desultory remark to one another; but thanks to the wonders of modern technology we can do it against a background of the same hundred-decibel racket we make when we're all on tip-top form.

Funny, says Rosi to Grazia after a bit. Are you watching the video? Look at us all! Every single person is talking, and not one of us is listening to anybody else! Amazing, says Grazia. So we are!

Back at the house I do some Christmas phone calls to my own family. Among them, a certain sister in Bulgaria. I alert her to the roof situation, and confess that Ciccio seems to have sort of moved in with me. She is annoyingly unsurprised by this. Was I the only person in the world who wasn't expecting it? Lucy thinks I may have been. Anyway, it's fine by her. She'll send me a share of the roof money. She'll be back by the end of next year, probably.

You don't sound much like a woman who wants to sell up her share in the house and groves to Ciccio, then, I say.

No, she certainly doesn't. And shouldn't I give it a year or so before I commit myself to anything permanent? she asks.

Just thought she might. Ah well, she may be right, it probably wouldn't have been a good idea anyway.

Bulgaria, she tells me, though charming in many ways, seems to have a serious problem with xenophobia. Her fellow teachers will sit chatting casually over dinner, for example, about how there would be no crime at all in their country if it were not for the Vietnamese.

The Vietnamese? I say.

Yes. Quite a community of Vietnamese grew up over there under communism. And when it isn't the Vietnamese, it's the gypsies or the Turks. You can hardly spend an evening anywhere, with anybody, and not be given a lecture on the genetic and/or cultural deficiencies of one or other of these groups. It rather spoils the whole thing. She is certainly coming back – and looking forward to it. But I needn't worry. We'll all fit in up at Besta de Zago.

So, on to the New Year. Ciccio and Franchino are open for New Year's Eve dinner: and they are booked solid. Friends and relations from all over the valley are being drafted in to help with the serving. We have a huge box of fireworks to let off down by the river at midnight. Ciccio has an idea: why don't I try waiting at table? I might enjoy it . . .

No. As it happens, I know that I would not enjoy it. I've had two jobs in my life that involved serving food or drink; and in both cases, I was sacked within a fortnight. Do I really have to publicly demonstrate, for the third time in my life, my inability to cope with the world of catering?

Yes. I do. It's easy: anyone can do it.

Well, be it on his own head.

The New Year's Dinner is composed of about three thousand different dishes, and, this being an upmarket sort of a soirée, each dish has its own type of plate. And knife, and fork, and glass and . . . once I've thoroughly demonstrated my inability to learn which type of fork goes with which dish, or to keep an eye on ten tables at once, seriously annoying some clients who needed another whatever-type-of-fork it was, I get a new job. I just have to stand at the front of the room and Be There for the diners, who can call me if they need something. This feels strangely like being made to stand in the dunce's corner; only rather a lot less private. I stand here trying to remember what I normally do with my hands when they are otherwise unoccupied, and wondering how you keep an eye on clients without seeming to be staring rudely, while the geniuses with the encyclopedic knowledge of the correct kit and the 360 degree vision dash back and forth doing the actual work at hectic pace. Eventually somebody calls me over to their table. Hooray. Will they be wanting an ashtray, a new glass, a spare napkin? No. They want to ask if I am French. French?? Are French waitresses especially known, perhaps, for standing about looking utterly gormless? An agonizing twenty minutes later, another table needs my services. They are extremely put out, they say, because their table is on the direct path to the loo, and people keep pushing past them all the time. I'll speak to the management, I say, scuttling off.

Ciccio can't believe it. That lot rang up this afternoon, desperate for a table for tonight, and he told them there wasn't one. They went on and on pleading, so in the end he said he'd squeeze them in somewhere. How can they possibly complain about where their table is? I return, quaking, to pass this on. The clients demand to see the Management personally. I set off to get Franchino, going over in my mind a lovely story of Ciccio's from when he worked in a *pizzeria* run by a large Neapolitan family: the tale of a pair of troublesome customers who sent back five pizzas, one after the other, and eventually asked to see the Management. The granny of the family, a tiny babuschka-like old lady, listened attentively to the woman's complaints, nodding away. Then, once the client had finished, all of a sudden the sweet little Granny from Naples reached down below the table, grabbed her by the crotch, dragged her to her feet by it, and told the pair of them to eff off out of her restaurant. Right away! Now!

Imagine that! By the crotch! Wonderful! I suppose this isn't the moment to try it out, though. I do a runner upstairs to the safety of Ciccio's flat instead. Extremely safe: positively nest-like, in fact. I'd forgotten that Pierino had transformed it into an Olive Net Experience. Nowhere to sit down except great dusty white rolls full of olive leaves and dried scratchy vegetation. I return chastened to the kitchens, which I now refuse to leave. I will wash saucepans for the rest of the night, I say. And this is what I do. So traumatic is this almost-waitressing experience that I will never have any recollection at all of any of the New Year's food. Must have been good though, because lots of people now come and stick their heads through the serving arch to congratulate the chef.

At last. Midnight. Quite enough of that Old Year, thank you. Time for the fireworks. Lovely fireworks. Big rockets. Lots more going off all across the valley, streaking across the skies: you can even see some shooting right up over the ridge from the Imperia valley next door. Now a spectacular display from down at the foot of the valley; strangely disjointed-looking at this distance, when you don't hear the bangs till several seconds after you've seen the pyrotechnics. At last the clients have all gone, and us staff go down to the town to relax. Here we set off loads more fireworks with lots of other people on the beach. Wonderful people with no interest in cutlery or seating arrangements. Somebody has a bag full of those big illegal fireworks they call *cipolle*, onions, things that go off with an almighty earth-shattering boom. Yes! That's more like it. *Buon Anno!*

37

A new Chicken Drama has broken out. Salvatore has taken to his bed with a terrible pain in his belly. What, he asks upon waking up next morning and drinking his stomach-healing cup of bitter *millefiori* tea (flowers gathered by Francesca herself) is going to happen to his chickens?

The chickens! Everyone has been so busy worrying about the human that nobody has thought of the chickens! What is to be done? Francesca can't go up to feed them; she's never learnt to drive, and the *campagna* is much too far for her to walk at her age. Nothing for it – Ciccio will have to go up and feed them till his father feels better. Ciccio throws a fit. From our house down to the bottom of the valley and back up the other side to his father's land, then home again; that'll be a good hour of travelling over rocky dirt tracks, a good twenty hairpin bends, all for a couple of dozen chickens! As if he didn't have enough to do already!

Maybe we could bring the chickens down from the *campagna*, I say, and Francesca could keep them in her garden for a few days? Certainly not; the place is too small, and with no space to scrabble about in they would destroy her flowers and vegetables in no time. They can't go in Marisa's garden; Marisa has a huge dog. Guisi is in the middle of moving house with two small children: no chance. Grazia and Rosi have flats without gardens; they're off the hook. Annetta too. We could have them at our house, couldn't we? I say. But no, apparently we couldn't; we'd need to build a chickenwire pen to protect them from foxes or wild boars or whatever, which would be as much work as plan A, if not more. Could they be put in with Auntie Apple's chickens up at Diano Borganzo? The younger generation all thinks this is a brilliant solution, but Francesca develops a strangely hunted look. Ciccio could just go on feeding them for a few days while we think the thing over, couldn't he? she says. Later Ciccio explains the problem to me; Francesca fears she would never get them back once they were ensconced at her cousin's place. They are Family Chickens: and *la Zia Mela* is, incontrovertibly, family. If Salvatore is ill for any length of time, the chickens might easily transmute, by right of length of residence, into her own property.

After several mornings of major agitation about which of the siblings' turn it is to feed the chickens, I volunteer to go. Anything for a quiet life. I now find myself confessing over the phone to Francesca the unbelievable and embarrassing fact that I've never fed a chicken before, and have no idea what they eat. Or how much of whatever-it-is. Francesca turns out to be as bad as her son at explaining recipes. Kitchen scraps, supplemented with grain and bran, she says, which I'll find in a couple of sacks in the *rustico*; they also like some fresh salad leaves. They'll need less grain but more greenery if you've given them a lot of bread: if, on the other hand . . .

But how much is a lot? What kind of kitchen scraps? I give up. I'll come and get her, I say, we'll drive up there and she can show me herself. I'm glad to get out of the house, anyway: Franco and his Albanians are banging about all around me, taking the tiles off the roof and stacking them neatly on the patio. There's still the wooden slat lining between me and the outside world: but not for long. And there's hardly a square foot left around the house that doesn't have a pile of something on it.

Francesca is glad I've come, too, because otherwise her leftovers would have gone to waste. She sits in the car clutching her recycled carrier bags and chuckling away. Whoever would have guessed that I'd never so much as fed a chicken! Living in the middle of the countryside the way I do! And I seem such an intelligent girl, too!

Now that Francesca has finally got me to herself, in a confined space, she can research my background in proper depth the way a good mother should. The interrogation begins. What do my parents do for a living? They're teachers. Not rich, then? No, they're not, I agree. How many brothers and sisters do I have? Three brothers, one sister. Ah. Francesca wrinkles her brow as she makes a few calculations about (I presume) teachers' incomes and potential lifetime savings; and divides them by five. So I won't be expecting any great inheritance to come, then? No, I won't. And the house and groves up at Besta are not all mine? No: they're half my sister's too. And how many olive trees do we have, exactly?

Ah, *bella mia*! says Francesca at last, having finished her calculations. No wonder you two haven't made the announcement we've all been waiting for, then! There's my son who can't settle down to work with his father, come what may, not that I can blame him. And you with hardly enough Plants to keep a dog! What would the pair of you live on?

I gather from this that Francesca still belongs, like her husband, to the old school. In spite of the clear evidence of her own children's ability to earn a perfectly good living in the modern market economy, she feels that a couple can't go settling down until they have the bit of land that will keep them if the worst comes to the worst. Still, I say to myself, none of her three married daughters seems to have any noticeable farming aspect to their lives, except on their father's land. But maybe it's different with sons? Yes, that must be it: I've been told that the sisters will inherit the house in Diano, while Ciccio will get the land. Evidently the restaurant counts for nothing.

Francesca says, half to herself, that she thinks she may have heard of something that might get us sorted out. Ivana – have I met her? Up in Cosio d'Arroscia? Still, we'll see about that later. She can hardly bear to think of such matters with her poor husband in the state he's in. Do I know that Salvatore has not Gone of his Body for almost a week?

Non e andato di corpo? I echo this gnomic utterance; but it must be obvious I'm not succeeding in extracting any sense from it. Francesca lets out a peal of laughter. What a simple girl I am! *Non ha cagato* – he hasn't had a shit – she explains. Going of your Body is a hospital euphemism, like Passing a Motion. That's why I've never heard of it.

Not for a week! I'm alarmed. Have they told Grazia? (Grazia works in the surgery ward of the Imperia hospital, and should be ideally placed to deal with this sort of thing.) But yes, they have. Salvatore has seen the doctor, who says the problem is definitely not his appendix; and he's scheduled to go into hospital for tests and a scan tomorrow.

No sooner have we parked up on the edge of the Devastation Zone than, out of one of the snazzy villas, pops the neighbour we met last time we were up here. Today she is wearing some type of floaty chiffon négligée. Francesca! she shouts as we head off towards the most expensive chicken run in the world. Come over for a coffee when you've finished?

We will, says Francesca, once we've got the chickens fed. She takes me off into the *rustico* and introduces me to various sacks and scoops – beautiful scoops hand-carved out of chunks of olive-branch, lustrous with age – and we get the trouble-some fowl fed and their eggs collected up. We'll let them run around a bit while we go and have our coffee with the Signora Elisabetta, says Francesca. She only wants to get a good look at you, anyway. We won't stay long.

And indeed we don't. Francesca doesn't even sit down to

drink her teaspoonful of espresso. I gather that she regards this woman, now draped elegantly across her wrought-iron garden furniture, as some sort of social superior: she is behaving in an extra-puzzled way around her. Here is our chiffon-clad and oddly plasticized hostess, crooking her little finger and drinking her coffee in exaggeratedly tiny sips while she makes polite conversation, as one who has never sunk to such chicken-feeding depths herself, about how Salvatore's fowls are doing. And there is Francesca, standing awkwardly in her lumpy home-made tubular skirt and ankle socks, crinkly kind eyes and untidy silver curls. I want to rush over and give her a protective hug. No need, though. As we are taking our leave, setting off to put our chickens back to roost, Francesca turns to me. You wouldn't believe it to look at us, would you, she says, but Signora Elisabetta's children were at primary school with mine. Think of that! And we're exactly the same age. Sixty-six.

Well done, Francesca. I manage not to start giggling till we've made it to Salvatore's rubble area. Did she do that on purpose? No idea. She's giggling too, though.

Ciccio is right: they really are amazingly well-behaved chickens. Just a few gentle hints, and they all rush clucking back home, no argument, and settle down to fluff and scratch. So will I come up again tomorrow? asks Francesca as we head off back downhill towards Diano Castello. All right. Why not? The roofing chaos is reaching a crescendo, there is no refuge up at Ciccio's among the olive nets, and it's impossible to get on with any writing, or anything else for that matter, in either place. Fine, I say, I can come by myself now I know what chickens like for lunch.

No. Francesca is not impressed. What about all her vegetable peelings and stale bread that will go to waste? Much better if I come down and get her first.

As we drive down through Castello, she decides to show me the house where Ciccio was born, the place that drove her, she says, to travelling half-way across the world. Following my orders, I squeeze the car along a narrow alley and out into a minute piazza. There it is! It's been done up now, but in those days. . . .! Do I see those two windows up there on the second floor, with the little balcony? One's the bedroom, the other the kitchen and living-room. If you could call it a kitchen. No sink in there, or cooker. No water tap, and no bathroom either. That's why Salvatore's still got it in for Carlo; he had other places to let, decent places to live, but he wouldn't let them to Southerners. Every drop of water dragged up in a bucket from the public fountain – for washing, for cleaning, for cooking. The laundry was a nightmare, a steep walk half a mile downhill to the communal wash-place, carrying the baby as well as the washing, no pushchairs round here in those days. Then back up that hill, worn out with the scrubbing, and the washing twice as heavy now it was wet. Francesca would light a charcoal fire in an enamel washing-up bowl and cook outside on that very balcony . . . and woe betide if it rained, they all just had to sit and get smoked while she made the dinner! And local people had the nerve to look down on you, as if you'd chosen to live like that! Her husband was earning twice what he got in Calabria, but everything else was worse. Much worse. People in Castello wouldn't even let their kids play with hers. Not until her daughters started at primary school, and rose like rockets to the top of the class. Then they were all coming round to ask if Rosi and Grazia could come out to play. Bad luck for those ones, she adds; good brains are no more contagious than bad housing! Much good it did them.

My chicken-feeding outing next day, supposedly a simple round trip – Francesca's leftovers, chickens, and home again

– expands to fill the whole afternoon and most of the evening. I am roped in to taking the suffering Salvatore to the clinic so as not to bother Marisa, who will be busy getting Alberto's lunch; while he's with the doctors we fit in a quick visit to the market in Imperia. Well, we're here anyway, aren't we? We may as well check out the cheese vendor with the extremely good bargains – the one who only comes to Diano once a month. Now back to the clinic to get Salvatore. But stop! We'd better go and buy a proper decent pair of pyjamas for him, hadn't we, because they might keep him in next week if he hasn't got better. We leave a strangely silent, pale and suffering Salvatore in the car – no, he doesn't want to come, he doesn't give a toss about pyjamas – to hunt for Special Offer nightwear. Why don't I stay to supper now it's this late anyway? I said I wanted to learn how to make that spare-rib pasta sauce, didn't I? Just chop those couple of onions over there . . . Poor Salvatore has eaten nothing but clear broth for two days, and retreats to bed so as not to have to witness the pasta. Giusi comes to dinner, along with Alberto and Marisa; she needs a hand to move her stove, a great big heavy cast iron thing that she can't shift on her own. It's only twenty minutes to her house in Civezza . . . As I am finally escaping bedwards, Francesca wants to know if I could get here nice and early, for eight maybe, instead of waiting till after lunch? Or seven thirty would be even better?

Next morning at breakfast – I am certainly not going anywhere for seven thirty – Ciccio, for a change, does not sit muttering darkly about his family over his cappuccino and threatening to take strike action. He doesn't need to. I am doing it in his stead, while steeling myself to make a stand against the tyranny of the De Gilio matriarch. As we eat our toast – yes, I have succeeded in recreating this great tradition, using a bit of expatriated Aga equipment, a thing like a metal tennis racquet that sits on the woodstove hotplate, and have succeeded in turning Ciccio into a toast-lover too – Ciccio and I enjoy the surprising spectacle of a small forest of beams and rafters rising from the ground, apparently of their own volition, and starting to move slowly hither and thither outside our windows. Presumably there are Albanians somewhere at the bottom of them. Ciccio goes to the window: they seem to have multiplied since we last saw them. There are half-a-dozen men out there now. Odd. Still, as long as Franco has them well briefed about delicacy when dealing with olive nets, it's fine by me. Ciccio goes off to chat to Albanians, and I am saved at the eleventh hour from making any awesome decisions about matriarchs by a phone call from Francesca herself. *La Zia Mela*, she tells me, has made a dastardly takeover bid on the chickens. She turned up at breakfast time with a neighbour in a van, and a set of crates to carry them off in! But Francesca has a brilliant plan that will not only foil Auntie Apple, putting the precious chickens well beyond her reach, but solve half-a-dozen other problems at a stroke. Am I ready? Am I listening? It is this: I shall go up and stay at the *taverna*; and I shall take the chickens with me. This will give me a proper roof over my head, where I will be safe from Frank the Knife and his Albanian hordes; and there is an old chicken run up there too, so the chickens will be safe as well. I can look after the chickens on my own, can't I, now I know how to do it? Meanwhile Ciccio, who should be able to make it up there most nights after work to keep me company, will be able to get on with bottling the rest of Salvatore's wine in his spare time. The family has run out, and Francesca needs it for the cooking. (Only two demijohns, a hundred-odd litres, have been bottled for family use so far; and demand for this year's vintage has been heavy, even though poor Salvatore's not drinking any at all at the moment.) Ciccio can also bring the eggs down every couple of days when he comes to work, and Annetta or Marisa or somebody can collect them from the restaurant. Or Patrizia can bring them down after work. Thus will Auntie Apple be confounded. It will be very handy all round; and I won't be alone too much, because there are the Cipollini next door, and anyway she and the family will come up to do the rest of the wine at the weekend, if Ciccio hasn't managed to finish. It'll be a weight off everybody's mind . . .

I put the phone down shell-shocked. So. I have a temporary home, willy-nilly; and a large number of clucking pets. Francesca's right, though: it's a brilliant plan. Peace and quiet at last. I can take my precious laptop up there and get on with some work. And with a few thousand litres of wine at my disposal, it won't even matter that it's rather a long way to the nearest bar.

Ciccio returns from the Albanians with the news that the last layer of roof will be coming off tomorrow, and the new beams going on in a day or two.

His mother's stepped in in the nick of time, then, I say, passing on the news of my imminent relocation, with chickens, some fifteen miles to the north. Ciccio bursts out laughing. It's my expression. And his mother's immense cunning. She suspected he might never get up there and sort out the wine at all, without his father to hassle him on. Now, with me up there, held captive by my chicken duties, he'll be bound to go. No doubt at all who Rosi and Grazia inherited their great brains from, is there?

38

I certainly can't pack the chickens into their crates and go quietly up to the *taverna* on my own. Think how tedious life would be if everyone settled for simple boring tasks when they could have interesting complicated ones. Since Francesca has to come up to the *campagna* to help me get my cargo loaded, she says, she may as well come the rest of the way to see them settled in, mayn't she? Otherwise she won't be at peace in her mind. And anyway, the chicken run may need fixing. She's organized Patrizia to join our outing, so as to have at least a hint of a convoy, as well as an extra pair of hands and a lift home: she was planning to drop in on Patrizia's cousin Ivana anyway, once she was up that far in the hills. Salvatore doesn't have to be in hospital till tomorrow morning for the next battery of tests anyway, and she's arranged a relay of daughters and grand-daughters to feed him his broth and keep him company till she gets back.

After a busy half-hour at the chicken run, involving much squawking and flapping and escaping from crates, Francesca announces that since I am practically family, and already have a surprising amount of chicken mess all over my clothing, the chickens and their sacks of grub may as well go in my car. She herself will be travelling in Patrizia's, so as to keep her company.

Within the hour we have the chickens in their new run, and some nice clean sheets on the old bedstead. We've cleaned the upstairs *taverna* window of dust and cobwebs, and I now have a stunning view of the rushing waters of the Arroscia from my sleeping quarters. The chicken run did need fixing; and I have impressed Francesca mightily by mending it in no time at all with a scrap of chickenwire and some bent nails dug out of a dusty corner of the wine *cantina*. Not so simple after all, see?

Francesca trots off to check out her lands, stopping to say hello to a pair of Spring Onions who are getting on with some pruning in their next-door vineyard. I'm rather pleased with this chickens-for-a-roof arrangement. I might have to move up here permanently, I tell Patrizia. Lovely crisp air. And wonderful to have a wild pebbly river just at the end of the path, instead of the over-civilized beaches of the Mediter-ranean with their militarized rows of sunbeds.

Much more exciting, Patrizia agrees. There's even a deep pool just under the humped Roman bridge that you can dive into, if you want. Her daughters stay up here with their granny for most of July and the whole of August. They love it. You may well find your dream come true if Francesca has her way, she says, with a grin and a nod of the head in the direction of the woman in question. She's got it all worked out, Patrizia adds. She's on a mission! Just you wait and see . . .

Got what worked out? I ask; but Francesca has already returned. She's asked the neighbours to keep an eye on me, she says. And on the chickens, of course. The Cipollini live in that clump of houses just behind the *taverna*, if I need anything. But we must all go now, she says, and check out Ivana's spare vineyard that she might be selling. Then we'll go up and pay our respects to her and Renzo, and maybe buy a *toma* or two. The vineyard could, she adds, be just what you and Ciccio need.

Could it? A vineyard? Patrizia is grinning away at me from behind Francesca's back. Yes, she says. It's close enough to her son's future inheritance – she crosses herself for Salvatore's benefit – to be neatly amalgamated one day with this one; but good enough for an independent living for the pair of us for the time being.

But might Ivana not want rather a lot of money for it?

Francesca thinks not: she also thinks Ivana, as a friend of the family, would let us pay in instalments. Moreover, Francesca has quite a bit of gold of her own she wouldn't object to investing in it.

Gold?

Yes, gold. We won't have seen her actually wearing her gold, because one of Salvatore's few defects as a husband is that he has never bought gold for her, the way he ought to have done, on birthdays and saints' days and anniversaries and suchlike. Not in all the years of their marriage. So she's just had to buy her own, with her housekeeping savings, bit by bit; which means, of course, that she can't wear it, can she? Because he'd want to know where it came from, and then he'd feel she'd given him a *brutta figura*, pointing out his shortcomings, and be embarrassed. Still, there it is. She's got it: and she could sell it off if we needed her to help us out.

I am completely out of my depth. I know nothing of a husband's duty to buy gold for his wife. And I can't see why Francesca is so set on us having a vineyard, either. It must show on my face. Patrizia, in the enviable position of straddling both cultures, is quietly killing herself laughing. She's not sure she'll remember which vineyard it is, anyway, Patrizia says. She hasn't been here for years. Cousin Ivana rents it out, because the one nearer her home is easily big enough for the family's wine needs these days. Half a mile later, she still isn't sure. Have we passed it already? We've been past four so far, all pretty similar to Salvatore and Francesca's own, all with the same sort of *taverna* on them. Francesca just wants to be sure it's one of the bigger ones, she says, the ones with the vegetable garden strips down at the river end. Yes, Patrizia's sure it's one of those.

Never mind then. We'll just go straight to Ivana's.

Off we set again, me driving along behind Patrizia and Francesca. It now dawns on me why Francesca is throwing herself with such energy into this vineyard plan. What an idiot I am. Not just because she'd like to see her son settled down. She's afraid that Salvatore's got something terminal, of course. He's nearly seventy, he's about to go into hospital suffering from some mystery disease, and Francesca's doing her best to pull the wool over Destiny's eyes. She's in denial, as the psychobabblers would say. Because Ciccio certainly wouldn't be short of land at all if Salvatore were to die, would he? She's hunting out another *campagna* for her son as a vote of confidence in her husband's survival. Poor Francesca! Better join in with a will for now, then, however unsure I am about this plan.

We wind on through endless vines, with the occasional mini olive grove in a sheltered patch, and pass the strange conical hill that announces Pieve di Teco. It always reminds me of some Chinese painting, ringed with terraces to its very top; even more so today with the bright shoots of the almond trees just coming out against their dark wood. On and up into high woodland and smooth green sheep country, distant glimpses of snow-covered Alps ahead.

Still, I say to myself, although we certainly couldn't be letting Francesca put her hard-won gold into it, a vineyard's not such a bad idea. It has a rather large *taverna* on it, too, if it's really one of the ones we walked past – a building that, as is the wont of Ligurians, nobody bothers to count for anything; it's just a necessary part of the facilities. But a house it is. And an extra house would certainly resolve any problems of overcrowding in the future, when Lucy comes back. We could live in it; or she could live in it; or we could take turns. Maybe we could run a bed-and-breakfast in it, even, in the summer months? I'm sure loads of other people would prefer ferny mountain pools to being broiled on the beaches of the Mediterranean in the August heat. Or whatever. Maybe a vineyard is just the thing to save Ciccio from his restaurant, too – if he really wants to be saved from it. Moot point. Still, he could cook the odd slap-up dinner for the bed-and-breakfast customers if he found he couldn't face a life without catering. And he could certainly put up his cherished basil greenhouses down by the river, which would be a much better bet than having them up at my place, in direct competition with Frank the Knife.

Ivana lives in a large rambling house down an alleyway on the edge of Cosio d'Arroscia. The air is even crisper up here, the sky full of scudding white clouds. You can actually tell it's winter for a change. This is serious sheep country, just below the immense pastures of Le Navette, and Ivana and her husband Renzo will be, I daresay, the direct descendants of those Ligurian cheese-makers so admired by Pliny. And how right Pliny was about that cheese! I must have eaten tons of Ivana's cheeses in my time; I can't resist buying two every time I pass, big kilo-sized pure white sheep's cheeses. The fresh *primo sale*, the 'first salting', is so fresh that it squeaks between your teeth, something like a solid round of cottage cheese, and it matures into a proper flavoursome buttery cheese with a rind if you can keep your hands off it for a month or so. Forty days, I mean, of course. But who could manage that? That's why I buy two: one fresh, one already matured in Ivana's own cheese cellars.

At the far end of the alleyway you can just glimpse a great expanse of gently-terraced grassland and grazing sheep. A steep path leads down from here to the Arroscia, sunk below in a rocky ravine. The pastures are dotted about, here and there, with low, bushy plants that sprout a head of long, reddish stalks. These are grown, I'm told, for making ties for the grapevines: and I happen to know that they are in fact seriously stunted almond trees. Amazing what you can do with Nature when you know it well. I found this out when I took a cutting from one several years ago and planted it back at my house. I wasn't quite sure how far to let it grow before I pollarded it; and suddenly I had an almond tree.

The cheese artist Ivana and her husband have that ageless farmers' look, healthy and bluff and weathered; you could drop them down on a farm in England and they'd hardly look out of place. Though their suntans are maybe a bit on the Mediterranean side. They come out of their kitchen to greet us as we go through a sort of tunnel into an inside courtyard; the next door along from the kitchen, on our right, is a very lopsided arch with a half-door in it. Through the door, a room full of sheep. There must be forty-odd of them today, haughty-looking creatures with black faces, high-curved noses and impressively curly horns. All of them baa-ing away like mad as we draw near. Ivana laughs at the panic, leans over the half-door to pet one, scratching it lovingly round the horns. Ewes in lamb, she says. And dying to get out to grass. The vineyard? Yes, she certainly does want to sell it. And a few cheeses too, why not? And how are Patrizia's girls? She and Patrizia launch into a session in the local highland version of Ligurian dialect, very hard work to understand. It has an American-style rolled 'r' in it, not a sound I've heard anywhere else in Italy. Ivana swaps to Italian to tell me that she'll pop over to the *taverna* in a couple of days to make sure I'm all right; and she'll give me a tour of the vineyard whenever I want. Would she mind checking out the chickens, too, when she goes? says Francesca. O ye of little faith! Still, it's nice to know I won't be short of people to keep an eye on me.

Soon we are sitting comfortably in Ivana's kitchen, with a little knee-high woodstove crackling away before us, a pan full of chestnuts bubbling away on one of its twin hotplates. For the *castagnaccia*, says Ivana, the chestnut cake. There's some left from the last lot she baked, if we'd like to try some? With a nice warm glass of wine? We certainly would. So would Renzo, even though he's meant to be taking the ewes up to pasture. Ivana pours a whole bottle out into a saucepan and sticks it on the stove next to the chestnuts: adds a strip of orange peel and a spoonful of brown sugar; scrapes some nutmeg into it with her knife. It will certainly keep off the *colpo d'aria*, we all agree: save us from being Hit by Air. It's from the same vine-stock as the vineyard she's selling, too, says Ivana, the Ormeasco variety, and the land's more or less the same, so that's the quality of wine we'd be getting from it. If we can tell past the spice. Oh, and this demijohn's had a touch of Lumassina grapes added to it as well, hasn't it, Renzo?

Confusing. Lumassina seems a very odd name for a vine cultivar. A *lumassa* is a snail in Ligurian dialect, so a *lumassina* would be a baby snail. A snail-ette. I think I'll leave all that to the experts, though. As we sip our hot snail wine and munch our chestnut cake, lovely biscuity autumn-flavoured stuff, Ivana tells me in a concerned, heart-to-heart way that she knows all about the terrible decisions a couple just starting out together has to make. Ciccio and I must think things over carefully. We mustn't rush into anything. Renzo nods wisely. She and Renzo, for example, when they got engaged, she says, had just enough money either to go on one of these fashionable honeymoon trip things that were supposed to give you a good start to your marriage without a load of in-laws and neighbours sniffing your armpits and watching your every move; or to buy a small starter flock of sheep. They were on the very brink of choosing the honeymoon when they stopped and looked around them. A neighbour was selling up a couple of dozen lambs, good milking stock, at a not-to-be-missed price. They got a grip. Honeymoons might sound good, but when you thought about it, foreign travel had had, if anything, an unsettling effect on the few of their neighbours who'd tried it. While there was definite, incontrovertible evidence all around them that life ran smoothly indeed if you owned a decent flock of sheep. So they went for the old-fashioned option – and rightly so, as it has finally turned out.

Still, says Patrizia the rebel, who knows what might have happened if you'd gone travelling?

Well, says Renzo, there was certainly a time when they thought they might just as well have done. Three or four years ago they were at their wits' end, he tells us. You couldn't make a *lira* from sheep – not the wool, not the cheese, not the meat. He and Ivana thought they were going to have to give the game up, slaughter the herd and think of something else to do if they wanted to keep the children clothed and fed.

Yes, but what could it be? says Ivana. Neither of them had ever done anything except sheep-farming and cheese-making; and once they'd cut the honeymoon, they'd never even been farther from home than forty miles. How could they, with beasts to keep? Still haven't, adds Renzo with great satisfaction from over in the corner, where he is getting his boots on.

It was terrifying, says his wife. They were just eating their own cheese and meat, drinking their own wine, and bartering with neighbours for other stuff they needed. Flour and clothing and what have you. As if they were living a hundred years ago. But in the nick of time some city man from Genoa turned up looking for cheese the way it had always been made, fresh milk, good grass, healthy animals, matured properly with nature and time, not by some strange industrial process. He bought up every single cheese they had, and rang a week later to place an order that kept them flat out for months; at a price worth the work, at last. What a relief! That man saved their lives. Nowadays, though, there seem to be plenty of people willing to pay more for genuine sheep's cheese than for the factory stuff, and all is well.

Hats off to the Sloffood movement, I say.

The what? Ivana ignores this senseless remark. Their meat is selling again too, she says, now lots of people don't want frozen factory-farmed stuff; but they still don't make any money from the wool. They just give it away to friends who get good sturdy mattresses made up from it, mattresses to store away for their children's wedding trousseaux.

Francesca gives me a meaningful look. Yes, I already know about this woollen mattress tradition, as it happens. Ciccio has one waiting for him, one that Francesca had made up for him when he reached marriageable age – about fifteen, I think – from wool provided by some Calabrian cousin. A de luxe version too, one side stuffed with cool cotton wadding for summer use. He's been trying to get Francesca to hand it over since before Christmas, not being too impressed with the only mattress I have to offer, but no dice. We have to get married, she says, or it will live forever in her attic.

Anyway, says Ivana, she herself has gone for sheep; but wine could be a good thing too. In these commercial times you have to concentrate on just the one thing, don't you, if you want to make a living? And Salvatore has the vineyard just along from theirs, so they could be worked together!

Yes, he does, says Francesca, but she's not so sure about us working them together. Not while her husband's still alive! She suddenly realizes what she's said, and looks desperate.

Decades to go yet! I say brightly, leaping into the breach.

Well, Ivana will be over to show us around as soon as I let her know Ciccio's up here. Though it's a bit of a long trip to see all of it.

All of it? What does she mean, see all of it? How much of it is there?

Didn't Patrizia tell us? There's a bit of woodland that goes with it – she's selling it all in one lot. Nearly a square kilometre of woodland pasture. Come outside, says Ivana, and she'll show us . . . We all trail out into the courtyard. At the top of that hill over there, about fifteen kilometres inland, Ivana says, pointing at something well on towards the snowline, something that to my mind is a lot more mountain than hill.

Patrizia certainly didn't tell us, she says, because she knew nothing about it. Patrizia is obviously thinking along the same lines as me: horrified. A square kilometre of land to keep clear, and a good hour's drive away from home! This is forest fire country, and if we owned a chunk of woodland we'd be responsible for the thing not catching fire and destroying the livelihood of everybody else for miles around. I've only just finished retelling, to my laptop, the tale of the horrible experience I had of forest fires in my early days here, when I didn't bother to clear my olive terraces properly due to a foolish foreign notion that the beautiful wildflowers growing upon them would be happier that way; and the awful consequences of that are fresh in my mind. Imagine how pleased Ciccio would be to have responsibility for a thrice-yearly clearing all the way up there added to his woes!

Would you not consider letting us buy the vineyard on its own, without the bit of mountain? I ask.

Why on earth would you want to do that? says Ivana, looking at me as if I was loopy. The woodland is essential to keep the vineyard going!

Is it? I shut up and wait for the explanation. It is as follows.

You need the woodland because you rent it out. Probably to the family that's been renting it out these last thirty years to keep their cows on. You don't need to go up and clear it, because the cows do it for you. And your tenants pay you not in money, but in cow manure; fifty *quintali* a year. To be well rotted down, and delivered to your vineyard each spring. Then you just dig it in, and bingo! Your crop grows big and fat and luscious.

I see. So we wouldn't just be buying a vineyard. We'd be buying an ecosystem. Irresistible. I seriously fancy becoming a cow-shit-rent property impresario. I can imagine myself pointing at that mountainside in years to come and going: See that bit of land up there? Guess how much we earn from that! Fifty *quintali* of manure!

Then there's the nice *taverna* full of arches. And the wine, too. We haven't discussed what the price might be, but something tells me that's best left to local experts to determine. A bit academic, too, since I'm going to be flat broke after the roof repair experience. But maybe I could raise some debt, if Ciccio's interested too? The list of things I'll do if only I get round to finishing that book seems to be escalating alarmingly . . .

As we're taking our leave of Ivana I notice, just outside the kitchen door, a funny little home-made-looking table; a foot-thick slice of tree trunk with four sturdy stripped branches fixed to its sides for legs. The legs have been painted white, and tipped with shiny black cloven toes at the bottom, sheep-style. Sweet! I exclaim. A sheep table! Yes, says Ivana. For cutting them up on, when we need some meat for the house.

Here we sit, Patrizia, Francesca and me, under the vaulted ceilings of the Albergo dell'Angelo, the Inn of the Angel, at Pieve di Teco. High above us on the vaulted ceiling are voluptuous frescoes of fruits and cherubs, representing the bounties of Spring, Summer, Autumn and Winter. Nothing too overtly religious, because these apartments were built as the headquarters of Napoleon's generals as they made their way south and east, trashing the remnants of the Kingdom of Savoy as they went. (Yes. The same lot who nipped the Italian Romantic movement in the bud with their treachery. Pity Annetta's not here to savour it.) The place has hardly been changed at all since then, you'd say. In the centre of the room, below the untouched frescoes, a massive barleysugar Venetian glass chandelier has been rewired for electricity in a half-hearted tangly sort of way. The tall narrow French windows opening on to the wrought-iron first-floor balcony, where we are sitting looking down on to a tiny grassy-cobbled piazza, look original, as do the glass-paned cupboard niches built into the walls. The only off-key note in the place is a small outbreak of lumpy brown plastic nineteen-seventies refurbishing on one side of the lobby as you come in. But then, this perfectly balances out the only other item that's a bit out of kilter, the carved slate well-head just inside the entrance that looks seriously medieval, way too old for the rest of the building, as if it were left over from some earlier incarnation.

Patrizia and I have mounted a pincer assault on Francesca, and dragged her off here for lunch on the way back down hill. Francesca is as excited as a kid disobeying parents' orders, and as convinced that she's doing something very naughty. She never eats out except at major events like christenings and weddings and first communions; and she can't believe it's all right to be doing this. The proprietor brings us a bottle of his own white wine, lovely slightly fizzy stuff with a hint of grape-pips to its aroma. Francesca is overwhelmed. Three women out on their own, eating and drinking wine together! How times have changed!

Ladies who Lunch, I tell her. It's an English tradition.

Francesca also can't believe my very peculiar, or very English, attempts to find out whether you could make a living, or at any rate earn some money, from a vineyard that size. She's laughing, in that puzzled way, at the very idea. Land isn't for earning money in her worldview: it's for saving money, or stopping you needing money, rather. Because you make your own supplies out of it, don't you, which you then don't have to buy. You make sure to have as many strings to your bow as possible; then the only question is one of time, of fitting all the work involved in your various enterprises into the hours of the day. Or the months of the year, I should say, since there are noticeable chunks of time where you're just waiting for stuff to grow or mature or whatever. How would you compute whether you were making a profit anyway, when you count your own labour as free? Maybe all this uncertainty built into their lives is why everyone in this country is so keen on games of chance? All completely alien to my own country's mindset, where you go to work and perform some specific task every day, for a set number of hours and a definite amount of money. Money that you can calculate perfectly easily whether you can manage on or not. I try Patrizia – though come to think of it, her work life is just a more modern version of Francesca's. Could we sell the wine? Is it a sensible business proposition? Is there a Slow Food type interest in locally-produced primitive wines? Patrizia thinks not. You couldn't establish any sort of reliable brand name. The quality of the wine is too different every year, too much at the mercy of the weather, unless you own thousands of hectares so the differences will all average out. She thinks we could sell the grapes, though, if we wanted, to Signor Feola in Diano, who has a commercial wine-producing plant there.

Francesca suddenly cheers up. She knows about selling

grapes. Of course she does! If you're short of money you can always just load your whole harvest on to a lorry and go and sell it at the Diano crossroads come *vendemmia*. She and Salvatore did that a couple of times when the children were young and they were in desperate straits. But then you have to drink bought wine for a whole year . . .

39

I'm going to spend my first night alone up here at the *taverna* tonight, unless I want to join Ciccio's fishing-and-bonfire party on the pebbly beach by Cervo. I think I'll give it a miss, though; I'll have a quiet night in up here with my laptop and the river, feed my chickens at dawn, and drive down to meet Ciccio later, at the poor roofless home, to check how the work's going.

We'll have lunch up there, then, says Ciccio, and eat whatever fish he's caught. We'll light a fire outside and cook *alla bracia* if the kitchen's still not usable. Maybe he'll invite Paletta too. Then he'll go off to work. Thinking of which, Ciccio says, he can hardly believe how much interest my notices on the restaurant wall are generating: how many foreign customers stand about reading the things, exclaiming to one another over them, even getting out notebooks and taking the phone number down, too. As if it wasn't in the phone book! What a weird lot they are! I should get a move on with that book of mine. If it's anything like as big a hit as my notices, I'm on to a winner.

Ciccio and I are sitting on the floor of the Christmas-tree bottle-holder room in the *taverna*, where we've spent the last three hours of another deliciously crisp blue-skied wintry morning siphoning Salvatore's wine into bottles. (I'm still loving this weather. Can it be the Scots blood in me? A genetic predisposition to needing more variety in my seasons than you get down in Diano's *conca d'oro*?) The least we can do for Salvatore, who's due back in hospital soon for an exploratory operation, his ailment still being a mystery, is to get a decent amount of his wine sorted out. It only took me two demijohns of bottling work to be converted utterly to Salvatore's way of thinking on bottle sizes. You only need thirty-three of Salvatore's nice big bottles to decant a fifty-six litre demijohn – the last few litres are the lees, to be chucked – instead of a never-ending sixty-six of those piffling fiddly normal-sized ones we're having to do for the sisters. More bottles to clean out first, more wine spilt as you change from one bottle to the next, more stirring up of the lees as you accidentally jiggle your siphon tube while changing over; and on top of that, sixty-six blinking corks to finish you off.

We got Mrs Spring Onion, also known as Maria della Nandina, to show us which was Ivana's vineyard yesterday (sweet, she must be eighty if she's a day, but she's still called after her mother, 'Nandina's Maria') and Ciccio was very pleased with the look of the place and the state of the vines, all in good heart; and very entertained to spot the Lumassina vines in the top corner, too. The old folks knew a trick or two, he says. The Lumassina is an ancient local cultivar of the Vermentino: a white grape they would grow to mix in with the red, to boost the strength of the wine dramatically; and it's a precious thing, almost dying out.

In spite of my ignorance of these matters – but don't worry, I shall learn – I was very pleased with the *taverna* at any rate, which is even bigger than this one, and even fuller of lovely arches, as far as I could tell by staring in through the dusty windows; though it is, it seems, of no interest to anybody except me.

Ciccio is waiting till Ivana tracks down a few bottles of last year's vintage from the place to be sure about the plan; but I can tell he's keen. He agrees, too, that the banks of a rushing river would be a better place for his basil greenhouse project than a dry hillside that suffers from water shortages and is, to boot, horribly near a famously knife-wielding competitor. Even if the competitor happens to be an employee of ours just at this moment.

Ciccio wonders, he says, avoiding my eye and concentrating hard on the corking machine, whether we shouldn't just get married? Because, he rushes on, that would produce easily enough money to buy the place up, without us having to do anything complicated like pressurize Franchino to buy his share of the restaurant from him immediately, or raise loans, or accept help from his mother.

What? Is this a proposal of marriage? Can this seriously be a good reason for taking the plunge?

Of course it can: especially if we went for a big old-style Southern Italian wedding, he says, looking positively inspired.

I await more information. Here it comes. At a Southern Italian wedding, you don't just get gifts. You also auction the bridegroom's tie. This is what produces the cash.

Would Ciccio perhaps like to fill me in on this?

He certainly would. After the boring bit in the church, you all go off for a huge banquet in some local hostelry. You invite all the wealthiest people you know, as well as the ones you really like, and of course even the most distant members of both families. After the meal, the best man (you have to choose one with the gift of the gab: Paletta would be great) removes the groom's tie, pulls out his pocket knife, and starts slicing it up into bits. And off goes the auction. Everyone being well mellowed out by now, a battle for *bella figura* will get going, with everyone, you hope, competing more and more wildly in their offers for tiny slivers of your tie to bring them luck and fertility. Some will be keen to go down in history as the most startlingly generous of the company. Others will feel obliged to avoid the embarrassment of offering less than someone else who is known, or suspected, to be poorer than them. If you're lucky, if you've chosen your food, your guests, and your wine well, you can end up with a fortune. We might get enough to pay Ivana twice over!

As I say, no romance in the man's soul. Is this the best he can do? Two can play at this game. Well, I say, I suppose getting married might be better than letting your poor old mum sell up all her gold.

What am I on about? What gold?

Whoops. I see that Francesca has shared a women-only secret with me.

Oh, nothing. Just a figure of speech, I say airily.

The trouble is, though, that his restaurant's been annoying Ciccio again, and I suspect he would be keen on any old escape plan at the moment. Even marriage. This time the problem is not the clients, who have been surprisingly well-behaved recently, but Pierino the landlord himself. He's getting on in years, isn't he, and Ciccio thinks maybe his mental health isn't all it could be. A couple of weeks ago he started to take violently against one of Ciccio's favourite regulars, a positively inspiring German who is, I'm told, a joy and a delight to cook for. Heinrich, he's called: an actor who has bought himself a holiday house in Moltedo. A man who really appreciates good food, and comes back week after week, in spite of Pierino's best efforts to alienate him. Although Heinrich has been coming to eat for a while, one evening last week Pierino suddenly took to sitting and glowering ferociously at him from his corner: then he appeared in the kitchens when they were closing up for the night, in a very disturbed state, announcing that he was sure, though the details wouldn't quite come back to him, that there was something terribly

wrong about that man. He couldn't quite put his finger on it
. . . but he was certain he'd had dealings with him before . . .
during the war, maybe? A few days later, he was certain it was
definitely during the war. Heinrich must have been here with
the occupying forces, he was some sort of high-up fascist,
Gestapo maybe . . . that was the image that kept coming back
to Pierino, anyway: the man strutting about the place in some
kind of German uniform, cold-eyed, dealing death.

Ciccio found himself unwilling to believe this. Still, he
began to worry. Was it possible? Could the man be older than
he looked? Were they going to end up with a War Crimes
arrest on the premises, if and when Pierino's memory finally
returned? Groups of unarmed villagers had certainly been put
up against the wall round here and shot, in retaliation for
Partisan actions against the German army. Would that count
as a War Crime, anyway, though? And even if it didn't, would
Ciccio actually want to be feeding a man who had participated
in such slaughter? Till now he'd been developing a beautiful
rapport with Heinrich, a man who so much appreciated the
wild mint sorbet he'd been given to cleanse his palate between
courses the first time he came that he instantly demanded to
meet the chef and shake his hand. Anyway, he looked a good
fifteen years too young to have possibly been involved in the
war. Ciccio tried walking unobtrusively right round Heinrich
to see if he looked the same age from every angle. Yes, he did.
No definite signs of plastic surgery, then.

Next time Heinrich came, bringing a large party of friends for
Sunday lunch, the gimleting hate rays being aimed at him
from Pierino's corner were so powerful that after a while he
swapped seats so as to turn his back to his persecutor.

There! See that? said Pierino to Franchino. Trying to avoid
my eye! Or to make sure I can't get a good look at him!

Pierino was now even more convinced that he was right. He'd known he recognized those pale, evil eyes, all along. The details would come back to him soon, and then they'd all be sorry. Far from being fed like a prince, the man ought to be shot like a dog. Why would no one trust Pierino's instinct?

Instead of joining his card-playing cronies that afternoon, Pierino stayed at his own table with his own litre-and-a-half of red wine and a fierce eye firmly fixed on Heinrich. The lower sank the level in the bottle, the louder grew the solo remarks about Nazifascist Barbarians emanating from the corner under the vines. Before long the half-dozen tables of Italians were muttering among themselves, staring covertly at the two tables of Germans and trying to work out which among them, if anyone, might be the Barbarian in question.

Ciccio crept out of his kitchens every now and then, to look on helplessly and wish he'd gone back to the land. Since Pierino was the legitimate owner of the place, and moreover was sitting in his own garden, there was no way they could possibly eject him. Or, more to the point, silence him. Equally obviously, thanks to the eccentricities of Pierino's unravelling-jumper dress code, and the fact that there was no visible barrier separating his terrace and the restaurant, none of this was at all clear to the customers, who couldn't imagine why this aged and possibly dangerous nut was being allowed to sit there and rave all afternoon.

When Heinrich and his friends finally got up to leave, Pierino rounded off his performance by coming and spitting loudly and spectacularly on the ground at their feet as they passed. The Germans politely ignored this odd behaviour; they sidestepped Pierino, and stopped to thank their hosts for a fine lunch. Now, one by one, they shook Ciccio's and Franchino's hands.

This was the last straw. Shaking hands with the man now, was it? shouted the enraged freeholder, coming right into the restaurant. Ciccio and Franchino were a pair of *bastardi* of *Nazifascista* collaborators! He'd had enough! If they ever let that man in here again, they would be evicted forthwith. No more restaurant for them! Got it?

Next lunchtime, which was yesterday, Heinrich appeared with a couple of videos in his hand. He had, he said, appeared in a couple of films set in Italy. They were war films, in which he was unfortunately somewhat typecast as the Evil Nazi. Still, perhaps their aged relative, the gentleman who sits in the corner, would enjoy watching them? Perhaps they might have a calming effect?

It was all Ciccio could do not to stuff those videos down Pierino's neck. Who wants a restaurant where they're at the mercy of a landlord who can't tell the difference between TV and reality, and who, when he's not busy filling your flat full of crap, lurks about on its confines day and night oppressing you with deranged threats to throw you out? Which, by the way, he does seriously have the right to do, if he gets mad enough. Roll on that vineyard, and death to all restaurants!

40

Arriving at the house, I find a cement-mixer and a chariot-like cart contraption occupying rather a lot of my parking place; and the two brown horses, very hot and sweaty-looking, drinking thirstily from buckets of water, tethered in the shade of a pair of olive trees on the terrace above. Olive trees that, as it happens, belong to my tragic beardy neighbour. Is this all right? Could it annoy people if you tether horses to their trees? O Lord, am I never going to have a moment's peace of mind again now that I'm the owner of a possibly-abusive roof, and hence at the mercy of my neighbours' every mood-swing?

This is, in any case, a mere foretaste of the scene of utter chaos at the house itself. Some of the chaos, such as the fact that there's no roof on the place, and that it's surrounded by a sea of rubble, is only to be expected. However, at the level I'm on, the path below the house, the main thing that strikes the eye is that the two big olive trees in front of it, the ones outside the bedroom door, have largely disappeared. Nothing is left of them but their big gnarled old trunks and a couple of miserably dangling branches. Massacred. Not a messy, casual massacre such as you might expect from, say, a passing rabid elephant. No, the job's been done systematically, clinically, with neat chainsaw strokes, by some member of the fundamentalist school of Drastic Pruning. There are great logs lying about all over the lower terrace, some even on the olive nets (growl); and several head-high piles of fronds piled up against the house wall, with a machete lying casually on top of the nearest one.

Drawing closer, I see that on the upstairs terrace, order reigns. Well, a sort of order, anyway. Ciccio, Paletta, Franco and three Albanians are milling rowdily around a bonfire they've lit on the barbecuing place by Bormano's oak tree, presumably preparing to cook fish. There are several empty wine bottles on the table near them, and judging by the level of hilarity prevailing, they're all three sheets to the wind. Ciccio hails me from above. Detects my eyeline. Casually announces, looking a tiny bit nervous, that he thought he might as well do a bit of pruning while he was up here, let some more light into the house . . . And there were hardly any olives on them anyhow . . . He trails off into silence. Franco and the Albanians snicker at his discomfiture. Paletta avoids my eye.

I can see exactly what's happened here. Ciccio and cousin were unable to resist the all-boys-together atmosphere of major works in progress, and had to find something major of their own to be getting on with, something with lots of loud sound-effects and much heaving and straining and a very noticeable outcome.

I don't really mind, I suppose. When we drastically pruned all the other trees, we left those two tall for beauty. But I've often thought myself that they were keeping a lot of light out of the house and could do with a prune. I stomp crossly up the stairs anyway – because how did Ciccio know I wouldn't mind, and now they'll grow into a weeping-willow shape when I might have wanted to keep them in the old apple-tree style, and why did he have to create even more mess at this precise moment on top of all the other mess anyway? – and I storm past the lot of them into the kitchen. There really is an awful lot more light in here than usual; but that's because there's no roof on the place, of course, only a skeleton of new beams.

Still, now that the trees have shrunk, you can see Diano Castello from up here as well as Arentino. And a lot more sea. I suppose it wasn't really such a bad idea. And now that I'm level with the cooking terrace I can see that they've made smoky-roasted peppers and slices of grilled aubergine tossed in olive oil and thyme for starters. I turn down the sulking and get busy with the wine; I'll need to put in some hard work to catch up with my dining partners. Who now reveal, once I've sat down with them, that they have been doing a lot more with their working day than simply destroying olive trees, cooking, and boozing. They have also been dashing up and down the hill on Franco's *baroccio*, the cart-thing I saw at the end of the path; while those of them who know how to ride – the Albanians and Franco – took turns to race against it on horseback. No wonder they're all looking so flushed and bright-eyed. Especially Franco, who seems to have got twenty years younger in this company; and who now takes me aside for a conspiratorial moment. The *Guardia Forestale*, he tells me, the Forest Guard police force, stopped their jeep this morning as he was collecting some stuff at the parking place and asked him what he was doing with all those tiles at the end of the road. But everything's all right: they were only passing by chance, and he told them that he was fixing the roof on an old cowshed of his own. Lucky, he says, that nobody would ever guess there was a house along a tiny path like ours.

What does this mean? Why did he have to conceal the roof from the *Guardia Forestale*? Is it, or isn't it, all right to be re-doing it? Is there any point in trying to make head or tail of the situation? I don't think I can stand much more of this. I sit down and try to get a grip. But it doesn't work: the panic sensation just keeps growing. What, I wonder, am I doing in this chaotic, senseless land, in this chaotic, senseless house?

And as for being in love with this chaotic, senseless man . . . !
I suddenly have a desperate desire to run away. What is to
stop me just giving up, packing my bags, and going back to
nice tidy, predictable England, where I know what's going
on? Nothing! In fact, I could get my suitcase out as soon as
we've finished lunch . . .

Now, as we start to eat, the truth about the trees comes out.
Franco, playing up delightedly to his audience of younger
men, makes a patently absurd remark about how annoyingly
loud the *grilli*, the grasshoppers, are; as if this was midsummer
with its great chorus of stereophonic trilling from the hills and
not a quiet January day. Paletta, grunting with suppressed
laughter, says that the unbearable racket is being caused not
by grasshoppers, but by tree crickets.

Ciccio tries staring at his plate, but his lips are twitching
too. I give him a sharp kick under the table; and he confesses
that perhaps a couple of those very noisy tree crickets, the
ones that sit there quacking like ducks on and on for hours
and hours, may have contributed to his pruning decision. He
and the boys had been trying to silence the creatures, he says,
by launching stones at them from up here during their coffee
break. (Wine break, more like, I would guess. What a bad
influence Franco is! This is what Luigi meant when he said
Franco 'led a disordered life'.) And when that didn't work,
Ciccio's blood now being up, he couldn't resist launching the
chainsaw attack. He had the chainsaw out anyway to slice up
the old infested beams ready to burn, and he was only going
to prune a couple of the highest branches, but then things got
a bit out of hand.

A bit? See what I mean! Can I seriously be thinking of setting up in agribusiness with a man who uses fifty nails to kill
one small beetle larva, and then chops twenty feet off a per-

330

fectly good olive tree just to get his own back on a tree cricket?

Still, Ciccio's made some perfect *trenette al nero di seppie*, black with cuttlefish-ink, for our pasta dish, so I suppose he must still own some shred of rationality. And it was nice of him to saw the beams up for me. Everyone around the table denies hotly that there is anything at all deranged about his behaviour. The moment may not have been best chosen, they say, but the effect is perfectly rational. The trees needed pruning. Moreover, an assortment of very pretty fish caught last night with his and Paletta's own hands is sitting grilling over the olive-wood *bracia*. Best fresh green olive wood, no doubt, given the circumstances.

Over the pasta, Remy, one of the Albanians, trying his hardest to improve my mood, compliments me on my *orto* down by the well. You can't have a vegetable garden like that in his own land these days, he says.

What does he mean? Why not?

That's how bad things have got, he says. There's no work at all, not in the whole country.

But why would that stop people having vegetable patches? You'd think it would have the opposite effect.

No, he says, because there are bands of people, landless people who've left the cities where there is no food and no work, who just roam the countryside, living off what they can steal. They make a camp for the women and children, and then go seeking food. With guns, often. As soon as anything pokes its head above ground, they will have it. Or before it pokes its head above ground, even. His father and grand-mother planted a plot of potatoes near their house, and some-one had dug the seed potatoes up within the week, to eat them. They only plant right outside the door, now; and his dad and uncle mount an armed guard day and night once the stuff gets anywhere near edible.

Poor Albanians. Even my wildest collapse-of-civilization nightmares couldn't match that. I settle down to revising my worst-case scenario while Ciccio bones and fillets the fish for us all with a series of snappy moves that make the job look absurdly easy. Of course, I say to myself: think of the fall of the Roman Empire. People don't just go quietly off and subsistence-farm. You get a century or two of roaming marauders first. I may as well give up worrying and live for today, then. Easily enough done with blue sky, warm springlike sunshine, and a lunch like this one. Ciccio generously gives me the *pesce di San Pietro*, which I happen to know is his favourite fish. For my beloved, he says, as he passes it across. Oh well, maybe he's not that senseless and chaotic. Or maybe he is, but I can't help being fond of him anyway. And I'd probably be bored to death in tidy, predictable England.

Once Ciccio's gone off to work, Paletta helps me clear the table and wash the dishes, to the great amusement of the Albanians, who come, I gather, from a culture similar to that of Salvatore's youth. Worse than that, says Paletta, piling plates fearless for his masculine *figura*. Remy, he says, told him a long, rambling story about having been given a lift by Franco, and Iole having got in the front of the car. Remy was seriously offended, because women are supposed to sit in the back of a car if there's a man there! He thought Franco had done it on purpose as a sign of disrespect! It will do the Albanians good, he says, to see how modern men behave.

Well done those Albanians! I've never known Paletta help with the dishes before, ever.

Enough worrying about the state of the world. Having decided against packing my bags, I collect a bucket instead. I may as well gather up some of those olives from Ciccio's frond collection below. I'll salt them *in salamoia*, rather than let them go to waste. Just as I'm setting off, Paletta's phone rings. Francesca. I can hear the panic in her voice from here. Salvatore has been taken into hospital a day early, and she wants the family to assemble at the hospital right away.

What, me too?

Especially you, says Paletta.

41

In the surgery ward at Imperia hospital, a long white building set high on a hill above the town with enormous plate-glass views of the Mediterranean, a great cluster of females sits closely packed around Salvatore's bed. We are keeping him company while he waits to be taken into the operating theatre; and devising an emergency rota. The sisters had everything worked out, but this change of plan has thrown it all into confusion. Apparently in this country a member of the family can sit by a patient's bedside all night if they want to; and Francesca will be taking the first shift. The first night after the operation is always the most dangerous, she says. She'll stay till three this morning. Then I will take over, since nobody can get hold of Annetta, the only other female without encumbrances, so Francesca can go and get some rest after her vigil. If all has gone well, that is, she adds, crossing herself. The sisters will have sorted out jobs and children by tomorrow morning, and one of them will take over at eight. Though I can go at seven, if I want, she says, because that's when Grazia starts her shift on the surgery ward anyway. And I'll need to be getting back up to the *taverna*, won't I, to see to the chickens?

At the moment the ratio of nurses to patients in this ward is a lot higher than anything I've ever seen in England – not that I would hold up the English system of lying about for days in lonely corridors for emulation – but in spite of this plethora of nurses, the need to keep a twenty-four-hour-a-day watch at Salvatore's bedside seems obvious to everybody here. Only the Simple Englishwoman is at all puzzled. Are there not usually this many nurses, I ask, or is it that we don't trust them?

What do I mean? (Very sharp look from Francesca.) Salvatore's own eldest daughter is a nurse here, isn't she? Of course we trust them! But imagine if a member of your family was the only patient without someone to look after them personally! *Che brutta figura!*

I see: so being allowed to have somebody by a patient's bed means, in practice, that you are obliged to have somebody by their bed, unless you want to look mean and uncaring.

Ciccio should be arriving any moment; Francesca's only just managed to get hold of him, she says, what with the way that telephone's always engaged up at the restaurant (thanks to my notices, I wonder?): but he can't be asked to take the night shift, of course he can't, because sitting by beds isn't a son's job, and his father would be mortified to see him there. Sons do have to go and water the *orto*, though, because it hasn't been done since last week; and they also have to pop in for a bedside visit, minimum once a day, whenever they can make it. Seems a bit of a soft option to me. Now we're all organized and the panic's over, the four of Salvatore's daughters here present, talking all at once in close counterpoint, turn to cheerful reassurance. Don't worry about a thing! It'll all be sorted out by this time tomorrow, whatever it is! Papa will soon be right as rain!

At last those of us on the later shifts take our leave, queuing to kiss first the invalid, then his wife; and we all squeak off in procession across the rubber-tiled floor.

Up at the restaurant, where I've gone to spend my next few hours chopping some stuff and maybe napping upon some nets until it's time for my stint back in Imperia, Ciccio returns horribly upset from the hospital. He got there just as they were about to take Salvatore off for the operation, he says; and when they were left alone for a moment, his father suddenly said he would help him buy that vineyard if he really wanted it, no strings attached. He would work it with him, too, if he wanted. Imagine that. Salvatore offering him help, instead of vice versa! The world turned upside down. Worse still, once they'd got him on the trolley thing, about to be wheeled off, he grabbed Ciccio's arm and pulled him down as if he wanted a last embrace; but instead, he croaked his secret wine recipe into Ciccio's ear. Something involving a branch from a peach tree, added to the *mosto* at a certain point in the fermentation. Slip it into the vat when nobody else is around; and never breathe a word to anyone, not even close family . . .

Ciccio can't believe a peach branch would make any difference. Though it is true that his father's wine never goes bad. But that's not the point. Salvatore would never have told him his forefathers' secret unless he thought he was on his deathbed.

A couple of hours later we hear by phone from Francesca that everything went fine. Of course Salvatore survived the operation! He was a wee bit pale and wan when he came round, but he already looks much better. There was no growth, no tumour, nothing at all to worry about, the surgeon says. Just a simple mechanical blockage, which he has removed.

Ciccio drives me down to Imperia for my night shift, and takes his mother home to bed: but of course he can't sleep anyway, and ends up back here, lurking about drinking coffee out of the thimble-sized plastic cups from the machine outside the bar in the hospital lobby. (A bar that serves espresso coffee, delicious filled *focaccia* sandwiches, and alcoholic beverages of every kind during opening hours: how's that for a hospital?)

I, on the other hand, spend a very peculiar night sitting at Salvatore's bedside in the low-lit ward, one among a dozen shadowy female figures keeping silent vigil over each of the twelve patients. When we meet outside the ward, on our way to the loo or the coffee machine, we exchange whispered information about our menfolk's innards; then we return to darkness and silence, only feet away from one another, watching and waiting.

By half past eight sunshine is blazing through the plate-glass windows. You'd pay a fortune for a hotel room with this view. If I ever need an operation, I'm going to make sure to come here. Just to be able to gaze at ships sailing past on a big blue Mediterranean from your sickbed, rather than stare at bricks and concrete, would have to be pretty therapeutic. Then there's the bar. And look how many people I'd have to sit round my bed. The bevy of daughters has regrouped around Salvatore, Annetta included now; all of them so relieved at the good news that they launch into a series of agitated contrapuntal lectures on his health. How many times they have told him off about drinking too much *vino d'uva*, about smoking too many cigarettes, about eating too much fatty food, especially cheese and salami; about gulping his food down without chewing it properly, about overdoing the chilli peppers. They've been telling him for years. Has he ever listened to a word? No! Poor Salvatore lies limp and ashen-faced, listening to the catalogue of his sins: for once without the strength to shout back. How lucky he is that it was nothing serious, he is told. Everything's turned out all right this time. But they hope he's learned his lesson!

My shift over and Salvatore safe (he certainly shouldn't have entrusted his son with that peach-branch secret, though, should he?), a happy Ciccio takes me off to Arentino. We'll buy some fresh rolls and go for breakfast with Marco and

Laura before he takes me back up to the *taverna* to get some sleep. He has a hunch there'll be a surprise for me up at Marco and Laura's, he says. There certainly is. Our hosts put the coffee on, and Ciccio and little Michele take me straight up on to the roof terrace. We look out across the valley. And yes! At last, now those olive trees have been cut down to size, you can see Besta de Zago perfectly. Unfortunately, though, just at the moment it looks more like a pile of rubble than the little gem I've always imagined seeing one day from afar. Still, half the roof is back on already, looking oddly speckly where a bright new tile has been added, here and there, among the faded originals. I'll come back next week and do some proper gloating.

Ciccio's father may be well on the road to recovery, but Marco's, we hear over breakfast, is not doing too well at all. Ciccio hasn't seen Marco for days, and now we find out why. One fine afternoon last week, a police car wailed to a halt outside Marco and Laura's door. The *carabinieri* had come with a warrant to search the house. They threw things about all over the place, made a terrible mess that, as Laura tells it, she still hasn't finished clearing up; and eventually found what they were looking for, stuffed into the electricity-meter cupboard outside the front door. A fat bundle of large-denomination banknotes. They waved it at Marco. Did he know anything about it? No he didn't: nor did his wife. They wished they did – they would certainly have known what to do with it. Imagine that, a fortune sitting right outside their door!

But, on closer inspection, most of the notes turned out to be false, just photocopies. Only the top and tail of the bundle were real. Even more mystifying. But this made no difference, said the police: it was what they'd expected. Who, apart from Marco and Laura, had a key to the cupboard? Nobody, they thought, except of course the ENEL, the electricity board.

But as Marco said this he realized with a sinking heart that his father, who has been behaving ever more strangely recently, had never given back the set of house-keys he was given when he was helping with the alterations.

And it turns out that Marco's dad has indeed seriously lost his marbles. He tried, the police said, to blackmail somebody, threatening to kidnap their son (a man of thirty-seven) if he wasn't paid some paltry amount – a couple of thousand pounds – not to do it. He did the job most incompetently, and the putative victims got in touch with the police as soon as they received the threatening note. The police provided the photocopied banknotes, suspecting, rightly, that the would-be perpetrator was too potty to notice.

Marco refused at first to believe this story – his father has always been a quiet, sober, hardworking man. Why would he do this out of the blue? Soon, though, the father, aged seventy-eight, was under arrest, and there was no denying the crime: his handwriting, and even his spelling mistakes, were identical to those on the blackmail note. Laura's good Ligurian family was mortified. Kidnapping and extortion! Exactly the sort of behaviour everyone expects of Calabresi!

Yes, it is, said Laura to her father: and after a lifetime of hearing about it from the likes of you, he's finally lost his sanity and done just what was expected of him! Are you all satisfied now?

Marco doesn't go along with his wife on this one, preferring the wandering-evil-spirit theory to the tediously socio-psychological. He is going to take his dad to see Padre Milingo on the next exorcism day, he says, and get the thing sent right back where it came from.

The law, meanwhile, says that a man of seventy-eight is too old to go to prison, even if he is in tip-top mental health; clearly not the case with Marco's dad. He can't go into a mental hospital, because the mental hospitals of Italy were all closed down some time in the seventies, to be replaced with Care in the Community. He won't stay at home with his wife, who is, he explains, a police spy. Which leaves Marco and Laura as the Community. They're going to have to convert the *cantina* into a grandad annexe; which will drastically curtail their storage space. Where will they keep those years' worth's of *passata*, of olive oil, of wine, of potted and bottled produce from the *orti*? Laura doesn't care, she says. Marco's dad has done her a favour. Marco should only bother to grow what they can eat fresh. She can buy tins of *passata*, bags of frozen peas, jars of roasted *peperoni* or pickled mushrooms, packets of dried beans: she's earning the money to do it, the stuff hardly costs anything compared to the hours of work you put into preparing it all yourself. Marco feels undermined; the older relatives so proud of him, and his wife counting it all as nothing. Laura, though, wants less unceasing work in their lives, and more quality time together, she says. The odd holiday abroad – or at least, away from home – and an occasional candlelit dinner together in some little intimate restaurant, maybe . . .

She's been watching too much American stuff on the telly, says Marco.

42

Back at the *taverna* among my feathered pets, and my manu-
script is finally finished. I've even come up with a good title
for it at last: *Extra Virgin*. Neatly covering both the main local
activity, and my own state of utter innocence when I first
arrived in these parts. Tomorrow I shall walk into Pieve di
Teco and post it off to Britain. A great weight off my shoulders.

I'm reading it through for the last time when I suddenly
feel sick. Very, very sick. O Lord, I hope it won't have this
effect on the literary agent I'm about to send it to. I spend all
evening throwing up, convinced I'm about to die all alone up
here. There's hardly any chance Ciccio will make it up to the
Arroscia valley after work to save me. It's Saturday night,
when restaurant customers are at their most demanding. By
three a.m., I've given up bothering to go back up the stairs to
my bed. I'm just lying on a pile of assorted drapery on the
kitchen floor so as to be close to the sink; I'm freezing cold,
too, weak as a kitten. No way could I find the strength to
rattle about with sticks and paper and matches to get the
woodstove lit. And I'm too scared to light the little round
sunray gas heater, having noticed, from this unusual position,
that it has a label on its base saying For Exterior Use Only. I
might die in its fumes, and nobody find me for days. Though
I may die of vomiting anyway, or of asphyxiation by the other
fumes, the powerful alcohol ones from the wine vats in the
back room that seem to be getting more and more nauseatingly
pervasive by the hour.

Dawn breaks and slivers of light begin to filter through the shutters; I can hear people outside banging buckets, or perhaps tin drums. Or is it bin-lids? The Cipollini must be very early risers. Will I call out to them? I haven't got the strength. I collapse back into delirious sleep instead, and wake up some time later still on the floor. No sound from the neighbours at all, now that I might just about make it to the door. I open the window, struggling with the complicated latches on the green slatted shutters, and finally get my head out. Nobody. The Cipollini's *Ape* is gone. The place looks deserted. I discover that the extra latch on the shutter belongs to a tiny, hinged section, in which you can actually swivel the slats up or down to change your viewing angle. Must be for following your neighbours' movements more closely without betraying yourself. Can't think what else it could be for. Fancy building nosiness into your very architecture! No use at the moment, anyway, with nobody at all to spy on. I shut the many latches again, drink a glass of water, throw it up immediately, and wend my wobbly-kneed way upstairs to bed at last. Only to be dragged back down within half an hour by a loud banging at the door. Leaning on the door jamb for support, I find myself face to face with an aged couple. The Cipollini. They've come to make sure I'm all right, they say.

But how on earth did they know? What made them suspect that I might not be all right?

They began to worry when they saw the house shutters still closed at half past eight, say the Spring Onions. When they still weren't open at ten, they thought they'd better come and check.

Well! Talk about keeping an eye on me! Imagine if I'd just been having a lie-in? And it's Sunday, too! Still, passing lightly over invasions of privacy, I've never been so glad to see anybody in my life.

There is an evil bug going round the village, the Cipollini

tell me, some kind of gastric flu: everybody's had it. They feared that might be the explanation for my non-appearance. Some people have even gone on vomiting for forty-eight hours.

No, please! I can't go on like this for another day and a half. I surrender to Signora Cipollini's expertise, and am put back to bed and plied with hourly cups of chamomile tea until lunchtime, when I am upgraded on to a ferocious bitter brew of sage, rosemary, lemon and honey, with a dash of some kind of super-alcoholic *digestivo* for good measure. One that Signora Cipollini makes herself, she tells me, out of gentian violets, gathered in the hills and macerated in pure alcohol. Evening comes, and I can still hardly manage to sit up in bed: possibly just because I'm dead drunk. Both Cipollini now come in to sit by my bed and keep me company while I drink my lamb broth, more of the hot, bitter herb stuff, and another, even more ferocious dose of the digestive gentian liquor, neat this time. Now, as I sink back into my pillows, it's time for my bedtime story: the strange and tragic tale of the Blue Blood of the Cipollini. Once upon a time, Maria della Nandina tells me, the Cipollini were great lords, and possessed a castle of their own, along with boundless lands lying around the village of Capra Una. Do I know the place?

I certainly do. Or I've driven through it, at any rate. Who could forget a village whose name, in translation, would be Goat Number One? Especially when they had driven through the villages of Armati and Ciccioni on their way to the place: the villages of Armed Folk and of Plump Folk respectively.

But alas, says Signor Cipollini, a century ago their claim to the inheritance was usurped by a cadet branch of the family. It is true that one of their ancestors did behave rather badly; but the thing might easily have been overlooked if a certain great-great-uncle had not taken advantage, fomenting discord

343

when he could have healed the breach. Sunk as I am in a haze of herbs and alcohol, the complexities of the great-great-uncle's dastardly activities escape me somewhat; but the outline is clear. The great expectations of the noble Spring Onions of Goat Number One were utterly destroyed, alas, by a certain late-nineteenth-century Onion, a man of intemperate habits, who disgraced himself and generations as yet unborn by throwing, in an unguarded moment, a bowl of piping hot minestrone into his mother-in-law's face . . .

Next day I am rescued by Patrizia's cousins: news of my plight has already percolated to Cosio d'Arroscia, and Renzo has come at dawn to get me in his *Ape*. I knew there were too many eyes being kept on me. An *Ape* is the last mode of transport I would have chosen in my current state, unless I could lie horizontally in its tiny truckbed. But Renzo has won the battle of wills with the Spring Onions, and I have no choice in the matter. Ivana says I have to be properly looked after. She promised Patrizia. I can't be left alone in the *taverna*. No hope for it. I squeeze pallidly into the tiny cockpit under Renzo's elbow and we are off.

In spite of the delicate state of my health, before I am allowed to take to my bed I am dragged off on a tour of a very confusing living-space. Through workrooms of every conceivable type, a pair of *cantine* packed to the gunwales with provisions, firewood, wine, you name it. A glimpse of a dark, damp cave-like room full of cheeses sitting like Tommaso's in their little muslin cages. Somehow we've ended up on the other side of the internal courtyard, opposite the lopsided arch with the sheep, in a room (a separate house, perhaps?) containing an ancient granny and a slightly less ancient aunt who is watching a TV of about her own vintage. This, it turns out, was the point of the trip. Houseguests must be presented to the matriarchs of the family before settling in, even if they are on their last legs. Now we pass back through the courtyard, and soon we are sitting comfortably in Ivana's kitchen, where I am sipping at Ivana's own solution to the illness gripping the region. Another powerful concoction, this time of lemon, honey and grappa. Soon I am feeling seriously befuddled again – a warm, glowing type of fuddle. As I sip, Ivana demonstrates to me the modern convenience she and her husband have just managed to add to their kitchen, thanks to the turn in their fortunes. Looks like a normal kitchen dresser set against the back wall, you'd say. But no. She pulls open a small curtain draped over what seems to be a mirror set into the back of it. Not a mirror. Come over and have a look. I drag myself from my very comfortable armchair and press my nose to it as instructed; to find myself gazing incredulously, through a pane of glass, at the forty haughty sheep in their living quarters beyond. A brilliant innovation, as Ivana explains. Now you no longer need to leave the warmth of your kitchen to go and check up on your beasts, as you did in the bad old days of windowless dressers. Especially handy when the creatures are lambing and it's freezing and blowing a gale outside. With this modern technology you hardly need to take more than a couple of steps from your armchair. I test this out by tottering backwards into mine; and sit down heavily just in time to catch Episode One in the saga of Ivana, Renzo and the sheep's yearly life-cycle.

They will soon be setting off, Ivana says, to walk the flock over the mule-tracks to another bit of land they have, a coastal pasture above the town of Cervo, perched on a rocky bit of shore not far from our house, where the spring grass is already coming up. I am momentarily amazed – Cervo must be a good thirty miles by road from here. But you can do it easily in a day on foot. Of course: the old trails go straight along the tops of ridges where no road could be driven. Then they will camp in their old *rustico* above Cervo, taking it in turns to stay with the animals while they eat the fresh spring grass; then, once the summer heat returns, it's time to trek back to the cool green heights of Cosio d'Arroscia. The flock is a couple of hundred strong these days, the great-grandchildren of the great-grandchildren of those first honeymoon lambs not merely keeping the family fed and clothed, but even, these days, producing that bit extra for the occasional luxury. Dresser with flock-viewing facility, for example.

Ivana does a monthly round-trip in the station wagon delivering her cheeses to restaurants and private clients, she tells me. Her husband can't go; he gets all tongue-tied and self-conscious when he has to meet customers. This supposedly shy man is at the moment busy chatting away in dialect in a very loud and lively manner with a pair of similarly large and loud men in Wellington boots who turned up just as he was leaving to take the sheep out, forcing him to sit down again at the kitchen table and put out a round of wine. Ivana spots my incredulous look and laughs. He's all right as long as he doesn't have to speak Italian, she says. That's what makes him clam up.

The hot topic at the men's table, just about understandable now I've got my ear into the pronunciation – the weird 'r', I've grasped, is standing in for an 'l' – is a neighbour who found himself with a ridiculously huge harvest of marrows this autumn. Think how much money he would save if he managed to live out the rest of the winter on nothing but marrow-based dishes! But could it be done? Renzo and guests have been running, with much hilarity, through all the possible recipes for marrow, *zucca*, and have now got on to impossible ones. *Focaccia di zucca!* Ha, ha! *Involtini di zucca!* Guffaw! *Torta di zucca!* Ho, ho! This last item meaning marrow tart, or cake,

I foolishly decide to tell them that I've heard that such a thing really exists. In America they make something they call pumpkin pie, I say: some sort of dessert dish.

A sweet made with marrows! Am I sure? Marrows and sugar?

I think so, I say. I know you can use them in sweet dishes – in England people make jam with them, marrow and ginger.

Why have I still not learnt to keep my mouth shut in this country when it comes to funny foreign food? Naturally, everyone is appalled. *Che schifo!* How revolting! Have I ever eaten any? Are they mad? The menfolk drain their glasses, still marvelling at the horror of marrow jam. Renzo comes over to give his wife a bearhug and a big smacking kiss, and all three stomp off sheepwards, while I get put to bed, at last, in a spacious spare room with a very comfortable mattress.

After a short period of luxuriating, I have to get back out of bed to check. Yes, it really is one of those hand-made sheep's-wool things. Lovely. A pure wool futon: I wonder if anyone's thought of importing them to England? I can imagine their creating a whole new generation of woollen futon fashion victims. Maybe Ciccio could add mattress export to his vast collection of careers? No. Delirium. But I shall certainly tell Ciccio to keep on at Francesca until she gives up the mattress that is his by rights. I drift off into beatific sleep. The thing might even be worth marrying for.

Incredibly early next morning, feeling a lot better, I am dragged awake. I thought the 7.30 olive-farming start was pretty serious stuff, but it has nothing on this – 6 a.m. and below me a cacophony of clattering pails, clanging churns, spraying water, baa-ing and shouting and barking. Renzo and Ivana seem to be enjoying themselves even at this hour, joking away and swearing amicably at one another and the beasts. They somehow strike me as being more like a pair of best mates than man and wife. Like a lot of the older couples in San Pietro, except that these two aren't old. I'm not sure they're even into their forties yet. Is it to do with having a project together that isn't just leisure-time, a home that is also a place of work? I straggle downstairs. Even the sight of Ivana doing all the milk-bucket-cleaning and cooking and washing-up doesn't look as backward and oppressive as it ought; not when you can see Renzo standing just outside the door doing all the chopping and stacking of the firewood, moving on to mucking out the sheep-room. I suppose it made sense when everyone lived like this.

Ludicrous though it may be – I know I wouldn't last five minutes in their shoes – all my Perfect Life fantasies have been activated by this pair. I want badly to mutate into half a simple sheep-farming couple. Why does everything have to be so complicated? It's not fair. I sip crossly at the giant *caffè latte* in a bowl that Ivana has given me, along with a pile of biscuits which I know I am supposed to crumble into it and stir about until they dissolve into sludge; the traditional Italian equivalent of breakfast cereal. Now who's talking about funny foreign food? The older folks even do it with bread. No way. I'll just eat the biscuits separately, nice and crunchy, thanks.

Is there some chance of me and Ciccio mutating into an olive-growing and vineyard-running couple, though? Something tells me it doesn't work unless you've never done anything else. Still, I may stop being so principled and start actively encouraging him to give up his restaurant. Or should I go and work there too, maybe? Perish the thought. I'm still busy being jealous when Ivana's eldest daughter comes into the kitchen and a simple sheep-farming row ensues about pocket money. Celestina spent all her savings on a pair of absurdly expensive trainers last week, it seems; now she wants to borrow more for an essential new computer game. Her mother is outraged. She never helps with the housework or the cheese-work, only with the sheep, if and when madam feels like it, says Ivana, and she hardly deserves pocket money at all, never mind extra for luxuries. Celestina hates her mother, she says, and storms off in a sulk, threatening never to return.

Ah, well. Maybe not so different after all, then.

Since I am feeling so much better this morning, and there is no hope for humanity anyway, I may as well go and buy a packet of fags. Cosio d'Arroscia turns out to be a beautiful place once you bother to investigate it by daylight, instead of just sitting stuffing yourself *da Maria* or nipping into Ivana's for a cheese. It is one of those once-prosperous medieval market towns slowly going to rack and ruin; down the hill its old centre is half-empty, several of its alleyways closed off with signs warning you of Danger from Falling Masonry; there are shops and bars, even a hotel, boarded up decades ago, bits of thirties-style signs and décor still visible. You can buy a beautiful pillared and porticoed house here for a song. But how would you live?

43

The doctors may have politely called it an intestinal blockage, but this is much too euphemistic an explanation for Salvatore's eldest daughter. A triumphant Grazia appears at Salvatore's seventieth birthday celebrations, which are taking place at his hospital bedside, with a small twiggy thing in a glass jar. The surgeon has given Grazia the offending innard-blocking object to show him. The source of all that agony was nothing more than a thyme twig, which Salvatore had somehow managed to swallow whole.

It's all down to not chewing your food properly, Papa, says the thankless child. How on earth did you manage to swallow a whole twig of thyme without noticing it? How often have we told you about gulping down your food?

Salvatore is mortified. Worse still, he has given away his great wine secret when he wasn't actually on his deathbed after all. He has years to live still, and his son knows all! He calls Ciccio over to sit close beside him, and it is obvious to those of us in the know – me, that is – that he is making his son promise all over again never to reveal the secret of the peach branch to anybody. Not even to closest family, he says, quite audibly now; because they can be the worst . . .

Now he does a thing unheard of in the annals of the De Gilio family. He takes Ciccio's hand in his own. And he lies like that, eyes half-closed, looking positively beatific. He certainly can't be allowed to get away scot-free with this, not after so many years of bad behaviour. Marisa leaps on to the other side of the bed and grabs his other hand. You see, she tells us all, it only took a near-death experience for Papa to realize that he loved his children. Come on now, Papa, say it! You've made it to three score years and ten! Old enough to say it out loud at last! You'll feel better if you get it over with! Come on, tell us you love us!

Of course I do, says Salvatore gruffly.

Not good enough! says Rosi. Come on! says Giusi. Say it! says Annetta. You know it's true! says Grazia.

I love you, says Salvatore, almost choking. All of you, he adds, with an extra squeeze to Ciccio's hand. A reward for his manly supportive silence, no doubt. And now poor Salvatore's eyes fill with tears. Love him!

Somehow, speaking of family love, we end up on the topic of Salvatore's own parents: between whom, he tells us, the bond was powerful. His children now find out, to their great amazement, that he is not, as they'd always thought, the first emigrant generation of his family. His own father left Calabria and came up to San Remo, he tells us, in a bid to earn his fortune, be able to buy his own bit of land back home and afford to get his kids schooled. He didn't want to have to send them away from home, hire them out to strangers, as soon as they were big enough to keep an eye on a goat. They deserved better. He couldn't find work in Liguria, though; moved on another hundred miles to the South of France. To Nice, Salvatore thinks. In those days, once you'd left the village, you looked like an idiot if you gave up and came home before you'd made your pile; you'd get less of a *brutta figura* if you never returned at all. But to Salvatore's father's great shame, he couldn't stick it at all. After a mere six months, he found someone to help him write a letter home to his wife. He hated this miserable exile's life, he told her. At this rate it would be another five years of loneliness in a strange land before he could return in triumph. He missed her terribly; he missed his family, he missed Santa Cristina; he didn't even care about his *figura* any more. Would she forgive him if he gave up and came home?

Back in Santa Cristina, the schoolteacher read the letter aloud to Salvatore's young *mamma*. She dictated her answer right away. No hesitation. Just two words: *Torna subito!* Come back right away! Two words that sealed Salvatore's fate. There was nothing she wanted more in the world than to have him back home. They would all manage somehow. She didn't care what people would think . . .

Francesca bustles in, bearing gifts, and breaks the spell. Hardly has Salvatore finished his unwrapping than Grazia is showing her the trophy in the jar.

The *lardo*! says Francesca. She distinctly remembers her husband wolfing a whole hundred grams of the stuff all in one go a few weeks ago, just swallowing it down, hardly chewing it at all! That's where the twig came from! She told him off about it at the time, she says.

Well, says Salvatore combatively, how was I supposed to guess you'd leave bits of old wood lying about in my food?

This is much better: Salvatore back to his old self. Soon he is pointing out to his daughters, cock-a-hoop, that he has proved them all wrong. A simple mechanical blockage! That's what the doctor said! Now they can all apologize, because his sufferings had nothing whatsoever to do with smoking! Or drinking! Or eating too much fat!

Unless you count the *lardo*, says Ciccio, with a nod towards the jar on the bedside table.

Mah! replies his father.

Birthday event over, Ciccio and I pop up to Besta de Zago to check on the roof. We find Franco in agitated conference with two of the Albanians. Remy and his cousin have been picked up by the police, they're telling him. And of course they have no documents. They're locked up down in Imperia jail; they will be deported back to Albania next week.

Terrible! Sent back to a place with no work, to sit guarding vegetable patches with guns against starving marauders!

Yes, says Franco. Still, it's not too bad. He was only paying for two, the ones with their papers in order, and the others were helping voluntarily, sharing the wages with their compatriots.

I glare at Franco. That was not the kind of terrible I meant. Can't we do anything about it?

Not unless you want to go to the police and say you'll employ them, he says. But we already are employing them! I say.

Doing what? says Franco. He certainly isn't employing them, because he would have had to ask to see their documents first.

Well, I shall go down and say I'm employing them myself, starting now, on the roof, I say.

Franco gives me a pitying look.

I see what he means. What roof? The roof replacement quite possibly doesn't exist, so obviously the job doesn't either. I've got nothing to employ them on.

A fortnight later, the roof is nearly finished and nothing more has been heard from Remy and cousin. They must have refused, heroically, to say how or where they were making a living. Which has saved their compatriots, and possibly us, from unwanted official attention, but means they will go down in the police annals as drug dealers or pimps. How else were they maintaining themselves? Doing them no favours if they're ever picked up in this country again. I knew I wanted to get proper planning permission. Look what happens when you don't.

Salvatore is still in hospital; and getting rather short-tempered from being kept in bed when he feels fit as a fiddle and wants to be out and about gardening and gossiping with the best of them. He'd certainly have been out on his ear by now if this was England.

I'm impressed, I say to Grazia. Do hospitals always give people this long to rest and recuperate in your country? There isn't some complication the hospital is keeping quiet, is there?

No, no, says Grazia. It's just that there are three empty beds in the ward already; it's a quiet period. And if there is no patient in a bed, no money is coming into the hospital for that bed, from the state or the insurance company or whatever. So they may as well keep him in as not. Anyway, a bit of enforced peace and quiet will do him good. Salvatore, looking very chipper and almost back to his old self, has worked out by now his preferred angle on the situation.

Look at this! he shouts, waving the offending thyme twig in the jar at the visiting Auntie Apple – and anyone else in the ward, patient or visitor, who cares to listen. Wood! he says. *Porca miseria!* They give me wood to eat! *Ah, si, si!* What do you expect when you've got a wife who feeds you on wood?

44

The roof is done at last. We're home again; and the chickens are back in their luxury pile across the valley. Only a couple of days' tidying up of spare piles of timber and tiles and bits of broken brick and sacks of cement ahead of us, and the place will look as it always did, ready for the roof closing party, our own official *chiusura*.

Tidying up? says Ciccio. Why? What's the matter with it?

Sometimes I worry about how much he has in common with his father.

Now, the night before our *chiusura*, once we have everybody invited, Franco and Iole, Anna and Tonino, Laura and Marco, Francesca and Salvatore, we discover that we've arranged the event on the very evening of a vital football match. Juve will be playing somebody-or-other, and the world will come to a sudden and ghastly end if the team should lose. According to a panic-stricken Paletta, the only thing that virtually guarantees a Juve win is for Marco, Ciccio and himself to be watching the game all together in the same place, with their traditional bunch of Juve-supporting mates. How could Ciccio even contemplate abandoning his team to the vagaries of mere fate now, when this system has been shown to work so perfectly the last three out of four games? Since the *chiusura* dinner can't be moved at this late date, we will simply have to have a *chiusura*-and-football match party. I am slightly worried by this plan. Might it not seem a bit disrespectful to the older members of the party? Of course not, say the Juve supporters. But they would, wouldn't they?

The stove is lit, hurricane lamps outside, candles in, big shadow-play from the bonfire as darkness begins to fall and the first half a dozen guests mill in and out against a luminous background of moonlit white olive netting, tending the food on the grill, carrying vessels and implements out on to the pair of tables we've joined together on the front terrace, arguing about recipes and cooking times as they go. The tables are already groaning under the weight of vast numbers of bottles of Fathers' Wines, now come to full maturity. Paletta and Marco have brought up a huge TV, an even huger generator, and a pair of young helpers, nephew Alberto and a spiky-haired friend of his named Luigi; and with much rushing up and down terraces and many *porca miseria*s and *madonna*s they have created a small but stylish outdoor cinema under the olive trees at the back of the house, with several rows of chairs facing the television, now perched high on the wall of the next terrace up. Now Anna and Tonino arrive, closely followed by Francesca and Salvatore. Salvatore, out of hospital and fully cured, is still making frequent remarks about being Fed on Wood, while firmly maintaining his see-how-wrong-you-all-were-about-my-lifestyle line. But we note that he hasn't so much as touched a cigarette since he came out of hospital. And though we're not allowed to mention this fact without getting our heads bitten off, we're all very proud of him.

Now the guests of honour, Iole and Franco, arrive, accompanied by Franco's favourite hunting dog, a large hairy creature named Rocky. Salvatore and Tonino have added even more wine to the table, and soon they and Franco have settled in among the comparative study youth group surrounding the bottles, Franco sipping away with great concentration, hat tipped back on head, holding forth passionately about something-or-other, glass waving wildly, to an impressed younger generation. Silly of me to worry about disrespect. Our older guests are positively charmed to find themselves in the middle of all these excitable young folk – though Salvatore is concealing it under a veneer of gruffness while he checks out the scenario. Now I feel guilty about not having arranged the encounter on purpose.

Except that we now discover that Franco doesn't like football. Amazing! Who ever heard of an Italian who doesn't like football? He has never bothered to watch it, he says. He's got better things to do with his time.

I have never thought about the progressive social possibilities inherent in football until now, my attention always having been grabbed by its more negative, hooliganistic side: but now I come to think of it, team games would of course be anathema to the ferociously I'm-all-right-Jack tradition from which Franco springs. Never mind, he says, he always goes to bed early anyway; he'll just go off home after dinner, when the match starts.

Francesca and Anna, meanwhile, have each brought us a large carrier bag full of nameless jars. In the nick of time. As winter has progressed, and I have learnt the uses of their various contents, my jar collection has been dwindling dramatically. The larder has begun to look quite bare. Iole helps us pack them away, and then we all go for a potter among the chairs of the outdoor cinema on the north-facing terrace, where my guests marvel, to my great smugness, over the floral delights I've managed to get growing out here, English-type plants that don't want to be shrivelled by too much sun. Iole is especially impressed by my English rose bush, an impulse purchase some ten years ago from Woolworth's gardening section. Once a small rooty stump in a plastic packet, it is now six feet wide and in full flower, covered in so many fat white blossoms that you can hardly see its leaves, and making a fine counterpoint to the cascade of bright egg-yolk-yellow crocuses all down the slope above it, provided by the hand of nature. Beautiful! You'd never get an Italian rose in flower at this time of year, she says. Nor an English one either, as it happens. The thing went completely haywire as soon as it met this unexpected climate, and never has realized that it ought to keep its vest on at this time of year.

Back indoors, tour completed, Francesca insists that we empty out a couple of those jars for *antipasti* snacks; her sun-dried tomatoes, plumped up by being brought to the simmer in half white wine and half water, then dressed with olive oil. I try one. Miraculous. Even more miraculous, and more intentionally so, is Francesca's other roof-warming gift; a pair of ceramic masks that will ward off the Evil Eye from our home, heirlooms from her granny, she tells us, to be hung above our external doors, facing outwards. Paletta will put them up immediately. Since Juve could only be beaten by the intervention of malevolent supernatural forces, it makes perfect sense to get them into position as soon as possible.

The masks, Francesca tells us as Paletta gets to work with hammer and nails, were a parting gift from her own mother; they came with her to Liguria, then all the way to Australia, and did their job perfectly all that time. But her children told her off, when she put them up outside her home in Diano, for giving the family the *figura* of ignorant superstitious Southerners, and made her take them down. Anyway, she says, up here in our dangerously isolated house Ciccio and I are a lot more in need of their help than she is down in the town. Destiny clearly intended them for this spot, too; the first, glazed in a murky, blotchy dark green with faun horns and wolf fangs half-hidden in wild hair and beard, is a Forest God without a doubt, Wild Nature to face uphill into the wilderness and the oak woods, while the other, a sort of laid-back Bacchus with big earrings, bunches of grapes and ears of corn in his hair, is a perfect Cultivator spirit, nature tamed, to deal with the olives and *orti* of the downhill slopes.

Triumph outside the front door: the first mask is up, big staring eyes now glowering fearsomely along our path, glinting in the firelight. I straighten him up admiringly. Bormano has come home at last, I say.

No, he hasn't. Paletta is having none of this. He may not be able to give the mask a name, but he can assure me that it is no vile weedy Ligurian deity, but a strong and noble Calabrian being, whose mystical power will have been immensely enhanced by his voyage right round the world. Britishly I start to bore Paletta to death with a short lecture on Pan-European worship of the Green Man in pre-Christian times, as described in *The Golden Bough*. Nobody's at all happy with this, though. Can I be suggesting that there is something un-Christian about the masks? Nonsense! They have nothing at all to do with religion.

Ciccio is now shouting to everybody to organize themselves to table: the first course is ready. Paletta, passing the plates along, suddenly realizes that there are thirteen of us to dinner. Thirteen! Catastrophe! He leaps to his feet in horror. Less than an hour to go till the match starts, and *thirteen* of us have sat down to eat! He will have to go and find someone else to join us . . . is no one else meant to be coming? Well, we say, the two remaining Albanians were invited, but if they haven't turned up by now, they're probably not coming.

Then would Alberto and his friend Luigi like to leave, maybe? asks Paletta. Alberto, who has just begun tucking into a bowl of the delicious *spaghetti alle vongole veraci* cooked by his uncle Ciccio, gives this out-of-order uncle an extremely filthy look. No, he says, they would not. Paletta has an inspiration. Rocky the dog! What if we put a chair out for him, and let him eat his dinner off the table? That should do it! A roar of outrage goes up all around the table; just as Paletta is poised to make a last impassioned plea for a dog's dinner on behalf of Juventus, the day is saved by the Albanians arriving late. Or in the nick of time, rather. Paletta rushes up to them, pumping their hands wildly in a great frenzy of relief, hugging them and slapping them on the back for joy. The Albanians are most startled by this unexpectedly rapturous welcome; and even more so by the discovery that they have secured Juve's victory tonight.

Soon we are all tucking in, a lucky fifteen now, the wine-tasters at the far end of the table managing to shout their heads off and eat at the same time, while down at this quieter end Marco and Laura are describing to us how much more entertaining little Michele's life has become since grandad came to stay. Michele's food-throwing and plate-hurling skills are coming along apace, it seems, under his grandfather's tuition.

We are idly gazing across the valley as we eat – a thing you can't avoid doing here, unless you're staring up at the stars – when a car, or rather a set of headlights, appears over there in the darkness, weaving its way in and out of the rocky hairpin bends towards the top of the ridge, lighting up sections of hillside first white, then red, then white again as it twists and turns. Not only is this car travelling strangely fast for such a bad road, its lights leaping as it bounces from rut to rock, but we now see that it is being followed, at equally hair-raising speed, by what is undoubtedly a police car. Blue-and-red lights flashing, the police are just a few hairpins below, and catching up fast. Or are they? Hard to tell in this terrain, where cars have to change direction every couple of hundred yards. Has the police car lost its quarry? It seems to be slowing to a stop . . . No, it's off on the chase again, the headlights were just momentarily concealed behind some rocky outcrop or clump of olives. Another police car appears below, heading up the valley from San Pietro, siren wailing. Silence falls for a moment at the far end of the table – the wine-tasters have heard the siren above their own racket at last, seen the police cars. A real-life cops and robbers show. Now everybody starts cheering the cars on, shouting advice. Naturally, it doesn't occur to anyone to take the side of the police.

Fermati! our guests roar. *Spenga le luci!* And it does look as though the fugitive would do best to take their advice, just turn off his lights and hide silently in an olive grove, invisible. But the driver, of course, can hear nothing of all this. Hunters and hunted career right over the ridge opposite and out of sight: darkness settles once more. Our guests return to their dinners, all agog with the *Miami Vice* car chase in the Ligurian hills. Has anyone ever seen such a thing? No, they haven't. You never see a police car this side of the Diano Marina crossroads at all, not unless someone's asked them to come, for an accident or something. Policemen are as *de trop* in San Pietro as beachwear. I have seen a pair of spotty young policemen, drifting slowly past Luigi's bar in a patrol car one afternoon, being told off in no uncertain terms by a bunch of aged gentlemen, knotted hankies on heads, sitting at the outside tables taking some air. Who, the policemen were asked, did they think they were? Why were they poking their noses in where they didn't belong and weren't wanted? Surprisingly (to me, at any rate) the policemen turned red, looked sheepish, and shot off down the back road past the olive mill towards Diano Marina and home, covering up their *brutta figura* with a burst of loud acceleration.

The next hour is devoted to wild speculation and to gluttony. Where was the escapee heading for? Does that road only lead to Moltedo, or is there a turn-off for Camporondo? Is either place at all a likely haven for desperate criminals? Are there any more of those fresh anchovies *in carpione*? Who caught the *branzino*, the huge sea bass that has greatly impressed Iole? They cost a fortune in the shops! Maybe she could learn to fish? Sandro, the Head of Fishing amongst our *compagnia*, has just arrived and immediately takes her up on this, much to Franco's disgust. She should come down to the breakwater by Cervo any Thursday night, he says; he always has a spare rod, she could learn in no time, he tells her.

Mah! says Franco.

Many fishy items later, football time is nearly upon us and the whole of the restaurant-sponsored football team has turned up and occupied the cinema terrace. We all straggle round to join them, bearing extra chairs. Franco now tries to carry out his threat to leave; but we can see Iole wavering. Does she like football, then? I ask, surprised.

She'd never watched it in her life, she says, until Lekbir came to stay. Her husband, to whom this name is anathema, gives a loud snort. But, she goes on, Lekbir used to love the game, he explained all the rules to her, and these days she enjoys it a lot. She got quite carried away, she says, during the World Cup.

Lekbir! Waste of space! says Franco, glowering as Iole, escorted by an attentive Sandro, takes her seat among the fans. Couldn't even ride a horse till I taught him. Had to have a *motorino* to come home on at nights! Ate us out of house and home, and now it turns out he was getting my wife hooked on that television nonsense into the bargain! We should mark Franco's words – that boy will come to a bad end! Franco gives us an evil leer, puts a finger under an eyeball, and wanders off towards the front of the house. Next time I catch sight of him, true to form, he has found himself an old sack – must have gone to his *Ape* to get it – and is spreading it out ostentatiously on the most lumpy and uncomfortable-looking bit of hillside above the TV terrace. He settles down on the sack, which he has taken care to put in an area from which the screen is not visible, calls his dog to him, and, using the creature as a pillow, has himself a nice nap while we all watch the match. Iole, I am pleased to say, is not at all unnerved by this behaviour, and has a lovely time oohing and aahing with the rest of us, while the hardcore supporters jump up and down, punch the air wildly, and shout their heads off. Needless to say, Juve wins.

Some days later we hear that the fugitive in the car was in fact our old friend Helmut/Mario, who had been spotted while removing a piece of broken marble shelving from a ruined chapel. The police have ransacked his home and sequestered his entire collection of kitsch ornaments – labouring under the delusion, the gossip has it, that he is an international trafficker in stolen works of art.

45

We're lying in bed under our newly safe beams a floor below our delightfully insect-free new roof, gloating over the fact that the restaurant's now closed for the month for the olive harvest, and over the other fact, that Ciccio may be leaving it for good soon anyway if we manage to get our vineyard and basil greenhouses. Suddenly some roaring-small-engine type noise erupts just to leeward of the house. Nino with some new piece of olive-farming machinery, we deduce. The only person still busying himself around his groves when all the rest of us are just waiting peacefully for the olives to start falling into our nets. I idly take my breakfast-in-bed cup out into the early spring sunshine and wander along the terrace to see what Nino's up to this time.

I see. And I run back indoors like the wind. He's got a rotovator ploughing thing, I say, a *motozappa*; and he's on the lower terrace.

So what? says Ciccio from the depths of the duvet. As I may have mentioned, he is not at his best in the mornings.

I am almost hysterical with panic. Well, I say, the only other terrace he hasn't laid any nets on yet is the one closest to here. So he'll be doing that next, won't he?

Of course he will, says the grumpy person, missing the point completely. He's just opening the surface up so the spring rain all gets absorbed into the ground instead of running off. Very sensible too. We ought to do it here, too, as soon as the harvest's up. Your land's hard as a rock.

What, I say, do you think he's going to be digging up when

he gets up there? Your buried rubbish, that's what! Great blobs of rotting mulch.

Maybe he'll think it was someone else, says Ciccio, after a short, thoughtful pause.

Like who? I say. Why would anyone else be coming up here to bury old vegetable peelings and fish bones on Nino's land? I can see the clods flying as he motozaps along the bottom *fascia*. Just think what will be flying when he gets on to Ciccio's favourite strip. Should I go out and make a clean breast of it?

Don't be daft, says Ciccio, finally getting a grip on the situation. There won't, he says, be any evidence left by now. The stuff will have biodegraded into the soil months ago.

Is he sure? I am momentarily calmed. It would be stupid to go and confess when likely enough there's no sign of the crime. There was plenty of rain last month, after all, though I don't have enough experience of these matters to know how long it would take for the evidence to vanish completely into the ecosystem. Maybe, though, Nino wouldn't be bothered, would just look on it as a fine bit of fertilizer? No. Because the problem about the flat stones was not our taking them, was it, but our not asking first? And he'll never believe I didn't know.

Now I think of eggshells. And bones! That's why Ciccio started burying the stuff in the first place, isn't it, because I wouldn't let him put meat leftovers on the compost? Then there's Ciccio's extreme unreliability in the matter of compost. I am always picking bits of cellophane and bottle-top and blister-pack and silver paper out of the compost since he's been participating. How could Nino miss them? What if he decides to denounce my new roof in revenge? There's certainly nobody better placed to know that I've got one.

I dither back out on to the terrace. Nino is just visible

between the farthest tree trunks. The moment of truth is coming: he is heaving his way up on to the danger terrace, his roaring machine trundling before him. I go up the steps and on to the scrubland above, where he wouldn't expect anyone to be; now I can peer through the vegetation unobserved and see what's going on. Heart thundering, still in Ciccio's stripy pyjamas and carrying my coffee for comfort, I creep stealthily along the hillside.

The end of Nino's terraces and the beginning of ours is marked, at this level, by a clump of broom bushes which we probably ought to have cut down but haven't quite got round to. I crouch down behind the screen of greenery as the teeth of the plough begin to bite, clods and pebbles flying. Was that a bit of pink-tinged papery stuff? Or just a bit of vegetation? As Nino slowly gyrates around the tree, I realize that he is wearing one of those protective visor things over his face. Of course, he is allergic to the *gamba rossa*, Red Leg, a weed that grows plentifully on the *fascie* around his ruin. The visor is already covered with quite a layer of specks of earth; maybe he can't see too much through it anyway?

I sip desperately at my coffee, hoping against hope. Nino goes stolidly on rotovating, noticing nothing. Maybe there's nothing to notice. Nature has done her work and saved our bacon. Greatly relieved, I shift position on the edge of the terrace, preparing to creep silently off the way I came. No such luck. Suddenly my foot slips from under me, causing me to leap into the air to try and keep my balance, skid on a loose stone on the top of the wall, and send the coffee cup flying through the air. It crash lands neatly just in front of Nino and the *motozappa* as they round the next tree.

Remember that this is the man I once tried shamelessly to entice into my lair when he was alone and defenceless; the man whose flat stones I stole, whose new nets I ripped; whose roof tiles I may well have wantonly broken, deny it though I may. Now I have crept up on him in my nightwear and, unprovoked, have senselessly hurled a cup of coffee at him.

Salve, says Nino politely, raising his visor and rotovating his way over to the cup, which he now picks up for me.

Salve, I say coolly, as one who quite often drinks her morning coffee while pottering around dangerously steep bits of hillside in her pyjamas. Nino holds the cup out to me. We can't possibly speak over the racket of the *motozappa*, so I am saved the trouble of making up an explanation for my extraordinary behaviour. I scramble down the wall, accompanied by a shower of small stones, and accept the cup with what I hope is a graceful nonchalance. I head back for the house along his terrace, feeling Nino's eyes boring into my back as I try desperately to remember how normal people walk. People, that is, who don't dispose of their household rubbish by burying it in their neighbours' olive groves.

Once Nino has rotovated his terraces to his satisfaction, he appears at our front door. How wrong I was to suspect him of un-neighbourly impulses. He has come to warn us. Do we know that you can see our new roof from right across the valley, now we've pruned back our trees like that?

We do.

But do we also know that panic-stricken rumours are going the rounds of our valley and its neighbouring ones about a *pazzo*, a madman on a *motorino*, who has been inspired by the fresh air of probity sweeping his land – or some twisted and tormented version of it – and has started combing the province of Imperia for abusive buildings to denounce to their local *comune*? For no reason at all!

Oh no! I can't believe I've managed to avoid getting embroiled in the local system of favours and obligations for all these years, only to finally take the plunge at the very moment when the whole Byzantine edifice has begun to develop serious structural faults. Who, in the good old days, could have imagined that an utterly motiveless denouncer – or at any rate, one motivated by planning principle rather than personal grudge – would ever appear on the scene?

But how accurate will the *pazzo*'s information be? If he spots our house from across the valley, and detects from afar its unofficial new roof, its possibly abusive porch, its dodgy larder, and its two sets of steps that nobody's actually mentioned yet, but about which I have strong suspicions, will he actually be able to track it down? Not too likely, says Nino. I agree; the closer you get to it, the harder it is to spy. You'd need a decent map to find it; and luckily there is no such thing. Unless, terrible thought, the *pazzo* has connections in the ENEL?

Ciccio now falls to devising a system whereby he could attach vast quantities of rolled-up olive net to the tops of the two trees in front of the house – or would it be better just to drape them over the roof like some sort of camouflage webbing? – to protect us from the spying eye of this evil busybody. Nino, sceptical at first, is soon gripped too, as Ciccio works out the finer detail of this plan. The colour scheme, in fact. That orange variety of olive net might be good, he says; they'd make it hard for the *pazzo* to tell from a distance if he was looking at a terracotta roof or just a tract of olive grove. Then rolls of the white could be tied to the trees in front. And where would we get all this netting?

Well, it just so happens that Ciccio has an entire flat full of the stuff.

I sit and gaze at the hills. Can this possibly be a sensible response to the situation? I suppose it's as sensible as anything else you could come up with.

Thank the Lord for Ivana's vineyard. At least we'll have a place of refuge if the worst comes to the worst. Though word has come back from London: the book is good. I can pay Franco the rest of his roof money; I can afford my share of the vineyard too. Maybe I could even buy my way out of my Sins of Abusiveness?

46

Here I stand high in one of Salvatore's olive trees, a three-legged ladder and a sea of silver-green leaves below me, wisps of February cloud in a bright sky above, glimpses of distant blue sea through the treetops. I give a quick rattle to my eight-foot pole among the tips of the branches, and a shower of shiny green-black olives cascades on to the nets beneath, scattering across the terrace. In the three nearest trees, Ciccio, Francesca and Salvatore are doing the same; the white of the net slowly disappearing under our fat falling harvest. Salvatore is supposed to be convalescing still, but the weather was perfect, he said, and he couldn't be doing with being fussed over. What was the point of waiting till the weekend when the rest of the clan were coming up? Just so he could listen to them telling him off about his lifestyle? *Mah!*

Naturally, though, where you have Salvatore and son, you have controversy. Ciccio has brought a load of crates up on Paletta's lorry for us to gather the olives up into later, instead of the traditional *quarto* sacks. One of the olive mills down in the valley has offered extra money for olives gathered like this; they're going for some sort of extra-extra virgin classification, and want the crop as little bruised as possible. We'll go up to the *taverna* when we break for lunch and collect a load more crates from there too, the ones we use for the grapes, and that should be enough to do the lot. But Salvatore is convinced there is something dodgy about this crate business, though he can't quite work out what it is. Olives are always measured by volume, not weight, as they go into the mill – no point in weighing them, because for a given weight of olives you'll get a different weight of oil every year anyway, depending on how the weather's been. But how will we know how many of these crate-things would make a *quarto*, anyway? Do we just take the miller's word for it? Is his son sure the man's honest? Why does he always fall for any old new-fangled fad he comes across? Still, the price is good, and Salvatore is going along with it, grumbling gently, for now.

Once we're up at the *taverna*, after a squashed and bone-rattling trip in the lorry, which is only meant to be a three-seater and has virtually no suspension as far as I can tell, we hurl a hundred-odd crates into the back; and now, of course, we all have to go and check on Ivana's spare vineyard. We'll cheer Salvatore up by showing him how endless the De Gilio lands will soon be. Straight away Salvatore notices, down at the river end of the vineyard, a few half-rows of *Grenaccine* vines that his son didn't spot on his own tour of inspection. I can't imagine how either of them recognizes anything at all about vines with no leaves on the plants, but then, as we know, I have a lot to learn. *Grenaccine*, they explain to me, are the sweet red grapes you use for making *sciac'e tra'*, the local *rosé* wine that you only leave to ferment with the grape skins for a single day – hence its strange name, which is dialect for 'crush and pull', or maybe it should translate 'crush and take a draught' – so it has a powerful fresh-grape flavour. And a kick like an ox, whenever I've tried it.

And there you were telling me there was only Ormeasco and Lumassina up here! announces Salvatore competitively to his son. He is drawing a deep breath with which to make a few rude remarks about Ciccio's incompetence at vine-spotting, when, with a visible effort, he catches himself and holds his tongue. Unbelievable . . . fancy such a transformation having been effected by a tiny thyme twig. A brand-new Salvatore.

So far Salvatore, distracted as he has been by his innards, hasn't paid too much attention to our vineyard-buying plan. Now, all of a sudden, he is fired with a wild enthusiasm for it. But he wants to see the bit of woodland up in the hills too, before he gives us his blessing. How could we have thought of putting an offer in for it before he'd checked it out properly for us? He is appalled to hear that we haven't even been to inspect it ourselves. Can we be serious?

Soon Ivana and daughter Celestina, dragged away by the power of Salvatore's personality from their curds and cheese-cloths, are leading the way uphill in Renzo's *Ape*. We follow our bone-shaking way on and on, higher and higher, the snowline drawing ever closer and the architecture getting ever more Alpine. The lorry may be the height of discomfort, but you get a great view from it, wide windscreen and several feet higher up than a car. Salvatore sits happily, wedged between Francesca and me, counting up in his head and on his fingers the vast numbers of vines and olive trees that will soon form part of our collective lives. How many Plants do I own, exactly? he asks me. He's not too impressed with my paltry total, not even a round hundred, but he adds it to his own anyway. Thanks, Salvatore. Yes, he finally concludes, Ciccio and I should easily be able to survive, even without the accursed restaurant.

We finally turn off down a dirt track and come to a halt behind a big blue truck. This isn't what you'd really call woodland in England at all – more like sloping meadowland with the odd tree dotted about on it. That explains how you can keep cows on it, then; I'd been finding it hard to imagine a wood full of cows. And here are a few of the cows now – huge smooth, beige, bony creatures with big horns that look more like Indian buffaloes than any cow you'd ever see in England.

If the truck's here, says Ivana, piling out of the *Ape* with Celestina, then Signor Ardissone, our putative cow-manure tenant, must be around somewhere. Yes, there he is, heading off down the path with natty hat and knobbly stick. Ivana calls out to him. No sooner has he finished shaking our hands and offering to take us to walk the boundaries, than there is a loud outbreak of shouting and mooing from a clump of hazels over to our left, and two youths appear heading our way fast, battling with a very large and wildly lunging horned cow. Salvatore, though he may have had plenty of experience with goats in his youth, has obviously had little truck with cows, and leaps back a nervous couple of feet at the sight of it.

Don't worry, says Signor Ardissone soothingly. They're just trying to put some drops in its eye.

Salvatore clearly feels he has not done his *figura* any good here, and spends some time, as Signor Ardissone takes us round, telling us rather rudely that keeping beasts is troublesome dirty work, and that's why he himself took to nice, civilized Plants. Except for the occasional chicken, of course, which doesn't count as an animal anyway, as Rose will tell you.

Tour over, we wander off towards the top of the ridge. You can see right down into both valleys from up here: the Arroscia winding down towards the sea at Albenga, and a hint though misty grey-green of the tiny San Pietro river running down to Diano Marina.

Perfect! says Ciccio, gazing around him like a man on top of the world. He spreads his arms wide. Ours as far as the eye can see! he says. (Well, someone had to, didn't they?) Or at any rate, he adds, a good few chunks of it here and there. Salvatore cackles delightedly and rests one wiry hand on his son's shoulder, the other on mine. Fantastic! I say. So, goodbye to the troublesome restaurant at last . . .

Well, I don't know, says Ciccio thoughtfully. When you think about it, vineyards don't really need a lot of work; not much more than olives, when all's said and done. And now you've finished with all that book-writing business, we've both got plenty of free time, haven't we? Maybe it would be foolish to go rushing into giving up a perfectly good restaurant.

Yes, says Salvatore. His son could be right. Especially, he adds, when he's around himself to give a hand with the pruning and manuring and suchlike. And the *vendemmia*, of course.

What? I turn to Francesca. Her puzzled look has multiplied a hundredfold. I can feel something very similar happening on my own face. I'm not sure which is more puzzle-worthy. Is it Salvatore offering to help his son even though he's no longer on his deathbed? Is it his agreeing with Ciccio about something for the first time in history? Or is it the fact that the pair of them have just undermined the entire point of this vineyard–purchasing project?

Francesca comes over and takes my arm. Never mind, she says. Think how much saving you'll be able to do while you're still young, with a vineyard as well as the olives and the restaurant! Then, if you manage to set up the bed and breakfast and the basil business too . . . !

Yes, I say, I'll be decking myself from head to toe in gold.

Francesca giggles, checks Salvatore to make sure he understood nothing of that last remark, and gives my arm a fond pinch.

Whatever happens, she says, she's going to hand over that woollen mattress right away. She can't keep it from me any longer. I deserve it.